JAPAN: Images and Realities

JAPAN:

IMAGES and REALITIES

Richard Halloran

ALFRED·A·KNOPF
New York 1969

For Carol and

    For Christopher, Laura, and Catherine

Who Shared the Adventure

Consider: is not to dream just this,
whether a man be asleep or awake, to
mistake the image for the reality?

—Plato, The Republic

ACKNOWLEDGMENTS

This book is a distillation of study, observation, and experience at various times over a period of twenty years. I am deeply indebted to many people for their help along the way. My father, RAdm Paul J. Halloran USN (ret.), and my mother, Catherine Lenihan Halloran, the daughter of an army officer, gave me their wanderlust and sense of curiosity about people in other lands. At Dartmouth College, the late Professor John Masland first piqued that curiosity about Japan. Later, the United States Army lived up to its recruiting posters and gave me a traveling introduction to Japan and other parts of East Asia.

At the University of Michigan's Center for Japanese Studies, Professor John Whitney Hall (now at Yale) and other fine teachers opened the door of Japan far wider than the Japanese did for Commodore Perry; I am especially grateful to all of them for two years of penetrating exposure to the realities of Japan. My employers at *Business Week* and McGraw-Hill World News allowed me three years of firsthand experience reporting in Japan, during which time some of the thoughts in this book began to take shape.

The Ford Foundation kindly provided the opportunity for further study as a Fellow in Advanced International Reporting at Columbia University's Graduate School of

Journalism. Though I concentrated on Chinese studies at the university's East Asia Institute, there was also time for more work on Japan. My employers at the Washington *Post* sent me back to Tokyo for two years, during which time I had the chance to refine the ideas I had earlier. In particular, J. R. Wiggins, former editor of the *Post*, showed an abiding interest in coverage of Japan.

During the years of involvement with Japan, I suppose I have met several tens of thousand Japanese, each of whom has taught me something about his homeland. To all, known and unknown, I am grateful. Two close friends, in particular, should be mentioned. Maruta Yasuko, my assistant for five years, was a constant source of valuable insight into the life of her country. Mrs. Maruta was especially helpful in explaining the myriad small things that add up to the immense differences between Japan and the West. Kamikawa Rikuzo, my language teacher, helped solve some of the mysteries of his mother tongue. More important, Kamikawa-*Sensei* patiently explained many of the hidden workings of Japanese thought and social practice.

In the preparation of the manuscript, I owe thanks to Professor Hans Baerwald, political scientist at the University of California at Los Angeles, and George Packard, author of books and articles on Japan. Longtime observers of life in Japan, both have read the manuscript and offered many excellent suggestions for its improvement, for which I am most appreciative. Hobart Rowen, Business Editor of the Washington *Post*, offered valuable advice on the chapter about Japanese economics. Harold Strauss, of Alfred A. Knopf, Inc., has been patiently encouraging ever since this book was in outline form.

Quotations from Ozaki Yukio, Ito Hirobumi, and several other Japanese are taken from *Sources of Japanese Tradition* (1958) with the permission of Columbia University Press.

Acknowledgments

It is standard for authors to absolve others for what appears in a book; it is even more imperative in this case, for no two people agree entirely about Japan. Thus, the final responsibility for the book is mine alone.

Lastly, my wife Carol and our children, Christy, Laurie-*chan*, and Catherine, suffered long while this book was being written. To them, it is dedicated with relief and affection.

—R. H.

Bethesda, Maryland
January 1, 1969

CONTENTS ◪

INTRODUCTION

Many Americans and Europeans today see Japan as the first genuinely Westernized nation in Asia. We see what appears to be the capacity of the Japanese to copy the ways and thought of the West. We are intrigued by the ability of the Japanese to reform a once-feudal political and social order into an apparently democratic society. We respect Japanese efforts to build an economy that rivals those of the West in organization and productivity. Looking at these and hundreds of other changes in Japan over the last century, many Westerners believe the Japanese themselves have changed and are now like us, remaining Japanese and Asian only by the accident of geography.

This image, however, is an illusion that is reflected from the surface of Japan. Beneath, the essence of Japanese life flows from ideas, ethics, customs, and institutions that are anchored deep in Japanese culture and history. The core of Japanese tradition guides the daily lives of the Japanese and directs the internal and external courses of their nation. That core has been little touched by incursions from the West.

Western influence has changed the face of Japan and the accoutrements of Japanese life, but it has not penetrated the minds and hearts of the Japanese people. Many centuries ago, Japanese culture was influenced by ideas from

China and, to a lesser extent, from Korea. The Chinese imprint is still visible today, particularly in the Japanese writing system. But many Chinese ways were tried, found unsuitable, and rejected. The Japanese, moreover, thoroughly modified those Chinese concepts that were retained as they assimilated and "Japanized" them. Similarly, the Japanese have taken from the West a few things whole (technology), adapted and made Japanese others (political forms, economic organization, and the press), and rejected outright still others (Western religions).

The fashioning of the myth about a Westernized Japan started during the decade of 1895–1905, when the Japanese first caught the general attention of the West. The Imperial Japanese military forces defeated the Chinese in 1895, participated alongside American and European troops in putting down the Boxer Rebellion in China in 1900, were recognized as a major new element in the Asian balance of power by the Anglo-Japanese Naval Alliance of 1902, and decisively defeated the forces of Czarist Russia in 1905. All this was achieved less than forty years after the Meiji Restoration in 1868, which marked the beginning of Japan's emergence into the modern world.

The Restoration had ended 250 years of Japan's seclusion, the long period of isolation that reduced to a minimum the nation's exposure to the profound political, economic, technical, and military changes in the West during the Industrial Revolution. Then the Japanese, with immense and deliberate effort, set about acquiring from the West knowledge to build the foundation of a modern economy, to use Western technology, to forge a respected military force, and to develop an apparently Western political structure. These innovations led Westerners to take serious notice of this faraway land and to acknowledge that Japan was due entry into the circle of major world powers.

From that time to this, the impression that Japan was

turning more and more to the West has become stronger and more widespread. There was a lapse before and during World War II, when Japanese propaganda emphasized an ultranationalist spirit to make both Westerners and Japanese believe that Japan had reverted to the older, feudal ways. But the illusion of a Westernized Japan has regained strength in the last twenty-five years. After the devastation of World War II and Japan's surrender, the American Occupation intended to bring to Japan the benefits of Western democracy, economic progress, and social equality. The stream of reports that issued from Occupation authorities once again spread the vision of a Japan on the march toward its destiny as a Westernized nation. Millions of American soldiers passing through Japan during the Occupation and the Korean War brought home the same descriptions.

In the past fifteen years, thousands of businessmen, tourists, politicians, and students who have visited Japan have seen and told of cities with big glassed office buildings and subways, of efficient shipyards and electronics factories and steel mills, of elections and business corporations, traffic jams and highspeed railways, jazz and television, Coca-Cola and Scotch whiskey. Perhaps most of all, the magnificently executed Olympic Games in October 1964 paraded before the world the panorama of a modern Japan technically, socially, and spiritually akin to the West.

Some prominent Western thinkers, too, have added to this image by contending that the basic pattern of Japanese life has been profoundly changed by the impact of the West. Historian Arnold Toynbee, in his study *The World and the West*, emphasized the penetrating effect of Western technology on Asian societies. He wrote: "In China and Korea and Japan today, a century or more after the date at which our modern technology first began to penetrate these countries, *we can see the revolutionary effects upon the whole of their culture taking place before our eyes.* Time, however, is of the essence in this process; and a revolutionary result that is so clearly manifest to all eyes today was not foreseen by the Far Eastern statesmen a hundred years ago, when they were reluctantly taking their decision to admit this foreign technology within their walls." (Italics mine.)

Similarly, author Arthur Koestler, writing in a September 11, 1964, special issue of *Life* Magazine on Japan, argued that "Japanese society is moving away from the Asian mainland and toward the West—in every domain, from foreign trade to life and letters. At worst, Japan might succumb to an Eastern version of 'Americanism' in its negative aspects. . . . At best, *it might achieve the first real synthesis in history between the essential values of East and West*—a synthesis which neither Alexander's conquering armies, nor the Mongol invasions, nor St. Francis Xavier's missionaries were able to achieve." (Italics mine.) Koestler concluded with this jingle:

> If East is East and West is West,
> Where will Japan come to rest?
> In the restless West.

Americans and Europeans, however, mistake the use of Western objects for a revision in the essence of Japanese values. Their interpretation overlooks the continuity in Japanese thought and the residual forces in Japanese life. It fails to take into account the selective nature of Japanese acquisitions from the West. More important, it underestimates the absorptive genius of the Japanese, who have taken *forms* from the West and molded them around the *substance* of Japan. The things Japan has borrowed from the West are changed by the Japanese—the borrowed items change the Japanese far less.

History shows that innovations originating within a society are far more telling and lasting than those coming from without. There is, of course, much interplay between internal and external cultural forces in Japan. But to say that basic Japanese culture is becoming a synthesis of East and West gives the impression that the mixture is equal parts Japanese and Western, or even more Western than Japanese. This is not so. Japan is still essentially Japanese—and very different from the West. Kawabata Yasunari, winner of the 1968 Nobel Prize for Literature, summed it up in an interview published in the French newspaper *Le Figaro.* Asked whether the Japanese tradition isn't in the process of extinction, Kawabata replied: "I don't think so. Despite industrial imperialism, despite television, despite the crush of urban life, the Japanese essence will remain. Don't look for the Japanese essence in society but in the individual." On the future of Japan, Kawabata said: "Every civilization fluctuates and experiences peaks and declines. The best works are produced after a peak has been reached. Japan is currently on the ascent. The best hasn't come yet."

The misconception that Japan is Westernized has spread for several reasons. All of us are ethnocentric to some extent and tend to see things abroad in the image and likeness of our own environment. We Westerners like to see in the Japanese and other non-Western peoples the outward appearances that are familiar. We recognize and more easily identify with people whose clothing, buildings, manners, and appurtenances like automobiles are similar to ours. If we visit Japan, we look for familiar objects as a guide to understanding a new and different environment. From a panorama of neon signs in English and Japanese, we focus on the known and block out the unknown. In sports, we see baseball but not *sumo* (wrestling); in a restaurant, we see Scotch but not *sake* (rice wine); in dress, we see Christian Dior gowns but not *kimono*; in manners, we see the handshake but not the bow. We are more comfortable with people whose things are like ours and who do the things we do, and we think then they must be like us. And if it is true that imitation is the sincerest form of flattery, we like to flatter ourselves that the Japanese have been wise in trying to copy our ways.

Western journals and newspapers have done little to correct this misleading picture. Those scholars versed in the Japanese language, history, and culture are few and, with a couple of notable exceptions, have concentrated on specialized academic research. In contrast, American and European journalists are not specialized enough. Most practicing the news craft in Asia know little of the language or background of the region. Editors, with several exceptions, insist that their correspondents in Asia cover only the violence and revolutions that produce thundering headlines, or else the exotica of the Fujiyama–geisha–cherry-blossom circuit. More subtle news from Japan often does not fit into the conventional treatment of the American press. So it has been ignored.

The Japanese themselves promote illusions about their country. The theme of modernization, industrialization, and Westernization has been a favorite of many Japanese as they have striven to "catch up" with the West. In the late nineteenth century, Japanese leaders stressed superficial Westernization as part of their effort to rid Japan of the "unequal treaties." Later, other Japanese emphasized abroad the Westernized features of their country to gain the respect of Westerners. Through much of the last century, a handful of Japanese intellectuals who were genuinely taken with Western thought have articulated their ideas to the Japanese people. Westerners hearing or reading these have concluded that Japan was truly and of its own will becoming Western.

This book seeks to dispel the illusion of a Westernized Japan. The Japanese have a concept called *kuromaku*, which means "black curtain" and is taken from the Kabuki theatre. It means that reality is not out front but behind the scenes. The book attempts to pull aside the black

curtain and to expose enough clues about the inner workings of Japan to indicate that the Japanese are themselves
and not us. The book, however, is far from a definitive
work. I have written about history, politics, economics,
social order, and the press but have not touched on
Japanese art, literature, theatre, music, and many other
facets about which I know little. I have also been selective
and have chosen those aspects of Japanese society that I
think show best the genuinely Japanese qualities of life.

The book is an effort to provide an interim report
from a way station in history. The late Sir George B. Sansom, the West's most thoughtful student of Japanese history, explored the question of Japan's Westernization in
his study *The Western World and Japan*. He analyzed the
effects of the Western thrust into Japan in the sixteenth
and nineteenth centuries. In the closing passages of his
long book, he wrote: "There is not evidence enough to
show that because she adopted Western machines and
commercial practices to her own uses, Japan became
Western in the essence of her national character by the
close of the nineteenth century. Whether a similar conclusion as to the first half of the twentieth century would
emerge from a survey of its cultural history is beyond
the scope of the present inquiry. Yet a study of the earlier
period raises doubts whether any of the chief civilizations
of Asia will, even if they voluntarily follow a Western
economic pattern, submit to Western precept in political,
social, or religious life."

This book ventures an answer to the question Sansom
raised and concludes that, no, Japan in the mid-twentieth
century has not become Western in the essence of its
national character. The book tentatively suggests that
Japan never will: Japan, rather, is heading into a time in
which traditional Japanese values and ways are becoming
even stronger in determining the course of the nation and
the lives of its people. Many analyses of Japan emphasize

the changes of the last century or more. Equal and perhaps greater emphasis should be given to the deep running continuities in the flow of Japanese history. There have been identifiable turning points in the evolution of Japanese life and institutions since the Restoration but they have been bends rather than sharp turns or breaks with the past.

Japan is perhaps the world's most fascinating social laboratory for the study of the effect of one culture on another. Beyond that, however, and of more immediate importance, the status of Japan today and the direction in which it will move tomorrow will have a direct impact on the national interests of America and other Western nations. Japan has again become the most powerful nation in Asia. It is potentially a major power equal to or surpassing those in Western Europe. Should it choose to exercise that power, it can have an influence in Asia second only to that of the American and Russian superpowers. This is directly pertinent to the maintenance of American security in the Pacific Ocean. It is axiomatic in political and diplomatic maneuvering, economic competition, and military combat that decisions should be based primarily on the most careful estimates of the other party's capabilities and secondarily on his intentions. In turn, this requires some understanding of another nation's fundamental motives, what its people hold to be valuable, how they make decisions, in what manner their political and economic institutions function. We in the West do not know much about these things Japanese, and this book, hopefully, will supply some basic explanations.

In a wider scope, I hope this book may be useful to Westerners in applying to other Asians some of the lessons that can be learned from developments in Japan. Just as Westerners have misjudged Japan, so it is likely that we have not understood the inner workings of other nations in Asia. Since the end of World War II, we have tried to transplant our ways to Asia. This attempt for years has pervaded the economic assistance, political advice, and military instruction that America has given to the developing nations of Asia. Much has been said about the influence of the American Occupation on Japan. Conversely, one wonders how the American mentality has been affected by the apparent achievements of the Occupation. Did it make Americans think that we have remade Japan from an aggressive, militaristic nation into a peaceful, democratic country imbued with Western ideals? Has the Occupation caused Americans to think that if we could reform Japan, we can make over other nations in Asia?

If it has, we have only been fooling ourselves. Americans should not expect Western ideas, especially those that touch the heart like religion, philosophy, and political thought, to penetrate the cultural consciousness of Asian peoples. Because Western forms may be adaptable to Asian needs, Western ideas might also appear to be applicable. But the evidence from the movements sweeping through Asia today shows rather clearly that Asian cultures, drawing upon thousands of years of tradition, are once more asserting themselves. Asians are not particularly interested in the teachings of Moses, Aristotle, or Thomas Aquinas. Nor are they likely to be long impressed with Marxism, also a Western philosophy. The attraction of Marxism in Japan has been limited to a relatively small group and has had little genuine appeal for the mass of the people. This gives rise to the hope that even in China we may one day see the diminution and then the passing of communism, despite the grip it seems to have on that unhappy nation today. Just as did the Mongol and Manchu conquerors in the thirteenth and seventeenth centuries before it, the Marxist river will probably drown in the Chinese ocean.

A final word on the nature of this book: It is intended for the general reader, not for the specialist, and presupposes no previous study or knowledge of Japan. It is a reporter's book and not a scholarly work. Historical facts come from standard works, though the interpretations of why events happened and what they meant are my own. For the most part, the observations recorded here are mine from firsthand experience.

The reader will find scattered through the book a number of Japanese words, which is not an affectation and for which I ask indulgence. The reason is that many Japanese words just do not translate well into English, the two languages being so dissimilar and the thinking of Japanese-speaking and English-speaking people being so different. Where I have thought it necessary to use a Japanese word, I have given the usual dictionary translation and then tried to explain more fully what it means. Because there is no plural form for most Japanese nouns, the reader will find the words used in both the singular and plural, depending on the context. Japanese names are given in Japanese fashion, family name first, to indicate, even in this small way, the differences between Japan and the West.

PART ONE

The
LAST HUNDRED
YEARS

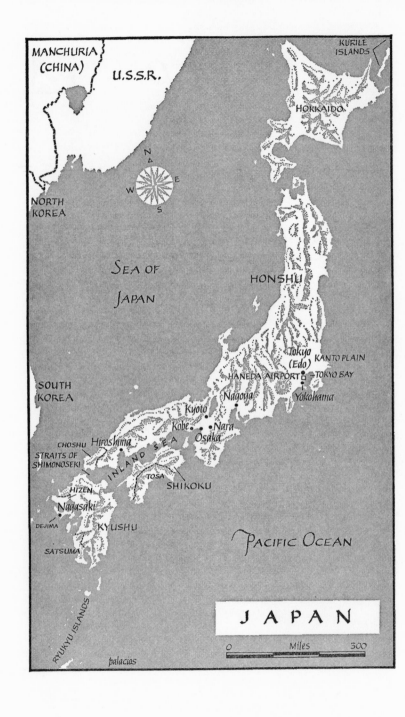

MANCHURIA
(CHINA)

U.S.S.R.

KURILE
ISLANDS

HOKKAIDO

NORTH
KOREA

N
W E
S

SEA OF
JAPAN

HONSHU

SOUTH
KOREA

Tokyo
(Edo)

KANTO PLAIN

HANEDA AIRPORT

TOKYO BAY

Nagoya

Yokohama

Kyoto

Kobe   Nara

CHOSHU   Hiroshima

Osaka

STRAITS OF
SHIMONOSEKI

INLAND SEA

TOSA

SHIKOKU

HIZEN

Nagasaki

DEJIMA

KYUSHU

PACIFIC OCEAN

SATSUMA

RYUKYU ISLANDS

JAPAN

0   Miles   300

palacias

Chapter I

MEN of MEIJI

Early in the morning on the Twentieth Day of the Ninth Month of the First Year of Meiji, the sixteen-year-old Emperor Mutsuhito stepped from under the sweeping eaves of the graceful wooden palace in Kyoto where his fathers had held court for a thousand years and was ushered by courtiers a few paces into a waiting palanquin. On signal from a court official, sixty bearers clad in yellow silk robes and black peaked caps carefully raised the ebony and gold-lacquered sedan, the rounded dome of which was topped with the golden Imperial Phoenix, and held it on an elaborate frame over their heads six feet above the white surface of the pebbled courtyard. From each of the upper four corners hung a thick red rope of silk that was pulled taut by three men to steady the swaying car. On another signal, the vanguard warriors, *samurai* from the clans of Choshu, Satsuma, and Tosa, began a slow march out of the palace grounds toward the outskirts of the ancient city. Behind them came bearers of the imperial belongings, borne in great treasure chests. Then followed the court nobles, seated on white horses and wearing the elegant, flowing *hitatare* robes and tall, black *kanmuri* hats that had been the style of the

Imperial Court since its early days. The aristocrats rode before, beside, and behind their Emperor. Bringing up the rear was another large body of Choshu and Hizen *samurai*, giving representation to the four clans from western Japan that had lately rallied to the imperial standard and restored to the Emperor the respect and prerogatives, if not the true power, due him as sovereign of Japan.

As the procession, which numbered between two thousand and three thousand, reached the edge of the city, it turned southeast toward Ise and the Imperial Shrines of Amaterasu-o-mi-kami, the Sun Goddess and mythical progenitrix of the imperial line. The caravan glided along at a leisurely pace and took four days to arrive at the shrine. There the young Emperor, who had come to the throne after the death of his father, the Emperor Komei, eighteen months before, reported to his imperial ancestors on the momentous changes of the times. Then the procession headed up the coast, boarded ferries to cross the bay below Nagoya, and turned east onto the Tokaido, the Eastern Sea Road, that was and is the main artery between central and eastern Japan. Stopping at castles and temples along the way, the procession moved toward the newly appointed capital in Tokyo. That city, previously known as Edo, had been the stronghold and headquarters of the shogun, or generalissimo, who had been actual ruler of Japan until a few months earlier.

On the Second Day of the Tenth Month, the entourage reached Hamamatsu, about halfway to its destination, and received news that the Wakamatsu Castle, far to the north of Tokyo, had fallen to imperial forces. Those warriors, led by other *samurai* from the clans supporting the imperial cause, were pursuing remnants of the army of the Tokugawa Shogun. The last Tokugawa Shogun, Keiki, whose family had ruled Japan for 265 years, had been turned out and the office of shogun abolished early in the year. Keiki decided to fight but his resistance was

4

sporadic and often desultory. The imperial *samurai* soon forced the surrender of Keiki's troops in Edo, sent him to incarceration in his family domain at Mito, on the edge of the plain north of Tokyo, and then marched north to rout the remaining Tokugawa troops. The fall of Wakamatsu was not the last battle, but it was good news and the Emperor was pleased. He ordered a halt and directed that *sake* be distributed to the bearers and warriors.

During the Eighth Day, the procession went through Hakone, the checkpoint in the mountains west of Tokyo that had been a vital Tokugawa outpost watching for guns going into Edo and women coming out, signs that a feudal baron might be in a troublemaking mood. On the Eleventh Day, it reached Kanagawa and passed before a covered stand erected so that foreigners living in the trading post at Yokohama could view the approach of the Emperor about whom they had heard but knew little. Their colony had grown up in the last ten years, following the opening of Japan by the black ships of Commodore Matthew Calbraith Perry and the commercial treaty signed by Townsend Harris on behalf of the United States. The behavior of the foreign spectators that day was in marked contrast to that of the Japanese citizenry. The Westerners, considered barbarians by the Japanese, kept on talking as the Emperor passed unseen in his curtained palanquin while the Japanese crouched low and were silent.

On the Twelfth Day, the Emperor reached Shinagawa, the last stop before entering Tokyo. Next day, the procession marched to Zozoji, a temple in the Shiba section of Tokyo, for a rest, then continued toward the center of the city, which had been spruced up a bit with repaved streets, new bridges, and freshly lacquered gates. The day was magnificently clear, a rare but good omen, and the Emperor and his escorts and guards entered not so much in triumph as in dignity and splendor. The streets were crowded with subdued but happy people whose voices ceased and whose heads bowed in awe as the Emperor passed. The population of the city, which had been a lively place, had decreased somewhat from its more than one million because the Shogun's warriors and bureaucrats had fled. The merchants and townspeople who stayed had not been much involved in the political struggle, as has always been true in Japan, but they were relieved that order was being restored.

After trooping across the Kyobashi and Gofukubashi bridges spanning the narrow channels that drained the swampy, low-lying city and through the Wadakuramon gate, the procession arrived at the Nishimaru donjon of Edo Castle, stronghold of the Tokugawa Shogun that had been surrendered to the imperial forces. A number of courtiers, lords, and *samurai* were on hand to receive the Emperor and to escort him into his new palace. There, at a little past two in the afternoon of the Thirteenth Day of the Tenth Month of the First Year of Meiji, which was November 26, 1868, in the Gregorian calendar, the Emperor took up residence in Tokyo and thus symbolized the opening of Japan's modern era.

The establishment of Tokyo as the new imperial capital and the arrival of the Emperor there to give it legitimacy marked the culmination of two compelling historical trends, one developing inside Japan, the other coming from without. As these two streams converged, they turned the course of Japan into a new historical channel, one in which it still moves. Life in Japan today is the direct consequence of events and developments during the last one hundred years and the influence of the people who directed them. Who they were and what they did, their hopes and motives, their successes and failures, and the manner in which they went about leading their nation, for better or worse, made Japan what it is today. Most of them are not well known in the West, especially those who carried on the work of the Restoration period. Yet their impact on the history of their nation equals that of the men who brought on the English, American, French, and Russian revolutions, though with markedly different results.

To pick up the currents of Japanese history, perhaps it is best to go back briefly to the turn of the seventeenth century. Japan at that time was in disorder and disunion. Three able generals successively subdued other warlords, with the Tokugawa clan becoming supreme. The Shogun set up his headquarters in the fishing village of Edo and built it into a bastion that commanded the Kanto Plain surrounding it. The Tokugawa rulers evolved a form of centralized feudalism in which they were the over-all masters and the *daimyo*, or feudal barons, maintained local control of their domains through their *samurai* retainers. The Shogunate imposed a strict hierarchical social order in which the descending scale ran from the warriors down through the peasants, artisans, to the merchants at the bottom. It put tax collecting and its finances in order, administered careful control of the population, and generally erected a viable dictatorship. This may well have been the world's most ambitious effort to make time stand still. To protect Japan from encroachment by Western missionaries and traders and the armies that followed them as they poked north from South and Southeast Asia, the Tokugawa rulers closed the country. No foreigner could come in, no Japanese could go out. As one scholar has written, it was a quarantine that makes the Iron Curtain look like a rusty sieve.

The Tokugawa rulers brought a reasonable degree of order and unity to Japan for almost two hundred years. About the turn of the nineteenth century, however, there were rumblings beneath the seemingly placid surface. The *daimyo* in western Japan who were not allied with the Tokugawa Shogunate were growing restless under its stern and increasingly inept rule. *Samurai*, who had little fighting to do except occasionally among themselves, were becoming indolent and impoverished. Artisans and merchants had started a mercantilist, money economy centered in towns around the feudal castles and they were becoming increasingly dissatisfied with the Shogunate's ever greater demands for tax revenues to fill coffers being emptied by mismanagement. The merchants were also unhappy with the loans they had to make to *daimyo* and *samurai* and with the inferior social position in which they remained despite their economic power. There were occasional rice shortages during which the peasants staged revolts, though these were easily put down.

At the same time, a distinct sense of nationalism developed. It focused on the emperor as the fount of political sovereignty, social order, and spiritual belief. This was accompanied and stimulated by a revival of interest in Shinto, the Way of the Gods that is the pantheistic and uniquely Japanese religion. Shinto beliefs did not clash with the neo-Confucianist doctrine of the Tokugawa regime. But they did emphasize the role of the emperor as the focal point of Japanese life—and he was living in genteel poverty in his secluded Kyoto court, ignored by Shogun and commoner alike. One of the early leaders among the Shinto revivalists was scholar Motoori Norinaga, who wrote: "Our country's Imperial Line, which casts its light over this world, represents the descendants of the Sky-Shining Goddess. And in accordance with that Goddess' mandate of reigning 'forever and ever, coeval with Heaven and earth,' the Imperial Line is destined to rule the nation for eons until the end of time and as long as the universe exists. That is the very basis of our Way. That our history has not deviated from the instructions of the divine mandate bears testimony to the infallibility of our ancient tradition." Other scholars echoed similar themes, and to their works Japanese nationalists later turned for inspiration and justification.

There was no cohesion or organized movement among the dissidents during the early part of the nineteenth century. It remained for the external current, the coming of the West and its threat of military imperialism, to coalesce the opponents of the Shogunate into the action that led to its downfall and the restoration of the Emperor. The Americans are usually given credit for prying open the doors of Japan, but the Dutch, Russians, and British were there knocking before them. When the Tokugawa Shogun closed the country in 1639, he allowed the Dutch to retain a trading factory in Dejima (sometimes written Deshima), a small island close to the shore in the bay of Nagasaki, a port city in Kyushu, Japan's southwestern island. Through this window came wisps of information about what was going on in Western industrial progress, medicine, and military prowess. The Russians entered the scene early in the eighteenth century as a logical extension of their push eastward across Siberia. In 1713, Russian explorers landed in the Kurile Islands, north of Japan, and in 1739 a Russian vessel nosed down the east coast of Honshu, Japan's main island, and put in at Shimoda. By 1768, the Russians had added a Japanese language course to their navigation school in Irkutsk. An expedition led by a Russian lieutenant, Adam Laxman, landed in Hokkaido, the northernmost Japanese island, in 1792 and spent the winter, but was then told it must leave and not return, except possibly to Nagasaki. In 1804, the *Nadiezhda*, commanded by a Captain Krusenstern and carrying an envoy named Rezanov, sailed into Nagasaki Bay. Rezanov tried for six months to negotiate a trading pact with the Japanese but got nowhere and left in a huff. Two years later, two of Rezanov's subordinates led raids on Japanese posts in the Kuriles and Hokkaido. That was followed in another two years by the call at Nagasaki of the British frigate *Phaeton*, whose captain demanded food and supplies and threatened to bombard the harbor if the Japanese did not accede. He got his food and sailed away, but not without shaking both the local authorities and the Tokugawa Shogunate. In 1811, Captain Golovin and some of the crew of the Russian warship *Diana* were captured in the Kuriles and held prisoner for two years. The prominent English colonialist Sir Thomas Stamford Raffles tried to take Dejima from the Dutch in 1813, as a result of European conflicts, but failed. Calls from ships of various nations, including a few American, continued until 1825, when the Shogunate issued an order that any foreign ship coming to Japan was to be destroyed and its crew arrested or killed without hesitation.

The Americans came into the picture after that. Just as the Russians were pushing east across Siberia, so the Americans were somewhat later pushing west toward the Pacific in the fulfillment of what some called Manifest Destiny. This led them to the China trade in the days of the clipper ships and to want ports of call and markets in Japan. If they were unlucky enough to be shipwrecked on the Japanese shore, the sailors also wanted safe haven instead of the ruthless treatment they received from the Japanese. In 1837, a small American ship called the *Morrison*, carrying trader Charles W. King, put into Edo Bay supposedly to return Japanese castaways but in hopes of opening up trade. The Japanese, however, fired on the unarmed ship. The captain sailed to Kagoshima but met with the same result. King went back to his home base in Canton, China, and recommended to the American government that an expedition be sent to pry Japan open and to insure humane treatment of American seamen.

Around 1840, the internal and external currents affecting the course of events in Japan began to flow together, and their speed quickened. The Shogunate didn't know about King's recommendation to the American government, but it did know about its internal troubles and the external pressures. In 1841, a high Tokugawa official,

Mizuno Tadakuni, undertook to reform the Shogunate, ordering strict discipline, tax and economic reforms, and tighter controls over the people. But things had gone too far, there was too much resistance, and Mizuno was forced to resign in 1844. Similarly, reports of the show of power by the British in the Opium War in China reached Edo and caused considerable consternation. In 1842, local authorities were instructed to treat foreign seamen with respect and to persuade them to go away, but not to harm them. This, too, was ineffective as the foreigners kept coming in increasing numbers.

Internally, scholars wrote more and more about the central role of the emperor on one hand and the need for fending off foreign incursions on the other. The teachings of Aizawa Seishisai began to gain interest. In 1825 he had written: "Since Heaven and earth were divided and mankind first appeared, the Imperial Line has surveyed the four seas generation after generation in the same dynasty. Never has any man dared to have designs on the Imperial position. That this has been so right down to our own time could scarcely have been by mere chance." Aizawa had some rather uncomplimentary words for the West, especially America. After writing that the world is in the form of a human body, with Japan as its head, he said: "The various countries of the West correspond to the feet and legs of the body. That is why their ships come from afar to visit Japan. As for the land amidst the seas which the Western barbarians call America, it occupies the hindmost region of the earth; thus, its people are stupid and simple, and are incapable of doing things." From writings such as this emerged the slogan of the times: "Revere the Emperor, Repel the Barbarian."

The court in Kyoto and the western clans, who were later to join forces to overthrow the Shogun, were moving toward that goal, though still without deliberate plan. With the accession to the throne of the Emperor Komei in 1846, the court began to revise its functions. The new Emperor issued orders to improve the discipline of the court and to eliminate some of its sloth. Among the clans, Satsuma strengthened its economy, learned to make cannon, and translated Dutch books on shipbuilding. In Nagasaki, in the Hizen domain, the Japanese learned more Western technology from the Dutch on Dejima. The clans of Choshu and Tosa did much the same.

Meantime, knocks on the door became more frequent, especially from the Americans. In June 1845, the administration of President James Polk authorized Commodore James Biddle, head of the East India Squadron, to attempt to open negotiations with the Japanese. He arrived with two ships in Edo Bay in July 1846. But Biddle was operating under restrictive instructions, having been told to be cautious and not to arouse Japanese hostility. Thus, when the Japanese physically pushed him around, he offered no resistance nor retaliation. The Japanese, having humiliated Biddle and having shown no respect for his mission, then sent him away.

Within a few years, however, the pressure to open Japan turned into a head-on competition between the Americans and the Russians. Both were by this time well into the contest for economic, military, and political advantage in Asia, mainly China. Moreover, the race to open Japan became something of a personal heat between Commodore Matthew Calbraith Perry and Admiral Count E. V. Putiatin.

President Millard Fillmore had agreed, at Secretary of State Daniel Webster's urging, that the United States should send an expedition to open Japan for trade, secure decent treatment for American seamen, and obtain coaling and supply stations. Commodore Perry was picked for the job. He wasn't happy, thinking it not an important assignment. But "Old Bruin," an arrogant and stern master, soon became interested and made it a point of personal pride to succeed and to be there first. He sailed from Norfolk in November 1852 for Hong Kong, the British colony on the South China coast, to rendezvous with the rest of his squadron.

Meantime, the government of Czar Nicholas II decided to try to establish relations with Japan as a check against American and British power in East Asia. The chief proponent of this policy was Count Nicholas Muraviev, governor-general of eastern Siberia and leading advocate of Russian expansion to the Far Eastern Maritime Provinces and the Pacific. Putiatin was Muraviev's man in this and other maneuvering in China later. The admiral left Russia for London in August 1852 and was picked up there by his flagship in October. He didn't know about Perry's mission until February 1853, when he put in at the Cape Verde Islands, off the west coast of Africa, and heard about it.

After Perry reached Hong Kong, he had to wait for another ship, and didn't depart until May 1853. He then sailed to Okinawa, in the island chain southwest of Japan, to establish a base where Europeans interested in Japan could not watch his movements. He put on a show of force and practiced landing manuevers there, thinking quite rightly that reports about them would reach the Japanese in Edo. Perry then left for Edo in June with two steam frigates towing two sailing sloops. They reached the mouth of Edo Bay on July 8 and sailed in past the Japanese guard boats that tried to stop them. Perry's ships, belching black smoke, were too fast and he simply ignored the Japanese protests. After anchoring, Perry didn't repeat Biddle's mistakes. Instead, he took a high posture and gave the Japanese three days to accept the letter from President Fillmore. The defenseless Japanese acceded to his demands. To emphasize that he was serious, Perry weighed anchor and instead of heading for open sea, steamed up the bay closer to Edo, much to the fright of the Shogunate. Finally, on July 17, he departed for Macao, near Hong

Kong, leaving behind a promise to return the following year for an answer.

Putiatin, having arrived in Canton, up the long bay from Hong Kong, only to hear that Perry was on his way to Japan, set sail for Nagasaki and put in there in August, a month after Perry had been in Edo. The Russian demanded that the Japanese recognize Russian claims to Sakhalin, the island north of Hokkaido, and the northern islands in the Kurile chain. He also asked for access to a trading port. But decisions weren't made in Nagasaki, and Putiatin shortly left for Shanghai. There he took some coal that Perry had set aside for himself and sent a message to his American competitor suggesting that they join forces when they returned to Japan.

Perry was furious. The last thing he wanted was to share the glory with anyone else, to say nothing of losing an important advantage for his country. He therefore moved up his sailing plans several months and headed back to Edo, arriving in February 1854. Putiatin beat him to Japan—only to make the same mistake of going to Nagasaki while Perry was making for Edo. Correcting himself, Putiatin sent an emissary overland from Nagasaki toward Edo. That unlucky chap was on the Tokaido road south of Edo just in time to see Perry anchor in the bay.

Between the time Perry and Putiatin had left Japan and returned, the Shogun and his advisers were caught in a vise. On one side was the demonstrated military power of the Americans (an impression that Putiatin's ships had reinforced) and the implied threat to use that power if American demands were not met. On the other side were the dissident western barons, by this time moving toward an alliance with the Kyoto court and having the backing of the scholars. They demanded that the Western barbarians be repelled. To ignore the barons, even though many of the Shogun's advisers saw that Japan was nearly powerless to refuse the American demands, would mean ever more active opposition to the Shogunate. Tokugawa officials, confronted with this dilemma, planned to play for time and try to send Perry away without a treaty. The American sailor had come with four ships the first time, but shrewdly arrived with eight the next time. Overawed and fearing an immediate attack, the Japanese agreed to negotiate. After several weeks of dickering, Shogunate officials signed the Treaty of Kanagawa, giving the Americans the right to call at Shimoda and Hakodate, on Hokkaido, for coal and provisions and insuring the fair treatment of crews in distress. No trade was allowed, but Perry insisted that an American consul be permitted to reside in Shimoda to negotiate a trade agreement later. The Japanese vaguely conceded.

Thus ended Japan's seclusion. Perry had won, but Putiatin didn't give up. Having learned that talking with officials in Nagasaki was useless, the Russian sailed to Osaka in November 1854, which the Japanese read as a threat to the Imperial Court not far away in Kyoto. Officials persuaded Putiatin to leave—which he did, but not for Nagasaki as the Japanese wanted. He went instead to Shimoda, closer to Edo. While negotiating there, an earthquake and subsequent tidal wave sank his ship. But he continued his mission while the Japanese built him another vessel. In February 1855 they signed the Treaty of Shimoda. The persistent Russian got more out of the Japanese than Perry had. Russia was given the right to trade at Nagasaki, while the Japanese gave up claims to the northern Kuriles and recognized Russian ownership of all of Sakhalin. Further, the Japanese conceded to the Russians the right to exempt Russian subjects from the jurisdiction of Japanese courts. This was the beginning of the unequal treaties and foreign extraterritorial rights that humiliated the Japanese for the next fifty years.

The Dutch and the French next negotiated treaties with the Shogunate, but it remained for the American consul Townsend Harris, who arrived in Shimoda in August 1856, to finish Perry's work. After two years of patient but persistent negotiations with the Shogunate, which procrastinated and obstructed him at every turn, Harris obtained a commercial treaty in July 1858. It opened more ports for trade, allowed Americans to reside in specified places, exempted them from Japanese courts and law, and gave them freedom of worship (Japan's Christian proscription of the early Tokuguawa days still being in effect). The following year, the foreign community in Yokohama started to take shape with the arrival of European consuls and traders.

That was the beginning of trouble. For the next ten years, Japan was the scene of intermittent and then steady turmoil. "Revere the Emperor, Repel the Barbarian" became the cry of the times. The *samurai* of the western clans, especially the able and vigorous young men who were rising to positions of leadership and responsibility, were enraged with the Shogunate for allowing foreigners on Japanese soil; they also saw this as an opportunity to exploit the evident weaknesses of the Shogunate. The Imperial Court was equally displeased with the Shogun and fearful of the approach of foreigners to Kyoto. Further, the court became increasingly anxious to regain some of the power and prestige that it considered the Shogun to have usurped. These two forces formed an alliance that received support of influential scholars. The court needed the power of the clans to oust the Shogun. The clans needed the court to give them legitimacy. Theoretically, the Shogun ruled in the name of the Emperor and the dissident clans wanted that blessing transferred to them.

From the beginning, Japan became a dangerous place for foreigners to live. Attacks on them were commonplace. A Russian officer and two seamen were among the first killed. The unassuming, scholarly Henry Heusken,

who spoke Japanese well and was secretary to Townsend
Harris, was cut down in the night shortly after New
Year's in 1861. An Englishman, C. L. Richardson, was
murdered by Satsuma *samurai* while on a horseback ride
in September 1862. This apparently drained the last of
the Westerners' patience, for in August of the following
year British ships bombarded the Satsuma headquarters
at Kagoshima in southern Kyushu and destroyed its shore
guns, arsenal, and ships—all of which had been painstakingly produced locally. The next summer, Choshu gunners
fired on an American ship in the Straits of Shimonoseki,
between Honshu and Kyushu. That brought retaliation
from a squadron of British, Dutch, French, and American
ships, which pounded the shore batteries into silence.

Seeing that the Shogunate could not expel the foreigners, the Emperor began stripping the Shogun of his powers.
In 1865, the Choshu clan went into open rebellion. The
finances of the Shogunate continued to deteriorate. Satsuma and Choshu lords, persuaded by some of their able
young *samurai*, agreed to an alliance to overthrow the
Shogun and to restore the Emperor to his rightful place.
Two final events brought the movement to a conclusion.
The Shogun Tokugawa Iemochi died in August 1866,
opening up new struggles within the Shogunate for his
replacement. Emperor Komei died in February 1867 and
was succeeded by Mutsuhito, giving even more impetus
to the Restoration movement. In November, the new
Shogun, Keiki, was forced to resign, and in January 1868,
the young Emperor proclaimed the Shogunate abolished
and the Restoration accomplished.

The men who quickly seized power in the new regime
were mostly the young *samurai* from the formerly dissident clans, sponsored by a few key nobles from the court
and abetted by their feudal barons. Calling the period
Meiji, or Enlightened Rule, they built the foundation,
then erected the structure of modern Japan that endures

today. It has been filled out and occasionally remodeled in the last hundred years. But the basic architecture and edifice stands and provides the framework within which Japan now lives.

The men of Meiji were a remarkable group, comparable to the men of the American Revolution in the number of energetic, zealous, and farsighted leaders who were all on the scene at about the same time. They were the grandfathers—in some cases the blood forebears, in all the spiritual precursors—of the men who govern Japan today. They were an oligarchy that later widened into the Establishment that now makes the major national decisions. The men of Meiji, as individuals, were an ambitious lot. The struggle for power among them was continuous except when they were threatened by the outside world or by other Japanese not of their group. But there was enough cohesion among them to succeed.

These men were all exposed to Westerners and Western ideas, both at home and during their overseas travels. But they sprouted from Japanese soil and their roots remained deep in Japanese tradition. The young *samurai* respected Western technology and military power and set about acquiring practical knowledge about these from the Western world. But they had no fawning admiration of the West. Indeed, antiforeign, meaning anti-Western, feelings continued long after the Restoration and can be found in no small measure today. A few were taken with Western philosophy and political thought, but they were on the fringe of the truly powerful group and did not have lasting influence.

Much more in the mainstream were the thoughts of scholar Sakuma Shozan. Sakuma's theme was: Eastern Ethics, Western Science. He taught that men should govern their lives according to the Confucian principles of loyalty, piety, and duty while using knowledge acquired from the West. He wrote that a gentleman "employs the ethics of the East and the scientific technique of the West, neglecting neither the spiritual nor material aspects of life, combining subjective and objective, and thus bringing benefit to the people and serving the nation."

The teaching of a disciple of Sakuma, Yoshida Shoin, caught even more the imagination of the young *samurai* before and after the Restoration. Yoshida was the adopted son of a poor *samurai* who ran a military school. From his father, Yoshida learned the code of the warrior and studied the Chinese classic, Sun Tzu's *Art of War*. He also went to Nagasaki to find out what he could about Western military power and methods. In his travels, he became aware of the weaknesses and ineptitude of the Tokugawa Shogunate and began writing about the need for "grass-roots heroes" and a "grass-roots uprising" to overthrow the corrupt dictator. Yoshida didn't envision a peasant uprising but a revolt by the poor *samurai* who remained close to the earth. He plotted to assassinate a shogunate official but was discovered, captured, and beheaded at the age of thirty in 1859. Before he died, he wrote a poem:

> That such an act
> Would have such a result
> I knew well enough.
> What made me do it anyhow
> Was the spirit of Yamato.

Yamato was an ancient clan, and the *Yamato damashii*, or Spirit of Japan, that Yoshida extolled became a watchword for later leaders of Japan.

A common denominator that permeated the oligarchy was their loyalty to the Emperor Mutsuhito, known posthumously as the Emperor Meiji. Not much is known about him personally because of his sacrosanct position. The oligarchs who met with him did not reveal much in their speeches or writing. The archives have not been opened to scholars by Imperial Household officials, palace guards whose major function is to protect the emperor from scrutiny. His chief tutor was a Confucian scholar, who presumably passed on his precepts. The Emperor was apparently a modest and reserved man, given to hard work and a conscientious devotion to his ceremonial and state duties. Though the real power of decision was in the hands of the oligarchs, he evidently made his views known and, having given careful thought to the problems at hand, had them respected. Most important, the Emperor was the symbol of Japan, its national unity and national character. As the source of sovereign power, he bestowed legitimacy in the eyes of his subjects to the acts of their rulers. He gave the new regime the mystique it needed to govern.

Several of the court nobles were active in the oligarchy. Foremost among these was Prince Iwakura Tomomi. One of the older of the new leaders, Iwakura was always close to the Emperor, a consistent and effective advocate of the imperial sovereign as the source of all authority. He distrusted popular government, especially in forms modeled on the English Parliament, and insisted that power remain in the hands of a small, elite group. But he urged the adoption of Western technology, having been mightily impressed with the railroads, factories, and communications he saw while leading a mission to Washington, London, Paris, and Berlin in 1871–3.

Three young *samurai* leaders of the early Meiji days were Kido Koin, Saigo Takamori, and Okubo Toshimichi. Kido was a frail young man, introspective, a student of Chinese classics and history and later of Western military science. A disciple of Yoshida Shoin, he drafted many of the imperial edicts and influenced the setting of priorities, which he said should allot three fifths of the nation's resources to building military strength, one fifth to organizing a political system, and one fifth to bettering the lot of the people.

Saigo made a sharp contrast with Kido. Perhaps the most colorful of the Meiji men, he was a huge, robust, booming man of action, violent in battle but compassionate in peace. He personified the old warrior spirit of Japan: courageous, loyal to his friends, willing to sacrifice himself for his cause. He was deeply troubled by his colleagues' interest in the West, fearing that the introduction of Western ways would destroy Japan's traditional values. In 1873, he withdrew from the government and returned to Satsuma, intending to retire from public life. Other *samurai*, equally fearful of change, persuaded him to lead a rebellion against the Meiji government in 1877. It failed, and with it went the last opposition to the new order. But the spirit that Saigo projected lived on, and even today he is considered a great hero.

Saigo's boyhood friend Okubo had a different outlook though he had the same dedication and tenacity. His talents ran to politics and economics. He had an ability to find capable people to staff the bureaucracy and left his stamp on that vital institution. In the early days, he helped restore order to the nation's finances, improving tax collection and arranging a loan in London. He accompanied Iwakura on a mission to the West and brought back vivid impressions of Western industrial and military strength. He stimulated the beginning of Western-style industry and opposed foreign adventures until Japan could put its domestic house right.

Kido, Saigo, and Okubo all died within a year of one another in the prime of their lives. Kido died in May 1877, of ill health. Saigo died the following September, after being wounded in the last battle of the Satsuma Rebellion. At his request, a friend decapitated him with a sword to preserve his honor. Okubo was assassinated in May 1878, ironically by a follower of his friend Saigo. The assassin said that Okubo was responsible for putting down the rebellion and thus for Saigo's death. But the three of them had left their mark, and the work of building the nation passed easily to other hands.

Chief among these was Ito Hirobumi, the towering figure of the Meiji period. Ito came from a poor *samurai* family in Choshu and, as a boy, studied under Yoshida Shoin. Yoshida taught Ito loyalty, self-discipline, service to the Emperor, and urged him to learn about the West. Ito went to Nagasaki, where he studied Dutch military science. Then, along with another young *samurai*, he smuggled himself aboard an English ship in defiance of the Tokugawa seclusion laws and worked as a deck hand to get to England, where he studied science. Returning to Choshu, he warned his clansmen about the overwhelming power of England and advised them, unsuccessfully, not to get into a fight with the English fleet. After the Restoration, Ito served as chief of staff on the 1871 Iwakura mission to the West and on his return to Japan was named to the ruling Council of State. He was then 33, remarkably young for such a high position.

Although Ito was active in the Meiji government's foreign affairs, finances, educational and industrialization policies and was four times prime minister, his lasting mark on Japan was his political thought and the Constitution of 1889. There is no better example of Japanese substance expressed in a Western form than this constitution. It crystallized Japanese concepts of national character, sovereignty, political and social order, and the function of government into a Western-style document not known before in Japan. The constitution embodied the spirit of Japan's unique *kokutai*, or national essence, with the emperor at its center. *Kokutai* was far more than a political philosophy; it embraced the sum of Japan's religious, moral, ethical, and social thought.

During the formulation of the constitution, Ito specifically rejected both Western democracy and Western absolutism and emphasized the need for a constitution based on Japanese ideals. In a memorandum to himself on Okubo's views, he wrote: "Democracy must not be adopted, nor should despotic monarchy be retained. In the framing of a constitution, our aims should be determined by the ideal of a government which conforms with our country's geography, customs and sentiments of the people, and the spirit of the times."

For years after the promulgation of the constitution, Ito explained and justified it and compared it with those of Western nations. In one speech immediately following its promulgation, he said: "The differences between our Constitution and their constitutions are considerable. For example, Chapter I which clarifies sovereignty in connection with the prerogative of the sovereign has no parallel in the constitutions of other countries. The reason for this difference can be understood at a moment's reflection. Our country was founded and ruled by the Emperor himself since the very beginning of history. Thus, to state this fact in the opening article of the Constitution is truly compatible with our *kokutai*."

Several months later, he told people in his home town: "Government is the prerogative of the Emperor. As you will be participating in government—which is the Emperor's prerogative—you must regard this right as the responsibility of the people, the honor of the people, and the glory of the people. . . . What all Japanese must bear in mind is Japan's *kokutai*. It is history which defines the *kokutai;* thus the Japanese people have a duty to know their history. . . . The *kokutai* of the various countries differs one from another, but it is the testimony of the history of Japan to this day that the unification of the country was achieved around the Imperial House."

Twenty years later, looking back on his constitutional work, Ito wrote: "It was evident from the outset that mere imitation of foreign models would not suffice, for there were historical peculiarities of our country which had to be taken into consideration. For example, the Crown was, with us, an institution far more deeply rooted in the national sentiment and in our history than in other countries. It was indeed the essence of a once theocratic state, so that in formulating the restrictions on its prerogatives in the new Constitution, we had to take care to safeguard the future realness or vitality of these prerogatives, and not to let the institution degenerate into an ornamental crowning piece of the edifice."

What Ito did for Japan's political order, Yamagata Aritomo did for the army. A Choshu *samurai*, he studied under Yoshida Shoin and later fought, as did Ito and Kido, alongside Saigo in defeating the Tokugawa forces. Like Saigo, he was a stern and fearless warrior, known as "the Wild One." But he learned prudence early, during the English bombardment of Shimonoseki.

Yamagata rejected outright imitation of Western military methods and took only what he thought Japan could use. The Military Conscription Ordnance of 1872 reflected his views. Noting the experience and detailed regulation of Occidental armies, the document said that "the difference in geography rules out their wholesale adoption here. We should now select only what is good in them, use them to supplement our traditional military system, establish an army and a navy, require all males who reach the age of twenty—irrespective of class—to register for military service, and have them in readiness for all emergencies."

In the conscript army, Yamagata raised the ordinary citizen to the level of *samurai* and imbued him with the Japanese warrior's code. The Imperial Rescript for Soldiers and Sailors, a clearly Confucian document drafted by Yamagata in 1882, admonished them "to consider loyalty their essential duty," to have "sound discrimination of right and wrong, cultivate self-possession, and form their

plans with deliberation," to "value faithfulness and righteousness," and to "make simplicity their aim."

In the traditional ideal of the *samurai*, Yamagata was a
man of culture and a lover of poetry. He recorded much
of his life in short poems that evinced his emotions and
sensibility. After his armies had defeated his old comrade
Saigo in the Satsuma Rebellion and Saigo had died,
Yamagata wrote:

> Mount Kidome looked white
> As if I had seen the smoke
> Of campfires.
> But it was cherry blossoms.

Kidome was where Saigo fell; cherry blossoms are signs
of the fleeting nature of life.

A third major Meiji figure was Okuma Shigenobu, a
samurai from Hizen, the province surrounding Nagasaki.
There, Okuma learned Dutch and English and picked up
some of the mercantile spirit of the town. He later became a forceful public speaker, which stood him in good
stead as he was among the first Japanese party politicians.
Okuma spent the early years following the Restoration
in foreign affairs and economic matters. But as the deliberations on the constitution progressed, he had a falling
out with his colleagues. Okuma, among the more receptive
of the Meiji leaders to Western ideas, wanted to move too
far and too fast toward representative government for
their likes. Further, the clansmen from Satsuma and
Choshu were consolidating their hold on the government
and Okuma was an outsider. Despite the changes in Japan,
personal and clan loyalties still counted heavily.

Okuma was forced out in 1881 and the following year
founded a political party. Though he was interested in
Western political systems, the party was as much a vehicle
for opposition as it was the symbol of what Okuma be-

lieved politically. Ito had the bureaucrats, Yamagata had the army, Okuma looked to political action. Thus began what today is a characteristic of Japanese politics: the faction, rather than political principle, as a fundamental motivating force. Though Okuma later returned to power, he spent much of his long career in opposition to the oligarchy.

There were many others who left their imprints on Japan during the Meiji period. Matsukata Masayoshi, another Satsuma *samurai*, went to Europe in 1878 to study financial and banking systems and returned to become Minister of Finance. He swept away the nation's archaic economic order, put it through a painful deflationary wringer, established the central Bank of Japan, and laid out the economic foundation on which Japan's present prosperous economy rests. Itagaki Taisuke, from Tosa, was often at odds with those in power and was a prime mover in organizing political parties. At times he and Okuma collaborated, at other times they competed. Itagaki and Okuma began the first ties between the political world and the business world. Goto Shojiro, a friend of Itagaki's from Tosa, was also an "out" and joined Itagaki in political opposition to the oligarchy. Mori Arinori, from Satsuma, studied in England and served as Japanese minister in Washington, where he surveyed the American educational system. But when he became Minister of Education, he swung over hard to emphasize traditional Japanese virtues as the substance of education, with a German system as the form.

A few men became prominent for their outspoken advocacy of Westernization. Probably the leading exponent of Western learning was Fukuzawa Yukichi, who wrote volumes on Western politics, economics, and society. He founded Keio University and a leading newspaper, the *Jiji Shimpo*. Others, especially converts to Christianity, were equally strong, if not such eloquent, advocates of Western ideas. But their influence was marginal. They did not have the political, economic, military, or social position from which to command the scene. Some of their ideas were found appealing, but most were diluted in the onrushing stream of forces based in tradition that were carrying Japan forward.

Chapter 2

NATION BUILDING

"Enrich the Nation, Strengthen Its Arms" was the avowed goal of Japan's new leaders. They made steady and sometimes spectacular progress toward it during the forty-five years of the Meiji period. The Meiji men set about building a nation capable of maintaining its independence and achieving prestige equal to that of Western powers. Their approach was pragmatic and devoid of ideology, except for their devotion to the Imperial Way. They moved deliberately but without an over-all, preconceived scheme, solving problems as they arose. There were no five-year plans, no grand designs. Had they known of it, they might simply have used John F. Kennedy's 1960 campaign pledge "to get the country moving again."

That the Meiji Restoration was called a restoration was not mere chance. It was not a revolution, despite the changes it wrought. The men of Meiji restored the emperor to his ancient place at the center of Japanese life and restored to Japan the sense of national unity he represented. They renewed the vitality of existing Japanese institutions and added new ones. The Restoration was engineered by the upper classes and it continued to be controlled from above, changes filtering down from the top.

The circumstances of the day dictated an order of priorities. The Meiji men first consolidated their power, gained control of the country, and mobilized the people. With Western imperialism in Asia reaching a peak, they put strenuous effort into assembling a military force while placating the Western nations. The perceptive young *samurai* quickly realized that a sound economy is the basis for military power, and they directed immediate attention to that. They further recognized that only an educated people could construct and operate the economy Japan required. They were painfully aware that Western nations were far ahead of Japan and put much energy into selecting and acquiring what they needed to know from the West.

The men of Meiji put off tasks that were not immediately imperative. They patched together a temporary political organization until they had time to think about a permanent, more carefully devised system. Other than defense, they paid little heed to foreign affairs until their domestic house was in order. They gave even less thought to social problems or the welfare of the people in their concentration on national power.

The process of nation building was not smooth. The leaders agreed among themselves on the general objective of a strong, unified nation but often disagreed on methods. They had endless political quarrels over who should have authority and how it should be exercised. Ito and Yamagata advocated that a small elite hold the reins of government. Okuma and Itagaki contended that power should be spread over a wider group, though not to the public. In foreign affairs, Saigo wanted to move immediately into Korea to secure it from Western incursions. Kido argued that domestic problems must be solved first. Those advocating restraint won out at first. But the group in authority was later enlarged, and Japan eventually conquered Korea.

The Emperor's Charter Oath, issued in April 1868, was among the regime's early moves. It set out the general intention of the new government but was vague and committed its authors to nothing. The Charter Oath allowed for a wide range of interpretations and adjustments, which followed over the years. But it allayed suspicion of the new government and contributed to bringing support from the *daimyo*, the *samurai* who had not participated in the Restoration, and the scholars. The five-clause oath assured that the new regime would not be arbitrary; called on rulers and ruled to unite to advance the nation; said the common people would not be discontent; promised that the evil and base customs of the Tokugawa era would be abolished; and pledged to seek knowledge the world over to strengthen the nation.

Choosing a capital came shortly after. Three possibilities were listed: Kyoto, ancient court of the emperors; Osaka, center of commerce and economic power; Edo, stronghold of the Tokugawa shoguns and political center of Japan. The regime picked Edo and changed its name to Tokyo, or Eastern Capital. Moving the Emperor to Tokyo would make clear his return to authority, taking physical control of the city would prevent a Tokugawa counterattack, and taking over the Shogunate's bureaucracy and facilities would be easier and cheaper than establishing new ones elsewhere.

Once in Tokyo, the new leaders held no grudges against the bureaucrats and drew them back to their jobs. Some, indeed, rose quite high in the new government. Katsu Awa, a Tokugawa retainer, was Navy Minister in an early council and later was noted for his negotiating skill. Enomoto Takeaki fought for the Tokugawa against the imperial forces but became an admiral and an ambassador. Katsu and Enomoto are credited with founding the Japanese navy. The reserve of trained and experienced

Tokugawa administrators was one reason the Meiji government was successful; the bureaucracy, with its origins deep in Japanese history, provided a major continuity with the past and is today a powerful force in Japanese life.

The new leaders, mostly *samurai*, knew that it would be impossible to organize a national government or to undertake national policies unless they took power away from their old feudal clan leaders, the *daimyo*. The artifice they used was a measure of their political dexterity. The barons were ensconced in their domains, and had their own *samurai*, tax collectors, and bureaucracies. To order the domains dismantled would cut sharply into the barons' vested interests and arouse resistance. The new leaders decided to persuade the barons voluntarily to surrender their domains to the Emperor for the sake of national unity. Once the *daimyo* who had supported the Restoration did so, the others would have to follow.

The key *daimyo* were those of Satsuma and Choshu, who were approached by high-level delegations. After an agreement was reached in Choshu, the barons petitioned the Emperor to accept the surrender of his property. The petition said, in part: "Now that we are about to establish an entirely new form of government, the *kokutai* [national essence] and the sovereign authority must not in the slightest degree be yielded to subordinates. The place where your servants live is the Emperor's land, and those whom they rule are the Emperor's people. How can these be the property of subjects? Your servants accordingly beg respectfully to surrender their fiefs to Your Majesty. They ask that the Court act on the basis of what is right, giving what should be given and taking away what should be taken away; and that Your Majesty issue edicts redisposing of the enfeoffed land of your clans. Furthermore, they ask that the Court lay down regulations regarding all things, from the administration of troops to uniform and military equipment, so that everyone in the empire, both great and small, shall be caused to submit to one authority."

It was a brilliant stroke. In one swipe, the antiquated feudal houses were cut down. Outlying centers of power and military forces were brought under centralized control, at least nominally. In another deft but conciliatory move, the Meiji leaders hastened to appoint the former barons as governors of newly defined provinces, which almost coincided with their previous domains. It took the government two years to make central authority a reality, but the new regime had made an auspicious beginning. The *daimyo* were given stipends, as were the unemployed *samurai*, to tide them over. These were taken away several years later, but they sufficed to keep most armed opposition from arising.

At the same time the new leaders were getting a grip on the country, they found it imperative to attend to the nation's economy. The Shogunate had left a huge deficit. The new government borrowed from rich merchants and issued more money to get back on its feet. (This was inflationary, but correcting that had to wait.) The new money in circulation stimulated industry. The government's policy was to give every benefit to industry and to encourage the *samurai* to go into business. Many plants and businesses were started by the government in the early years, then sold to entrepreneurs at low prices. The Meiji government put a good bit of attention and money into "infrastructure," if that term could be used for those days. They sensed quickly that railroads, telegraph communications, lighthouses for harbors and the like would be needed if industry was to be nurtured. It was slow progress, because experience was lacking. But within ten years of the Restoration, Tokyo and Yokohama and several other cities were linked by railroad and a telegraph line ran through major Japanese cities. Other reforms included standardizing the currency in *yen* and putting tax collections in order.

The absence of foreign capital was a striking phenomenon in Meiji economic growth. The Japanese floated only two loans abroad, both in London. Foreign investment in Japan was also small. Foreigners came to trade, not to invest. Moreover, the Japanese did not want major segments of their economy controlled by foreigners, as was the case in China and Southeast Asia. Japan's efforts to build its economy largely out of the sweat of its own labor force seem all the more remarkable in today's world of foreign economic aid.

In contrast, foreign technical assistance was immense and was by far the greatest Western influence on Japan. Here again is a marked difference between then and now. Industrialized Western countries showed no interest in aiding an underdeveloped Japan. Instead, the Japanese sought out across the face of the globe the technicians and knowledge they needed. They sent missions and individuals abroad for surveys and studies and hired Westerners to come to Japan. But the Japanese made sure that the Westerners stayed only so long as they were needed. As soon as Japanese technicians acquired the skills to replace Westerners, they were thanked, paid off, and sent home.

The mission to America and Europe led by Prince Iwakura in 1871 was the most extensive single effort after the Restoration. It spent two years abroad, having gone ostensibly to ask for revision of the unequal treaties forced on the Tokugawa Shogunate, but in this it was not successful. The members of the mission learned, however, a tremendous amount about Western technology. They spent more time in factories, shipyards, telegraph offices, railroad yards, and textile mills than in the ministries of their host governments.

Japanese participation in the 1873 Vienna International Exposition was another major undertaking. It was the first advertising and trade promotion abroad for Japanese products. More important, it gave the Japanese an opportunity to observe European manufactures. After the exposition, Japanese officials traveled throughout the Continent to see how Europeans manufactured and marketed their products. Following these initial missions, soldiers, businessmen, engineers, and students went abroad to pick up specialized knowledge.

In turn, hundreds of Westerners hired by government or industry went to Japan. Others came on their own, mostly as traders, but stayed to contribute to Japanese economic development. The Ministry of Industry had about one hundred and thirty foreigners on its payroll by the end of Meiji's first decade.

A British engineer named Morrel came in 1870 to supervise the construction of the Tokyo-Yokohama railroad. Other English technicians helped build the first telegraph lines. Richard Henry Brunton became Japan's first lighthouse builder and erected beacons over much of the coastline. In agriculture, two Americans, General Horace Capron, the U.S. Commissioner of Agriculture, and Dr. William Clark, president of Massachusetts Agricultural College, were important advisers. Industrialists imported entire textile mills from France and brought in French technicians to set them up and to teach Japanese girls how to run them. Later in the Meiji period, German technicians helped to start the Japanese steel industry. Among the private citizens who taught the Japanese much were Englishmen Thomas Glover, who built shipyards and opened mines in Kyushu, and John Black, a newspaperman who was singularly influential in establishing the Japanese press.

Concurrent with industrialization, the Meiji government started educating its people. It had a fair base from which to push forward. During the Tokugawa period, each of the domains had schools to educate *samurai* and their sons. Many temples and shrines also had schools. An estimated 40 per cent of the adult male population could read at the time of the Restoration.

Education under the Meiji government was another example of Western form and Japanese substance. A French model was used to write the Education Law of 1872, establishing compulsory elementary education. It took many years before this could be implemented, however, as buildings had to be built, teachers trained, textbooks written and printed. An American, Professor David Murray of Rutgers University, went to Tokyo in 1873 to serve as an adviser to the Ministry of Education. He was particularly influential in setting curriculum standards for training teachers. Another American, Marion M. Scott, trained the first teachers. American textbooks were translated for school use. At one time, some five thousand foreigners were either teaching or training Japanese teachers.

But the foreign influence was limited mostly to techniques. The Japanese quickly imposed their own views on the curriculum and the underlying purpose of education. They relied heavily on Confucian concepts and saw education as a means to train the people for service to the state. Morality, patriotism, loyalty were stressed; individual attainment and fulfillment ignored.

The Imperial Rescript on Education, promulgated in 1890, was the best evidence of the tenor in Japanese education. It was more than a guide to educational principles; it was a precept for all Japanese social and political behavior. A classic in Confucian thought and language, it was devoid of any taint from the West. In its entirety, it read:

Know ye, Our subjects:
Our Imperial Ancestors have founded our Empire

on a basis broad and everlasting, and have deeply and firmly implanted virtue; Our subjects ever united in loyalty and filial piety have from generation to generation illustrated the beauty thereof. This is the glory of the fundamental character of Our Empire, and herein also lies the source of Our education. Ye, Our subjects, be filial to your parents, affectionate to your brothers and sisters; as husbands and wives be harmonious, as friends true; bear yourselves in modesty and moderation; extend your benevolence to all; pursue learning and cultivate arts, and thereby develop intellectual faculties and perfect moral powers; furthermore, advance public good and promote common interests; always respect the Constitution and observe the laws; should emergency arise, offer yourselves courageously to the State; and thus guard and maintain the prosperity of Our Imperial Throne coeval with heaven and earth. So shall ye not only be Our good and faithful subjects, but render illustrious the best traditions of your forefathers.

The Way here set forth is indeed the teaching bequeathed by Our Imperial Ancestors, to be observed alike by Their Descendants and the subjects, infallible for all ages and true in all places. It is Our wish to lay it to heart in all reverence, in common with you, Our subjects, that we may all attain to the same virtue.

In retrospect, it seems safe to say that the rescript on education was the single most influential document to come out of the Meiji period. It touched the life of every child who attended school, and it was held up to him as an ethical guide throughout his life.

On the military front, the Japanese had learned well from the West the value of military power. The new leaders could see the expansion of the British into India, Burma, and the Malay Peninsula; the Dutch in the East Indies; the French in Indochina; the Spanish (later to be replaced by the Americans) in the Philippines; and, to the north, the Russians in Siberia. In China, all the major Western powers were contesting for spheres of influence and special privileges. The Japanese themselves felt the indignities of the unequal treaties and feared that further direct incursions were on the way.

Shortly after helping to defeat the Tokugawa forces, Yamagata Aritomo went to France and Prussia to study modern military organization. He returned to Japan to set up an army that was a melding of the *samurai* warrior of Japan and the mass, conscripted soldier of the West. This army was first tried in a punitive expedition to Taiwan in 1875, then against Saigo Takamori's Satsuma rebels in 1877. Based on those experiences, Yamagata in 1878 organized a general staff on the Prussian model and undertook a ten-year expansion plan. A war college was set up in 1883 so that young officers no longer had to be sent abroad to study. At the same time, island Japan's navy took shape. A naval construction program began, with the Japanese building their own hulls but relying on imported machinery and ordinance to equip them. Progress was hindered, however, by limited budgets and the lack of a heavy industrial base. The Japanese continued to build and play for time.

By 1880, the Meiji leaders had consolidated their position, had economic and educational progress under way, and had the beginnings of a modern armed force. They gradually turned their attention to the things they had originally delayed, particularly politics, law, and financial reform.

The men of Meiji looked to statesmen in Europe and America for advice on formulating a political system. But they relied on their own instincts and Japanese political precedent in making the final decisions. The net result was a political order that was mostly Japanese in content, though it resembled Western systems in form.

The oligarchs began assembling their ideas in 1878 for a constitution that would be the basis for the new political order. Former U.S. President Ulysses S. Grant stopped in

Tokyo on a world tour the next year and met with the Emperor and other leaders. They asked his advice on representative institutions. Grant, aware the Japanese had had no experience with elections and parliaments, advised caution and a gradual approach. In 1881, Ito Hirobumi was given the responsibility for writing the constitution, which was to be drafted in secret and promulgated by the Emperor without public participation.

Ideas on the constitution came from memorials submitted by each of the very top men. Ito sifted through them, injected his own thoughts, and determined the basic outlines. All authority would reside in the emperor and would be implemented by his closest advisers. The constitution would allow for a parliament, but its function would be to serve the emperor and not to obstruct the rule of imperial advisers, ministers, and the bureaucracy. The military would not be responsible to the civil arm of the government but directly to the emperor. The duties rather than the rights of citizens would be stressed.

Ito had already decided most of these major points when he went to Europe in 1882 to study constitutions there and to find a suitable framework on which to mold the Japanese constitution. Among those with whom he conferred, the German Chancellor, Count Otto von Bismarck, and several noted German political scientists made the deepest impressions. They confirmed Ito's ideas and gave him arguments to use in refuting opponents. After he returned to Japan in 1883, Ito and three trusted assistants began putting the constitution together with the help of a German jurist.

In the spring and summer of 1888, the newly formed Privy Council, led by Ito and including the top oligarchs, debated the draft but made few changes in Ito's version. The Emperor promulgated the constitution on February 11, 1889. This was Kigensetsu, or Empire Day, anniversary of the mythical ascent to the throne of the first ruler, the

Emperor Jimmu, in 660 B.C. The ceremony took only ten minutes in the Emperor's palace. The Emperor rose from the throne, read a short proclamation recalling his ancestor's virtues and his subjects' duties, took the parchment scroll on which the constitution was written from a prince of the court, handed it to another official, and left the room. The constitution, which came into force twenty-one years after the Restoration, remained unchanged until the American Occupation decreed that it be abolished.

Drawing up laws and a legal system to implement the constitution resulted in a much greater clash between Japanese and Western concepts. This was a long, complicated procedure because the Japanese simply had no legal precedents, no concept of what law is. From time immemorial, Japanese government had been government of men, not government by law. The Japanese people respected authority and obeyed it. They had no concept of individual rights and laws to protect them. Custom, which was unwritten and which evolved with time, determined how men lived with one another. Disputes were resolved by conciliation and compromise between those of the same class and by the power and position of a superior in conflict with an inferior. Various codes laid down ethical principles and preserved class privileges but contained little legal procedure. Even the codes were scant. An 1892 compilation of all the codes from the seventh century to the Restoration came to but a thousand pages.

Moreover, the Japanese had to conform to certain Western legal standards if they were to persuade the Western powers to revoke the unequal treaties. These treaties were based on the premise that Japanese custom was unfit to be applied to foreign residents. The Western powers insisted on the right to try their citizens in consular courts according to their own national laws. They further insisted on controlling Japanese import and export tariffs. The Japanese found the treaties an indignity to their pride and national sovereignty and a hindrance to economic development. Further, opponents of the Meiji regime tried to use the treaties as a political weapon much the same way the opponents of the Tokugawa Shogunate had used the breakdown of seclusion. The Meiji government began asking that the treaties be revised shortly after the Restoration. But the Western powers said it would not be possible until the Japanese had brought their laws up to Western standards. The Meiji oligarchy had no way to force the Westerners to give up their special privileges other than to do as they were bid.

The Meiji rulers were too preoccupied to give this high priority until they started thinking about a constitution. Not until 1886 did the government put its full attention on a new legal system. It set up a Bureau of Study and Legal Codes, which drafted a stricter criminal law, reworked the civil code, and wrote a commercial code. A German jurist helped write the commercial code and influenced work on the others. These versions, however, still did not satisfy the Western powers. Ito Hirobumi set up a revising committee that included prominent jurists who had studied English, French, and German law. They produced, after many changes, final versions that were an amalgam of Japanese and Western laws.

Economic changes in Japan, which brought new forms of property ownership in corporations and the accumulation of money wealth, required Western-style laws. But the Meiji government made sure that laws pertaining to the family, such as marriage and private property, did not tamper with the household as the basic unit of Japanese society. This was particularly true in ensuring that nothing disturbed the continuation of the family line. It was important to all Japanese that provision be made for the reverence of ancestors, which could be accomplished only by having the family name carried on either by blood or adopted descendants.

The Meiji laws complemented the constitution and the educational system in giving the state control over Japanese citizens, which was not a great departure from the feudal tradition. They did little to introduce Western concepts of individual human, civil, or political rights. The concept that law rather than custom, or law rather than men, should govern did not penetrate far.

Finance Minister Matsukata Masayoshi's economic reforms, begun in 1881, were a contrast to the Japanese essence in the constitution and the mix of Japanese and Western concepts in the legal system. Matsukata's fundamental restructuring of the nation's finances was based heavily on European models.

Japan's finances were in disorder in 1880 due to the disruptions and changes of the previous decade. The banking system was not working, currency values fluctuated sharply, inflation sapped what little purchasing power the common people had. To put the nation into sound financial order, Matsukata instructed that the national budget be frozen, a fund be established to service and reduce the public debt from loans incurred ten years earlier, and new taxes be imposed. He further enforced a stringent deflationary policy. Over the next ten years, and later as prime minister and concurrently finance minister, Matsukata founded the central Bank of Japan, had the banking laws rewritten, and set up special banks to stimulate Japan's economic growth. The Yokohama Specie Bank became Japan's main foreign-exchange bank, financing trade and enabling Japanese importers and exporters to bypass foreigners in the port cities. Nippon Kangyo Ginko, usually translated "Japan Hypothec Bank," made long-term loans to aid industrial development. The ultimate in European influence came in 1897 when Japan adopted the gold standard.

Three major trends marked the second half of the Meiji period, beginning in 1889 with the promulgation of the constitution. Internally, leaders of political parties forced the oligarchy to share some power with them. This was the first enlargement of the ruling group and the first step toward the Establishment that runs Japan today. Along with that went the rise of the *zaibatsu*, the great business combines that dominated the economy. Anxious to share in the power held by the oligarchy and the politicians, business leaders took their first steps toward membership in the Establishment. Most important was the elevation of Japan to first-class international status and admittance to the circle of major world powers.

The leaders of the political party movement were Okuma Shigenobu, of Hizen, and Itagaki Taisuke, of Tosa. Of the original Meiji leaders, they were the "outs," the "ins" being men from Satsuma and Choshu. Okuma and Itagaki organized political parties as a power base to get into the government, or at least to participate in the exercise of power. The political parties were not mass parties in the Western sense, formed by common ideological and policy beliefs, appealing for wide public support, and encouraging popular participation. They were, rather, small elite factions held together by the leadership of the organizers, personal loyalties, common interest in acquiring power, but not by principle or ideology. Parties had a tentative start in the 1880's. The real beginning was made in preparation for the first election for the Diet in July 1890. Okuma had founded the Progressive Party and Itagaki the Liberal Party. These two and a smaller third party made a good showing in the election, in which about 500,000 of a population of 40,000,000 were eligible to vote. But the oligarchs continued to control the government. Okuma and Itagaki joined forces in June 1898 to form a cabinet, but were out by November. The parties, however, had made enough of an impact to jolt the oligarchs.

In 1900, Ito Hirobumi founded the Political Friends Association to counter the party movement. This was a maneuver to get rid of opposition by making it a part of the mainstream.

The *zaibatsu*, usually translated "financial cliques," were clusters of financial, commercial, and industrial firms centered on a bank at first and later on holding companies. They were tied together by joint stockholding, interlocking directorates, and personal relationships. They contributed money to politicians in return for influence in national decisions. The Big Four were Mitsui, Mitsubishi, Sumitomo, and Yasuda. The Mitsui family had started in the rice and moneylending business in Osaka in mid-Tokugawa days. Mitsubishi was the firm of Iwasaki Yataro, a *samurai* who had been business manager for the Tosa clan. The Sumitomo family started mining in Kyushu during the seventeenth century. Yasuda was the firm of a lower-class *samurai* from the Japan Sea coast who came to Edo to set up a money-exchange shop just before the Tokugawa fell. Each of the firms had put its capital into new and expanding ventures, often with government help as part of the Meiji policy of fostering industry and trade.

Japan gained its ranking among the world powers during this period by ridding itself of the unequal treaties and by war. Political and economic developments by 1890 gave the Japanese enough national strength to negotiate an end to the unequal treaties imposed during the last days of the Tokugawa regime. They succeeded first with Great Britain, which agreed in 1894 that by 1899 its subjects would no longer be exempt from Japanese law. Other nations followed the British lead, but it was not until 1911 that the Japanese finally gained control of their own customs administration.

Of the few things that Japan learned well from the West, technology stood first. Military aggression and imperialism was a close second. Before its exposure to the

West, military expansion overseas was practically unknown to the Japanese. The exception was Korea, supposedly invaded in the misty days before recorded history by the Empress Jingo (hence the term *jingoistic*). Japan actually ruled part of Korea from the fourth to the seventh centuries, and invaded and was repulsed at the end of the sixteenth century. Japanese pirates marauded along the coasts of Korea and China at other times. Japan's only foreign threat, prior to the modern era, was from the Mongols in 1274 and 1281. The mighty armies of Kublai Khan gave up on the first try because bad weather endangered the fleet, and were destroyed the second time when a typhoon smashed their armada. This was the *kamikaze*, the Wind of the Gods or Divine Wind of later fame.

The Japanese had had internal wars, some prolonged and bloody, but most of the fighting was limited to that small class of professional warriors, the *samurai*. There was no military tradition among the mass of the peasantry. Neither were there Japanese explorers and seafarers, traders and missionaries, nor armies that built empires in the European fashion, until the Japanese learned these things from the West.

The Japanese military expansion that started in 1895 was centered in Korea, which accounts for much of the ill feeling between the two peoples today. The Japanese have contempt for their former colonial subjects, and the Koreans have bitterness for the sufferings they endured during forty years of harsh rule. The Japanese defeated a weak Chinese dynasty in 1895 and took away its sphere of influence in Korea, which brought Japan notice in the West. The Japanese also demanded portions of Chinese territory and an indemnity. The Russians, however, were alarmed by the Japanese success and, backed by the French and Germans, forced the Japanese to retract part of their

demands. Three years later, the Russians took for themselves that which they had denied to the Japanese.

Infuriated, the Japanese made careful plans to eliminate
future Russian threats. Meanwhile, Japanese troops participated alongside European and American soldiers in putting
down the Boxer Rebellion in China in 1900 and brought
themselves new prestige. In 1902, Japan and Britain concluded the Anglo-Japanese naval alliance, which gave the
Japanese a free hand to attack the Russians and the British
a new weight to place in the European balance of power.
The Japanese, in 1904–5, destroyed two Russian fleets and
drove the Russian army from Korea, which now became
a Japanese protectorate. Japan also won special rights in
Manchuria and control of the southern half of Sakhalin,
the island off the Russian Far Eastern coast. Japan quietly
annexed Korea in 1910 and made it part of its empire.

The Meiji period came to a close when Emperor Mutsuhito died on July 30, 1912. The man who had ridden in
a lacquered palanquin carried by silk-robed bearers through
fiefs and rice fields had lived to see his countrymen build
railroads across a united, economically advancing land. He
had seen a Japan that lagged far behind the West become
an equal among the world's major powers. He had seen
his people select what they wanted from the West and
graft it on to their own society without much change in
their national essence. He had seen Japan begin to take on
the appearances of a Western nation but remain true to
its own fundamental values and ways and beliefs. It had
not been easy, and not all of the results were good. The
people of Japan had not shared much in their nation's
progress, and other Asians had begun to feel the heel of
Japanese aggression. But by the imperfect standards of
historical achievement, it had been a great age.

Chapter 3

DISTORTION and
RENEWAL

Emperor Yoshihito's ascension to the throne after the death of his father was not a good omen for the three decades ahead. He was an unhappy figure, mentally incompetent, who proved to be a tarnished emblem for the nation. The years between 1912 and 1945 were a sorry contrast to the Meiji era. New leaders rose to steer the country into turmoil at home and violence abroad instead of turning the hard-earned Meiji progress to the benefit of the people. Western influences continued, particularly in technology, but the selective and regulated borrowing ceased. The assimilation of Western forms, especially political, was a disruptive process. During the confusion, a reaction set in and the Japanese betrayed the ideals and ways of their own tradition. It was a time of duplicity and expedience, of political assassination and economic exploitation, of ultranationalism and aggression. In retrospect, it was a deviation from the mainstream flow of Japanese history. The distortion was aggravated by the West itself, which came to the end of the century-long Pax Britannica and blundered into an age of ravaging conflict. The democratic nations of the West bungled and failed to stop Japanese militancy before war became inevitable.

Disaster was the result for Japan. The devastation and defeat of World War II left the Japanese political order shattered, the nation's economy and industry in ruins, its dream of national purpose and international prestige gone aglimmering. The Japanese sank into despair and struggled just to stay alive. But they are a resilient and determined people. They picked up the pieces of their lives, their economy, their politics, and their own social institutions and rebuilt them in remarkably short order, considering the damage that had been done. Like their Meiji forefathers, their approach was pragmatic and they did whatever was immediately necessary to get the country functioning again. Then this ever-introspective people began questioning what had gone wrong and why; who and what kind of people they are; what sort of nation theirs should be and how could they make it so. The search has taken more than two decades and has not yet produced all the answers. But a renewal of Japanese identity and pride is taking place. Where it will take Japan in coming years, no one can say with certainty. It seems clear, however, that the Japanese will be guided by their own values and will make their decisions their own way, without much influence from the West.

In the course of events that led to the disaster of 1945, the men at the top made the decisions and determined the character of the country. The Japanese people, for the most part, followed obediently as they always have. But the leaders who replaced the men of Meiji were not of Meiji caliber. They lacked the charisma, the talent, and the vision of their predecessors. Moreover, the new leadership comprised men of disparate origins and lacked the underlying cohesion the men of Meiji had had despite their continual struggles among themselves. The new men included aristocrats from the old court families, peers named to give recognition to prestige in various fields, sons of *samurai*, a second and third generation of bureaucrats turned out by Tokyo Imperial University and other schools, soldiers from the rural areas, politicians from the cities, businessmen gaining influence because they produced the economic power of the nation. With this widening of the top class and the absence of strong personalities, those with power reverted to more traditional patterns of collective leadership. Four major groups contended for supremacy, the military eventually winning out. The bureaucracy steadily accumulated power through its day-to-day administration of the country. The politicians, in loose alliance with the businessmen, made their bid in the years immediately following World War I but were not long successful. The military, by contrast, became increasingly powerful from World War I on and came out on top in the late 1920's and early 1930's. Never, however, was any one group in absolute control, even during World War II. There was always a certain amount of give-and-take and adjustment in the power balance. To tip the balance in its favor the military finally resorted to force in the late 1930's.

The imperial role changed due to both succession and the aims of the new leaders. The Emperor Meiji had participated less and less in affairs of state toward the end of his reign, resuming a much more symbolic role as the father of the national family. Emperor Yoshihito, known after his death as Emperor Taisho (Great Righteousness), was only a figurehead until his death in 1926. His son, Crown Prince Hirohito, had been named Prince Regent several years earlier. When he became Emperor, the ultranationalists and militarists were moving to take over control of the government. Emperor Hirohito, calling his reign Showa (Radiant Peace), is a mild and retiring man more interested in marine biology than government; he shortly became little more than a ceremonial pawn of the militarists.

The two most prominent aristocrats of the period tried but failed to halt the ominous growth of militarism. Saionji Kimmochi, a protégé of Ito Hirobumi, became Prime Minister and head of Ito's party in 1906 and was again Prime Minister for several months in 1912. Saionji was a moderate and prudent man who opposed oppression at home and adventures abroad. But he did not have Ito's dynamic qualities and, in the years close to his death in 1940, he was in frail health and could not control the militarists. Prince Konoye Fumimaro, in turn a protégé of Saionji, was a member of the upper House of Peers in the prewar Diet, was three times Prime Minister, and became president of the Privy Council advising the Emperor in 1939–40. He, too, was no leader and appears to have made his thinking and action conform to whatever suggestions were made by the last person to talk with him. His positions vacillated from moderation to extremism. He committed suicide shortly after the war's end when he received news that he would be charged as a war criminal.

Of the new breed of professional politicians, Hara Kei, Kato Komei, and Hamaguchi Osachi were representative. Hara was a newsman and government official before the turn of the century, became executive secretary of Ito's party in 1900, was appointed to an Ito cabinet, and was elected to the Diet in 1902. He served in two later cabinets before becoming party president in 1914 and Prime Minister in 1918. He set a route through the bureaucracy, party, and Diet that is commonplace for today's politicians. Hara, the first prime minister who was not a noble, *samurai*, or military officer, was a tough and able politician. He believed in parliamentary government, reform of Japan's rule over its colonies in Taiwan and Korea, and curbing military influence in politics. He had close ties with the Mitsui combine.

Kato Komei graduated from law school, studied in England and Europe, and married an Iwasaki, the family of the Mitsubishi combine. He entered the Foreign Ministry and rose to be ambassador to London in 1908. Kato became president of the Constitutional Party and Prime Minister in 1924. He cut the military budget and advocated a conciliatory policy toward Russia and China, though he wanted to see China under Japanese influence. Kato pushed through a bill giving all Japanese males over the age of twenty-five the vote. At the same time, he had the Peace Preservation Law adopted to counterbalance the widening of popular rights. Kato died in office in 1926.

Hamaguchi Osachi, known as "The Lion," was a civil servant who came up through the bureaucracy and became Prime Minister in 1929. Hamaguchi believed that the cabinet, with the support of the Diet, should run the government. He worked for fiscal stability, limitation on arms and arms expenditures, and restraint in foreign policy. His business backing came from Mitsubishi.

Hara, Kato, and Hamaguchi were political practitioners striving to make viable a political system that was not yet fitted to Japanese political realities. But they lacked the power of the military and the prestige of the nobility. They had some support from intellectuals and they were appealing to the public. The people, however, were not a solid base on which to build policy and programs.

Indeed, a major group opposing the politicians came from the lower reaches of the population. These were the discontented young men from the rural areas who felt a deep alienation from the political, economic, and social developments they saw in an industrializing Japan. Economic progress at that time was concentrated in the industrial sector, while the farm areas had been left behind. The young men from the countryside believed that the *zaibatsu* businessmen were exploiting the country for their own profit and not for the benefit of the common people. They considered all politicians corrupt and self-seeking and scorned any thought of democracy. They believed that Western ideas and institutions were demoralizing Japan, especially the imperial institution, and they decried the loss of Japan's unique way. Many of these young men, especially the second sons of farm families whose first son inherited the land, went into the army. The new officer corps of the Japanese Army was staffed heavily with these young men, who took with them their discontent and added to it in the army the mystique of having risen to *samurai* status. They became ultranationalistic and were easily enlisted by those advocating military expansion into supporting the concept that Japan should drive the West from Asia and replace Western colonialism with Japanese imperialism.

These young men, many of them members of secret societies and ultranationalistic factions within the military service, had a marked impact on events during this era. The impact was often violent. Assassination had long been a part of the Japanese political scene, both ancient and modern; there were a number of assassinations and attempts in the Meiji period. Then, in 1921, Prime Minister Hara was murdered in front of the Tokyo railroad station. The same year Yasuda Zenjiro, founder of the Yasuda *zaibatsu*, fell at the hands of the assassin. Hara was killed by fanatics who feared that politicians were succumbing to Western influence, Yasuda by fanatics who believed that he and other businessmen opposed military expansion because they were interested only in profit and not in the glory of Japan. Other politicians and businessmen were threatened, and in 1923 there was even a plot against Crown Prince Hirohito.

The wave broke, however, with the murder of Prime Minister Hamaguchi in 1930 by assassins who later said they acted in the name of the Emperor to preserve Japan's unique national essence. Hamaguchi was shot at the same place as Hara, but lingered on for a year. Finance Minister Inouye Junnosuke was killed in February 1932, for opposing arms expenditures. Dan Takuma, managing director of the Mitsui *zaibatsu*, was cut down the next month. Prime Minister Inukai Tsuyoshi was killed in his official residence on May 15 in the "5/15 incident" by young naval officers.

Forty young army officers organized themselves into the Shimpeitai (Heaven-sent-soldiers) in 1933 and intended to assassinate imperial advisers who opposed their ultranationalistic aims and even possibly the Emperor himself. Their plans were discovered and they were arrested. When a faction in the army caused a shuffle of army commanders in 1935, a young colonel murdered one general and failed in his attempt to kill another. More threats were made against politicians, scholars, and moderates.

The great slaughter came on February 26, 1936, in the "2/26 incident" when fourteen hundred young officers and their troops attempted a coup, took control of key government buildings in downtown Tokyo, and murdered Finance Minister Takahashi Korekiyo, Lord Keeper of the Privy Seal Saito Makoto, Inspector General of Military Training Watanabe Jotaro, and Colonel Matsuo Denzo, who deliberately misled the assassins into thinking he was Prime Minister Okada Keisuke. Grand Chamberlain Suzuki Kantaro was wounded and Prince Saionji Kimmochi and Count Makino Nobuaki escaped.

Even the ultranationalists in high military places could not stomach this outrage, although they were sympathetic with its motivation. Seventeen of the assassins were tried and executed. The militarists, however, had gained the upper hand. The frightened moderates appeased the military command in hopes that the senior officers would henceforth keep their juniors under better control.

The careers and ideas of the militarists were reflected

in Tanaka Giichi, Araki Sadao, and Tojo Hideki. They were among those who marched Japan down the road to military ventures abroad, then aggression, and finally to full-scale war. They began by taking over German concessions in China during World War I and by sending an expedition into Siberia between 1918 and 1922 to penetrate as far west as Lake Baikal. The invasion of Manchuria was engineered on a flimsy pretext in 1931 and was followed by the war in China in 1937. They sent troops to Indochina after the fall of France in 1940 and finally ordered their planes to bomb Pearl Harbor and open World War II in December 1941.

Tanaka Giichi came from Choshu, attended the military staff college, rose to be the army's leading specialist on Russia, and became Minister of War in 1918. He became Prime Minister and Foreign Minister in 1927 and pursued an active policy in China, especially in trying to stop the unification drive led by Generalissimo Chiang Kai-shek. But he was forced out in 1929 and retired from public life to die shortly after in the arms of his mistress, possibly by suicide. Tanaka's name was associated after his death with a mysterious document known as the Tanaka Memorial. It purportedly was a plan for the conquest of Manchuria, China, and the rest of Asia, possibly even the world. The authenticity of the memorial is doubted today, even though a text was published in an English-language paper in Shanghai in 1931.

Another professional soldier, Araki Sadao, became Minister of War in 1932 and was more powerful than the Prime Minister. Araki was a latter-day *samurai*, a man who lived simply and had no personal ambitions for wealth or power. He was dedicated to *Kodo*, the Imperial Way, and a leading advocate of expanding Japan's domination of Asia and throwing out the Western powers. Araki carried his plans forward until 1935, when he was forced out temporarily during a war struggle between two army factions.

But he returned as Minister of Education in 1938 to prepare Japan psychologically and emotionally for all-out aggression. He was convicted as a war criminal by the Allied tribunal in 1948 and sentenced to life imprisonment.

Tojo Hideki, Japan's wartime leader, was a curiously unprepossessing man, short, skinny, bald, and wearing round eyeglasses. But he was a skilled organizer and administrator known as "The Razor" in the Kwangtung Army, his base of power in Manchuria. Tojo was that army's chief of military policy, then its chief of staff, finally its commander. He returned to Tokyo in 1938 to be Inspector General of Military Aviation, became Vice-Minister of War in 1939, Minister of War in 1940, and Prime Minister in October 1941, just before the December 7 attack on Pearl Harbor. Tojo either won over the last opposing elements to expansion or forced them into submission. He had the backing of businessmen who had made their fortunes in Manchurian exploitation but not the support of the older *zaibatsu* houses. Many *zaibatsu* executives thought Japan could do just as well through trade and investment without the necessity of military expenditures and the risk of war. Tojo was convinced that Japan could succeed only by driving the West from Asia and by going to war with the United States, a course he had already decided before he took office. By 1944, however, the war was going badly for Japan, and he was dismissed. He retired to his Tokyo home and was occasionally consulted about the war. He attempted suicide in 1945 when American troops came to arrest him, but survived, was tried as a war criminal, and executed by hanging in 1948.

The intellectuals of the prewar period provided all groups aspiring to lead Japan with a mélange of justification and rationalization. Moderates argued that Western-style institutions could be made to work in Japan in harmony with Japanese thought and practice. Ultranationalists advocated a complete disdain for the West and a return to what they saw as the pure essence of the true Japan. Marxist and non-Marxist leftists looked for an entirely new communist or socialist society.

Yoshino Sakuzo, professor of political theory at Tokyo Imperial University, wrote long essays to show that Western-style democracy was not incompatible with Japan's Imperial Way. In 1916, he defined "democracy as the policy in exercising political power of valuing the profit, happiness, and opinions of the people." He used somewhat Confucian arguments to show that "since the Imperial Family is the unique head of the national family, it is utterly unthinkable that it should become necessary in the interest of the Imperial Family to disregard the interest of the people." He further said that even if there were conflicts between the two, the emperor's benevolence would resolve them. "Since democracy relates to the sovereign's way of using his powers," he wrote, "there is nothing to prevent him from establishing the basic principle that he will not arbitrarily disregard the welfare of the people."

Perhaps the most controversial of the constitutionalist theories was Minobe Tatsukichi's belief that the emperor was an organ of the state. Minobe, professor of constitutional law at Tokyo Imperial University, wrote that "if the nation is likened to the human body, the Emperor occupies the position of its head." He said the emperor, like the brain, "is the pivotal and paramount organ." Minobe came under attack in 1934 for heresy. He defended himself in the House of Peers, the upper house of the Diet of which he was a member, by upholding the unique qualities of Japan. "I am second to none," he said, "in my deeply rooted conviction that our unique *kokutai* [national essence] is our people's greatest glory and that therein partly lies the strength of our nation. The greatest duty of the people is to clarify the concept of our *kokutai* and to support and uphold it." Minobe denied that incursions from the West were undermining the *kokutai*. He said that "one does not have to go to the length of studying foreign countries in order to see that a nation's law is transformed and changed by the influence of actual circumstances." Minobe's most telling rebuttal to his attackers, and perhaps the most telling commentary on the day, was: "Even though they style themselves believers in the Japanese principles, that gang which wantonly prides itself upon attacking and entrapping others is at great variance with the true Japanese spirit."

Among the leading ultranationalistic writers from the rural areas was Kita Ikki, whose writings reflected their violent discontent. The son of a Sado Island *sake* brewer, he associated with members of the Amur Society (sometimes called the Black Dragon Society), and drifted into a belief that was both radical and reactionary at the same time. He wanted changes that would eliminate what he believed to be *zaibatsu* exploitation, corrupt politicking, and bureaucratic restrictions on the Imperial House. Japan, in Kita's view, must rule Asia for Asia's own good. He praised the assassin of Yasuda Zenjiro and participated in the assassination and the coup attempted by army extremists on February 26, 1936. He was executed for that in 1937.

Kita showed a nationalistic paranoia in his "Outline Plan for the Reorganization of Japan." He wrote: "At present the Japanese Empire is faced with a national crisis unparalleled in its history; it faces dilemmas at home and abroad. The vast majority of the people feel insecure in their livelihood and they are on the point of taking a lesson from the collapse of European societies, while those who monopolize political, military, and economic power simply hide themselves and, quaking with fear, try to maintain their unjust position. Abroad, neither England, America, Germany, nor Russia has kept its word, and even our neighbor China, which long benefited from the protection we provided through the Russo-Japanese war, not only failed to repay us but instead despises us."

The official doctrine of the militarists was the *Kokutai no Hongi*, or Fundamentals of Our National Essence, published by the Ministry of Education in 1937. The book was a course in national ideology for schools and study groups to discuss and bring about a national uniformity. It reaffirmed Japan's unique *kokutai*, warned against Western influences, and stressed the overriding importance of the nation, not the individual. It dwelt on the virtues of loyalty and patriotism, filial piety, harmony (meaning conformity), the martial spirit of *bushido* (way of the warrior), selflessness, and devotion to the emperor. It called on the Japanese people "to build up a new Japanese culture by adopting and sublimating Western cultures with our national essence as the basis."

It has been fashionable for Japanese leftist critics in recent years to point to the Meiji men as the originators of Japan's woes during the wars, defeat, occupation, and recovery of 1931–1951. They laid the responsibility on Ito Hirobumi, Yamagata Aritomo, and their colleagues, whom they regard as reactionary and dictatorial. History would seem to show, however, that they are mistaken. Authoritarian as the men of Meiji were, they were not the ones who led Japan to the trials and ruin of this century. Rather, those responsible were the ultranationalist thinkers and militaristic aggressors of the 1930's, who distorted the best ideals and traditions of Japan. It might be added, too, that many of the critics today were young adults during that period and did little or nothing to stop Tanaka, Araki, Tojo, and their cohorts.

Every American and European who has visited Japan in the postwar era and seen the diligent and orderly Japanese going about their normal lives must have asked himself: How could these people have started the war? There is no single or simple answer, but with the passage of time and the advantage of perspective, several fundamental, interrelated motives suggest themselves.

The imperialism learned from the West is surely one. This was particularly true in Manchuria and China, where the Japanese felt they had a special position and were deep in trade and investment. Japan had come late to the imperialist race, but was determined to have its share of the spoils.

Fear of the West, not just in cultural but in military terms, was another motive that loomed large in the Japanese mind. The Japanese believed themselves to be surrounded and threatened by the Americans, the British, and the Russians, and to a lesser extent by the Dutch and French in Southeast Asia. The rising power of Russian communism, which the Japanese conservatives loathed, added to this.

Nationalism and the right to an equal place in the sun with the Western powers was an ever-growing sentiment of the 1930's—and not just among the militarists. The Japanese were led to see themselves as the deliverers of Asia from the West. Okawa Shumei, organizer of an ultranationalistic society, wrote: "The words 'East-West' struggle, however, simply states a concept and it does not follow from this that a united Asia will be pitted against a united Europe. Actually, there will be one country acting as the champion of Asia and one country acting as the champion of Europe, and it is these who must fight in order that a new world may be realized. It is my belief that Heaven has decided on Japan as its champion of the East."

The specter of racial inequality, real and imagined, stared deep into the Japanese soul. It was rooted in the Gentlemen's Agreement to prohibit Japanese immigration into the United States in 1907, the exclusion policy of "white" Australia, what the Japanese considered condescending slurs such as the phrase "little brown brothers," failure to have a racial equality clause written into the League of Nations Charter, and the American exclusion law in 1924. Colonel Hashimoto Kingoro, one of the army's extremist agitators in the 1930's, expressed the bitterness many Japanese felt: "It is just since the [Western] powers have suppressed the circulation of Japanese materials and merchandise abroad, we are looking for some place overseas where Japanese capital, Japanese skills and Japanese labor can have free play, free from the oppression of the white race." He continued to justify military expansion: "And if it is still protested that our actions in Manchuria were excessively violent, we may wish to ask the white race just which country it was that sent warships and troops to India, South Africa, and Australia and slaughtered innocent natives, bound their hands and feet with iron chains, lashed their backs with iron whips, proclaimed these territories as their own, and still continues to hold them to this very day?"

The state of both the Japanese and world economies had much to do with Japan's decisions leading to war. The depression of the 1930's sapped the economies of most nations and disrupted international trade. Japan's exports, vital to the resource-poor nation, were not providing the earnings needed to build its economy. Later this was compounded by American and Dutch embargoes against shipment of steel and oil to Japan. In simplest terms, the Japanese decided to take by force the markets and sources of supply they could not win peacefully. This was the basic justification for the Greater East Asia Co-Prosperity Sphere, which envisioned three concentric spheres of economic blocs. The Inner Sphere would include Japan, the Russian Maritime Provinces, Manchuria, North China, and the lower Yangtze River area in China. The Smaller Sphere included Eastern Siberia, the rest of China, Indochina, the Dutch East Indies, and the Philippines. The

Greater Sphere wrapped in India, Australia, and the South Pacific Islands.

Events in Europe contributed to Japan's move toward war. The rise of Adolf Hitler in Germany and Benito Mussolini in Italy, their rampant expansion and conquest, and the appeasement of the Allied nations served to persuade the Japanese leaders that they could move against the Western powers in Asia with impunity. This belief was reinforced by the failure of the League of Nations and the Western nations to stop the Japanese invasion of Manchuria in 1931 and of North China in 1937. These factors, in turn, led to the great mistake in judgment that directly brought on the war.

Miscalculation was perhaps the crucial cause of the outbreak of World War II in the Pacific, the point on which all others turned. The prewar leaders of Japan committed the classic blunder in geopolitics, an error that Ito Hirobumi and the men of Meiji assiduously avoided: Tojo and his colleagues failed to estimate correctly the capabilities of an enemy, in this case the United States. An axiom of war, from planning national strategy to leading an infantry platoon, is to determine first what an opponent can do, and to prepare accordingly. The Japanese badly underestimated the ability of the Americans to put together a war machine of overwhelming power. They committed a second error by focusing on what they thought the Americans would do. But they completely failed to understand American intentions, which was more a cultural than a strategic lapse. The insular, parochial Japanese leaders with their narrow vision did not understand the West any more than the West understood them. This was particularly true of the Kwangtung Army clique led by Tojo that was composed of men who had not been much exposed to Western thinking. Their ignorance of American history and national psychology led them to assume that the Americans would fold up and sue for a negotiated peace after the lightning strikes at Hawaii and into South-east Asia. Events showed how wrong they were.

Tojo and those around him were not madmen. They were products of their own history, culture, and experience. That they were so badly informed about the West, and especially America, would seem to be clear evidence of how little from the West had penetrated into the Japanese cultural consciousness, or at least into one large sector of Japanese leadership. Some Japanese understood the outside world and opposed the course Tojo had chosen. Few disagreed with the objective of driving the West from Asia and having Japan assume the dominant role in the region; but some did not go along with the methods. A few *zaibatsu* businessmen preferred economic to military imperialism, and they resented the military controls over their industrial, commercial, and financial operations. Some bureaucrats, particularly diplomats, believed that Japan could gain its ends through diplomacy rather than risk war. They also knew something of the basic economic weakness of Japan compared with the United States. Moderate politicians opposed war because it put the militarists in control and left them out. A few also had ideological reservations. Even within the military, there was opposition. Some naval officers, who had seen more of the West than Tojo's landlocked and isolated Kwangtung Army, doubted that Japan had the staying power to defeat America. But the extremists in the army had forcibly taken the upper hand and with the imperial authority behind them, the others followed. The Japanese people had little to say about it, and did as they were told. Finally, despite the reservations or opposition any Japanese had, when the struggle came it was Japan against the world. The feeling of national unity, or simply of being Japanese, was stronger than anything else.

Another question that has occurred to many Westerners is: How could the Japanese have committed the atrocities of the war? In the carefully ordered life of a Japanese, courtesy and decorum are required virtues. How, then, can the paradox of the Rape of Nanking, the wanton slaughter in the Philippines, the beheading of helpless American captives be explained? These went beyond the ferocity of war. Again, only a couple of basic clues can be offered in tentative answer:

In the Japanese mind, "a man away from home has no neighbors." The ethical guidelines and the rigid code of social behavior in Japan come from society itself, not from within the inner man. As long as the Japanese is functioning within the rules set by his society, and has the social pressures of other Japanese to enforce those rules, he knows how to conduct himself. Once those rules are gone, he is lost. Because Japanese society is unique, outside it the Japanese has few signposts to show him the way. Further, the Japanese at home lives in an environment where no two people are equal. Everyone is superior or inferior to everyone else, one way or another. The conquering Japanese saw himself as the superior, the Filipino or the Indonesian as the inferior. When the inferior did not show proper respect or keep his place, the Japanese felt compelled and righteous in putting him down. Compound all this with the stress of war and the danger in a foreign land, and the Japanese, who has a thinly covered streak of violence in him, could go berserk.

Further, the Japanese leaders truly believed in their mission to liberate Asia from the white man's colonial rule. They saw themselves as the heroes of their race. The training and inculcation of the average soldier made him also believe this. He therefore expected to be welcomed by other Asians as the Japanese forces drove into China and later swept through Southeast Asia. When the Japanese soldier was not welcomed but was treated merely as one tyrant substituting for another, he was stunned. The passive or armed resistance he met stunned him even further.

Unprepared, the Japanese soldier and his commanders struck out to subdue by force the populations of their subject lands. The Japanese demonstrated that as products of a carefully ordered society, wherein everything is done deliberately, they did not know how to cope with an unknown and unexpected situation except by resorting to brute force.

By the end of the war, the Japanese had failed to gain any of their objectives, save one. They had broken the back of the white man's colonialism in Asia. They had intended, of course, to replace it with their own rule, which was short-lived. Nationalistic movements in Southeast Asia were already underway when the Japanese arrived and tried to use these local nationalists to rule their conquered territories. This, however, had a catalytic effect and stimulated nationalism all the more. The American, British, Dutch, and French armies that returned to their colonies after the defeat of the Japanese found themselves confronted with people who would no longer accept their rule. They had been shown by the Japanese that the yellow or brown man need no longer knuckle under to the white man. The Filipinos had been promised independence before the war broke out; this allowed the Americans to bow out gracefully. The British left Malaya, Burma, and India without much trouble. But the French and Dutch tried to reimpose colonial rule in Indochina and the East Indies and shortly became embroiled in bloody conflicts. The Vietnam war involving America was a direct, if delayed, consequence.

The atomic bombings of Hiroshima and Nagasaki in August 1945 were the catalysts that forced Japan to surrender, but defeat had been ordained before that. American bombers had severely damaged Japanese war industry and fire-bomb raids on Tokyo and other cities had taken even greater tolls than the atomic bombs. American submarines had cut the Japanese sea lanes and reduced shipments of oil and other strategic materials almost to nothing. The Japanese navy lay either at the bottom of the sea or anchored in Japanese bays, too crippled and too short of fuel to move. American troops had battled their way north from New Guinea to Okinawa and were within invading range of the Japanese homeland.

Even so, the Japanese militarists were split on whether to continue the war or to surrender. Emperor Hirohito, however, resolved the issue in one shining moment of courage and decision. He alone determined that Japan would accept the Allied terms of unconditional surrender. He said he could no longer see his people in distress and agony; and his decision was accepted by those opposing it when he summoned up more than a thousand years of tradition that no loyal subject, except a few fanatics, could defy. The Emperor showed his compassion in an August 15 broadcast announcing the surrender. After enumerating the hardships the people had undergone and the trials of the days ahead, the Emperor said: "We are keenly aware of ye, Our subjects. However, it is according to the dictate of time and fate that We have resolved to pave the way for a grand peace for all generations to come by enduring the un-endurable and suffering the insufferable."

The Allied Occupation, realistically the American Oc-cupation, was intended to be the second great infusion of Western ideas and practices into Japan since the Meiji Restoration. But there were two basic differences. The Japanese studied the West of their own accord during Meiji. They were forced to open the country, but nobody said they had to borrow anything from the West. During the Occupation, Japan was force-fed by the Americans. The Japanese had no choice so long as the Occupation authorities governed the country. Moreover, the Japanese borrowing from the West during Meiji was highly selec-tive. The Occupation, instead, was an attempt to make over the whole of Japanese society. Hardly a facet of the entire nation was not scrutinized and some sort of reform ordered.

The Occupation was surely the most benevolent tyranny installed by a victor over a vanquished in the history of man. General Douglas MacArthur, the Supreme Commander, was a brilliant soldier, a charismatic leader who gained the full respect of the Japanese, a dedicated man who fulfilled his mission with justice and compassion. His staff went about its multitude of tasks with zeal, good will, and genuine hope for the future of the Japanese people.

The Occupation, however, was an inherent contradiction, being a military dictatorship administered by a proconsul. (It was and still is known to some as the MacArthur Shogunate.) A dictatorship cannot order a nation to become a democracy, with all that entails in free choice, individual rights and responsibility, parliamentary government, economic opportunity, and a myriad attitudes and practices among the citizenry. If a man is a democrat, he does not have to be told to be one. If a man is not a democrat, he cannot be ordered to become one. A people can be taught democracy, perhaps, but surely not in the short time of the Occupation. Seven tutorial years could not be expected to change a people whose society had been formed over a thousand years of history.

The Occupation attempted to revise the fundamental nature of the Imperial House, install a political system based on American and British models, instill legal concepts of individual rights, decentralize the economy, orient education toward individual attainment, organize a labor union movement, give equal rights to women, return land to the tiller, teach freedom of the press, eliminate military power, insure freedom of religion, and in general prevent the resurrection of a police state. The Occupation authorities started on this idealistic course but had to modify it to meet the exigencies of the outside world. Nearby Korea had been divided in half at the end of the war, and no agreement was being reached with the Russians on reunification. The Cold War between the two superpowers was well under way by 1948. A year later, the Chinese mainland came under the domination of the Chinese Communists. The Korean War broke out in June 1950. These events gave the Americans pause and caused them to reverse some Occupation policies. The priorities of the Occupation were reordered to make Japan into a strong and useful ally against the spread of communism in Asia. The breakup of the *zaibatsu* ceased, and a number of purged leaders were "depurged." Rehabilitation of the economy, including revival of heavy industry, became a priority. Controls on communists were partially reinstated. The labor movement, to which General MacArthur had earlier given almost free rein, was subject to some restriction. The need for internal security brought about the beginning of a police reserve force that eventually was expanded into today's Self-Defense Force.

Nonetheless, the Occupation was effective in many of its policies, but with results that it did not foresee. The Americans were successful in half of their mission: in destroying the ultranationalism and militarism of the prewar era. They tore up the distortions and aberrations into which the prewar leaders had twisted Japanese society, demolishing the militaristic controls over politics, economic enterprise, education, the press, and the rest of society. The Occupation was like a cleansing tidal wave that washed across the surface of Japan, clearing away the deviations and perversions of the 1930's. But the Occupation did not accomplish the other half of its mission, that of constructing a new Japan that conformed to the ideals and practices of a Western democracy. Few of its substantive reforms were permanent, excepting women's rights and land reform, which the Japanese appear to have assimilated. As soon as the Occupation relaxed, the Japanese revived their institutions according to their own traditions. When the Occupation was over, they quickly rebuilt in Japanese patterns, especially in the organization and operation of the economy, corporations, and commerce. The net effect of the Occupation was to eliminate the contortions of the previous twenty years and to make it possible for the Japanese themselves to return to the mainstream of their own historical development, picking up where they had left off in the post-World War I days before the militarists took over.

The Japanese spent the Occupation years and the first few years thereafter in the struggle to stay alive, to put the pieces of their shattered lives back together, and to recover economically. As that progressed, they slowly turned to thinking about themselves and their nation. They looked mostly into their own history and culture to recover their pride and sense of national destiny, although they looked again to the West for technology and ideas with the careful selectivity of the Meiji years.

The turning point in the psychological and emotional recovery process was the Tokyo Olympic Games of 1964. To the rest of the world, it was a spectacular and exciting athletic meet. To the Japanese, for whom symbolism and nuance are everything, the Olympics represented their nation's re-emergence into the world of self-respecting people. No Japanese missed the implications in the choice of the lad who ran into the stadium carrying the torch to light the Olympic flame during the opening ceremonies. He had been born in Hiroshima nineteen years before—the day the atomic bomb was dropped on that city. It was an expression of the Japanese saying to themselves: "We have done it. We have wiped away the shame. We are ourselves again."

PART TWO

The DYNAMICS of the NATION

Chapter **4**

The

ESTABLISHMENT

and CONSENSUS

 The best description of the way Japan is run today is a pithy Tokyo saying: "Japan is governed by the rolling consensus of the Establishment."

The Japanese Establishment is an elite of senior bureaucrats, businessmen, and politicians, plus a handful of prominent intellectuals and men of special prestige. They determine Japan's course in every sphere of society— politics, diplomacy, economics, education. The Establishment, like every Japanese group, makes its decisions not by majority will but by a consensus that is reached through an intricate and laborious process. The Japanese call this an adjustment of views; Westerners might call it an interwoven collection of compromises. The consensus is never static but is forever rolling, a dynamic and endless revision of agreements, sometimes only by the slightest refinement in nuance.

The Japanese Establishment has no close parallel in the West because Japanese and Western concepts of a nation are basically different. The modern Western nation-state has been derived from political theories and institutions evolved over the last three hundred years. The Japanese nation-family, in contrast, has evolved from

71

earliest times as families joined into clans and clans into a national family. The Japanese social order, based in the Shinto religion and Confucian philosophy, is intensely personal and intuitive rather than contractual and rational. Japanese society is authoritarian rather than egalitarian, oriented to the group rather than the individual, and, being the product of a tight island country, is homogeneous rather than diverse.

In the Japanese nation-family, the emperor is the father, the chief priest of the Shinto religion, the arbiter of ethics and beauty, the fount of political legitimacy, the focus of national unity. But he does not govern directly. The Establishment, the elder brothers of the nation-family, are given the responsibility for governing and seeing to the welfare of the people, who are the children of the nation-family. In the ideals of the nation-family, if not always in practice, the Establishment preserves the social order and makes it function for the common good. It is obliged to be benevolent and paternal. The people, in turn, are obliged to show respect and to be obedient. And all are obliged to be loyal, first to the emperor, then to one another. Despite all the changes on the surface of industrial, modern Japan, these tenets are accepted as natural, right, and proper by the farmer in Kyushu, the shipbuilder in Kobe, the bureaucrat in Tokyo, and the fisherman in Hokkaido.

Today's Establishment is the direct descendant of the governing class of premodern Japan and the Meiji oligarchy. It is the result of a slow widening of the elite to include the bureaucracy, military, the business executives, and the politicians. The Occupation eliminated the military, for the moment at least, and helped elevate the politicians to full membership in the Establishment. The businessmen came to the fore in the economic reconstruction and expansion of the postwar period. The bureaucracy, which survived the vagaries of the Restoration and the militaristic upheavals, has simply continued along its way.

The bureaucracy today, being the oldest of the three main Establishment groups, perhaps best reflects traditional Japanese values. The Japanese bureaucrat is something of a cousin of the ancient Chinese mandarin. He is imbued with the Confucian ethic of authority, benevolence, and paternal responsibility. The bureaucracy has lost some of its earlier semireligious aura, and bureaucrats no longer openly consider themselves servants of the emperor. But the mystique lingers and tinges the tone of bureaucratic influence.

Japanese society assigns high prestige to the government official, making the bureaucracy attractive to the best brains in the nation. It has many of the brightest and best educated men in Japan, especially in choice agencies such as the Finance Ministry and the Foreign Ministry. The bureaucrats are thoroughly and carefully trained, both in their formal education and in the bureaucracy itself. The bureaucracy is fully staffed, which gives each man the time to develop an expertise in a specific area of operation. Moreover, the Japanese government has over the years built up an incomparable reservoir of statistics and information on every conceivable aspect of Japanese society and on pertinent subjects abroad. The bureaucrat has access to these research facilities, plus anything connected with his work that has been accumulated in universities and private institutions.

The combination of intelligence, training, time to think, facilities, and prestige makes the bureaucrat a formidable power in the decision-making machinery. When he does his job well, which is the usual case, anyone disposed to disagree with him finds it difficult to dispute his findings. Foreign diplomats going into a negotiating session with officials of the Japanese bureaucracy have found that they had best come thoroughly prepared as they will face a squad of experts armed with an overwhelming array of data and well-grounded arguments. Moreover, the bureaucracy has been entrusted by custom and law with implementing policy, which means that the bureaucracy can modify political and economic decisions to fit more closely to the needs of the country as it sees them. The bureaucracy has such broad responsibilities that few areas of Japanese society are left untouched. In the Ministry of Education, for instance, sits a specialist in mathematics education whose desk, crammed into a long line of other specialists' desks, is laden with reports. He studies every detail of math teaching in Japanese schools, looks into developments in other countries, and formulates a standard for all math teachers in Japan. This appears to pay off: a 1967 Swedish survey of math education around the world concluded that the teaching of math in Japan is the best in the world.

The Japanese business community also has its roots fairly deep in Japanese tradition. The present-day big businessman's predecessors were the merchant class that evolved in the last half of the Tokugawa period and the *samurai* who became industrialists, bankers, and traders after the Meiji Restoration. The business community was fostered by the government in the Meiji period but gradually developed its own power as an equal partner in constructing Japan's industrial economy. The business community came into its own in the postwar period, first by reconstructing the heavily damaged economy, then by pushing it to new highs of industrialization, and finally by giving the Japanese the beginnings of a consumer economy and their first taste of the affluent society.

The financiers, industrialists, and traders wield power largely because they hold the keys to wealth and economic prosperity. The bankers are the most influential because they control the sources of money for investment and for financing business operations. The banks are the main suppliers of funds, as Japan has not yet fully developed a public capital market. Trading company executives control the major portion of sales in both domestic and foreign markets. They are especially important as the earners of Japan's vital foreign exchange needed to pay for imports into a nation that lacks rich natural resources. The industrialists are the producers, the makers of national wealth. Small businessmen, for the most part, do not have much influence on the national scene.

The Japanese businessman, like any in a semicapitalistic economy, works to make a profit. He is motivated, however, by the same Confucian ethic that guides the bureaucrat. He is responsible to the shareholders for the efficient and profitable operation of his corporation but also feels a responsibility to help provide for the welfare of the nation. He works closely with the bureaucracy and the politicians to decide what is best for his country, even though a particular action may not be immediately best for his business. The businessman has inherited a tradition of service from the *samurai* who became businessmen a hundred years ago and brought their ethics with them. Putting down the sword and picking up the abacus changed their way of life but did not change their mode of thought.

The third major group in today's Establishment are the professional politicians of the ruling conservative party that has held power, except for one brief period, since the end of the war. This is the newest group in the Establishment, the least rooted in Japanese tradition, and the one in which the greatest frictions occur in the adaptation of Western forms to Japanese practice. The conservative politicians are organized into the small, elite Liberal Democratic Party, which has an enduring structure instead of the loose organization that American politicians put together for elections. Party officials, even when not in elective or appointive office, have considerable influence. The members of the House of Representatives (the lower house of the Diet) are the hard core of the party. From among them are drawn the prime minister and most

Cabinet officers, though occasionally one from the House of Councillors, the now less powerful upper house, is selected for the Cabinet.

The politicians are perhaps the least influential members of the Establishment because they have little precedent behind them. The concept of party politics was not introduced until the latter half of the Meiji era and did not really take hold until the Occupation gave politicians the chance. The politicians, moreover, are dependent on businessmen for political funds and on the bureaucracy for the implementation of policy. But the politicians have legal control of the government and a public forum in the Diet. More important, many experienced postwar politicians have come from the bureaucracy or the business community and have maintained their personal ties with their associates, exercising influence through them. An increasing number of politicians, however, are making their careers solely in politics and developing sturdy bases of power both in their home electoral districts and with other politicians. The key to this is a strong political organization. One young (50, which is young for Japan) and ambitious politician who aspires to be prime minister has organized associations for older people, white-collar workers, farmers, housewives, university students, and even youngsters under voting age. He pays professional political workers to maintain these leagues and meets with them himself on a regular basis. He has fashioned such a well-knit political mechanism that he spent only one day campaigning in his own district during a recent national election. The rest of the time he was elsewhere electioneering for his political allies.

Beyond the three major Establishment groups are a number of individuals who have influence. Some operate in the shadows behind the scenes, rarely appearing in public. One such is Kodama Yoshio, who made a small fortune in China during the war, was convicted and imprisoned as a war criminal, and emerged from prison to become a powerful manipulator in conservative politics. Kodama holds no public office and his name rarely is mentioned in the press, but he is consulted on most major political decisions. Money is the source of his power. He uses some of his own to finance the conservative party and knows where in the business community to get more.

Other key figures are the elder statesmen who have retired from day-to-day politics, the bureaucracy, or business. Certainly the best known in the postwar period was the late Prime Minister Yoshida Shigeru, who led Japan's recovery from the war. Yoshida had been a diplomat before the war, was arrested by the militarists on suspicion of "plotting peace," and was brought out of retirement to go into politics during the Occupation. He was prime minister for most of the difficult and sometimes stormy days of Japan's rehabilitation and earned himself the unflattering title of "One-Man Yoshida" for his determined and often autocratic ways. After he retired again to his seaside home in Oiso, on Sagami Bay southwest of Tokyo, no major decision was taken without his tacit, and often his explicit, approval.

A particular place in the Establishment is reserved for the intellectual community, except the outright Marxists. In the Confucian ethic, the *sensei*, or teacher, is accorded the highest esteem. His counsel is heeded because he has taken the time to become an expert and, as with the bureaucrat, is hard to dispute when he has set out a solid case. The intellectual, too, is bound by the moral responsibility to use his knowledge for the benefit of society. The intellectual community is not limited to the university but includes at least two other categories. One is the *jyogensha*, or wise man, who has few counterparts in America. His advice is sought because he has knowledge and experience in special fields. Some of these men have retired from one of the Establishment groups; others head small, privately financed research institutes.

Another Establishment intellectual is the journalist. Newspaper editors, magazine commentators, and social critics are consulted in return for their public support of a decision when it comes out. The distinction between scholars and journalists is much more fuzzy in Japan than in America. Scholars often write for the public prints, and journalists associate closely with those in the academic circle. *Bungei Shunju,* a mass-circulation monthly magazine, published a survey in October 1967 entitled "A Hundred Men of Culture Who Move Japan." It included a wide range of scholars, male and female social critics, students of ancient Japan and the modern West, journalists of the major newspapers and independent free-lancers, avant-garde novelists and writers steeped in traditional Japanese themes, even two Chinese and an American who are versed in Japanese life and letters.

In the making of the Japanese consensus, even those not clearly identified with the Establishment have a voice. They must be heard even if their views count for little in the final decision. The opposition socialist party leaders, labor union chiefs, and leftist intellectuals are the main outsiders. They can delay a decision and possibly force a compromise by protest. But their influence is marginal because it is negative and they have no base for affirmative action. The opposition, however, can be an asset to the Establishment, which uses it as a judo wrestler uses his opponent. The judoist attempts to defeat his opponent not by meeting him head-on but by side-stepping and turning the opponent's thrusts and momentum to his own advantage. The Establishment allows the opposition to push it in directions it wants to move without admitting so. Some members of the Establishment have argued that Japan should move toward closer relations with Communist

78

China, especially in trade. The official American policy opposes this, and American diplomats have been instructed to make these views known to Japanese authorities. The Japanese reply by contending that they are being pressed by the opposition and must make some concession or risk political disruption.

The opposition also provides the Establishment with an excuse for not doing something it does not want to do. The United States has for several years been urging Japan to take greater responsibility for its own defense. The Establishment has resisted because it has not wanted to spend the necessary funds. But the argument the Establishment has used with American officials is that a greater defense effort would draw too much political fire from the neutralist opposition and would threaten political tranquility.

Almost completely outside the Establishment are the farmers, whose voice is becoming weaker every year as Japan becomes more industrial. They have some influence with the conservative politicians for whom they provide considerable electoral support. The Japanese election system, like those in most formerly agrarian countries, is weighted in favor of rural areas. Japanese farmers can influence policies that directly affect the production or price of food, particularly the price of rice, but not much else.

The military is the group most notably excluded from the decision-making process. It was discredited by the wartime defeat and has recovered from that only slightly. The present Japanese Self-Defense Forces operate under the restraint of public antipathy for war and fear of any action that might involve Japan in hostilities. As the wartime generation passes, however, and this sentiment wears off, the military may regain part of its former influence.

Public opinion, which in the West is an effective, if elusive, element in the governing process, is even more elusive and formless in Japan and plays little part in decision making. The Japanese historically have deferred to authority and have been willing, with a few individual exceptions, to allow the leaders to run the country. Every nation, however, is ultimately governed by the consent of the governed. The most absolute totalitarian regime cannot force people to do what they refuse to do if they are willing to suffer whatever consequences their rulers might inflict on them. In Japan, the Establishment knows there are limits beyond which the Japanese people would either not follow it or would actively oppose it. It is most doubtful that any leader in Japan today could propose overseas military ventures that risk war and survive in power, so strong is the antiwar feeling among the mass of the people. The Japanese public is docile, but it must be led, guided, and persuaded. Not only must the Establishment reach a consensus within itself but it must pull the Japanese people together in a national consensus on the broad and basic questions of national policy. Prime Minister Sato Eisaku started a drive in 1967 toward a fundamental consensus on the issue of Japanese security. He wanted the Japanese people to agree that Japan must bear the basic responsibility for its own defense, a question on which there was a wide range of diverse views. More than a year later, there was still no consensus in sight, and it may be several years before one comes about. Until then, neither Sato nor any other prime minister will be able to force Japan into an assertive, positive security policy.

The Japanese Establishment is found almost entirely in Tokyo. People in other cities and the rural areas have influence only if they go to Tokyo or have their representatives there. Tokyo is the Japanese combination of Washington, New York, Chicago, and Los Angeles, with the Ivy League and the major state universities included. It is the site of all government ministries and agencies, the headquarters of nearly all big business corporations (those with headquarters in Osaka or elsewhere have senior repre-

sentatives and permanent offices in Tokyo), the headquarters of all political parties, the home of most major
universities, the head offices of the national newspapers, the
residence of most of the intellectual community.

The size of the Establishment is difficult to estimate as
it starts with the top men who clearly belong and shades
away to people of lesser importance. A rough guess is that
about three thousand men and a very few women are in
the Establishment. In the bureaucracy, the career vice-
ministers are the senior establishmentarians, each being the
top bureaucrat in his ministry. Below them are senior
advisers and heads of major bureaus who hold ranks
equivalent to assistant secretary in an American department of government. Their deputies and counselors, equal
to deputy assistant secretaries, are also members. In business, the chairman of the board, the president, vice presidents, managing directors, senior advisers, major operating
department heads, and their primary deputies are in the
Establishment. In the conservative political party, the prime
minister, Cabinet officers, Diet members, senior party
officials, and special advisers are members. The intellectual
establishmentarians include full professors and lower-
ranking scholars who have made a reputation by publishing. In the press, publishers and senior editors, department
heads, specialists in particular fields, and senior reporters
are members. In age, a few of the Establishment are
younger than fifty, the majority are between fifty and
sixty, and the most prominent are almost always over sixty.

The Establishment is essentially an elite of brains, education, and merit. A Japanese can make it all the way to
the top from the most humble origins if he starts early
enough, follows the prescribed route, and conforms to the
system as he progresses. If men from socially prominent or
historically prestigious families are ineffective, they are
shunted aside with sinecures. The same is true of a man
from a wealthy family or the son of the owner of a busi-

ness. The Establishment is no longer aristocratic, though families of noble background are still prominent. The peerage that was adapted to the Japanese social stratification in the Meiji period was abolished by the Occupation but has resumed some activity in recent years. The former aristocrats can make their influence felt, however, only if they have merit, not because they once had proud titles.

The routes an individual must follow to get into the Establishment are well defined. Most important, by far, is the educational path. This route can start as early as the first grade, the selection of a primary school being important for prominent families. For most, passing the middle-school examination and being accepted into a prestigious school is the first move onto the track. The second is passing the examination and entering the right high school. After that, passing another examination and entering one of several national or private universities marks the man as a potential businessman or bureaucratic official. Tokyo University, formerly Tokyo Imperial University, is at the apex of this scheme, with the Tokyo Law Faculty at the very peak. The university was founded by Ito Hirobumi during the Meiji era to train men for the bureaucracy. He imbued it with his thinking, and it has turned out generations of bureaucrats in his mold. Other prestigious universities are Waseda, Keio, Hitotsubashi, and to a lesser degree, Meiji and Hosei. Outside Tokyo, Kyoto University, also formerly an imperial university, has considerable stature. Unless a young man has graduated from one of the top schools, his chances of gaining the upper reaches of the Establishment are small. But the schools, excepting the private universities, are public and open to all by examination. This puts tremendous pressure at an early age on the man who is ambitious or, more accurately, on parents who are ambitious for their sons. A favorite admonition from parents at examination time is: "Four hours sleep, pass; six hours sleep, fail."

Young men with fathers already in the Establishment have a better chance of getting onto the track and staying on it than those from families outside the Establishment. The insiders are more aware of the rules of the game, and these young men from their tender years are inculcated with the necessity of doing the right things. Further, the competition for entrance to schools and universities becomes tougher each year as the population grows but educational facilities do not expand proportionately. A university has only so many places in each entering class, and a young man from a known family will get the nod over one from an unknown family if all other things are equal. There are other breaks along the way, which the sons of the privileged have always enjoyed. But the original outsider can still make his way to the inside by intelligence, diligence, and hard work.

The Establishment is held together by formal, visible organizational ties that are much the same as in other leadership groups around the world. But there are unspoken, intangible ties that are unique to Japan and often unseen by the foreigner. No tie is more important to the Japanese than the interwoven personal relationships that define his place in the web of society. This sense of personal loyalty and obligation is considered a prime virtue and permeates Japanese society. It governs every facet of one person's relations with others in the family, marriage, school, work, and play. Those in the Establishment have personal obligations to the Emperor and the Imperial Household, to their own families and through members of the family to others, to their wives and their wives' families and through them to still others, to their classmates and schoolmates, to their business or bureaucratic associates, to people in a wider circle with whom they have become associated one way or another, down to the young girls who caddy for them on the golf course.

The Japanese take great pains to delineate personal

relationships and have a register, called *inseki*, that tells who is related to whom and how, whether by blood, marriage, school, or professional association. Japan's three most recent prime ministers were all *deshi*, or protégés, of the late Prime Minister Yoshida Shigeru. Kishi Nobusuke and Sato Eisaku are brothers, Sato having been adopted into his wife's family to continue the family line. Sato and the late Ikeda Hayato were schoolmates a year apart in the Kumamoto Fifth Higher School in western Honshu. Sato's son Shinki is married to the daughter of Anzai Hiroshi, vice president of the Tokyo Gas Company, a major utility. Anzai's brother is Anzai Masao, president of Showa Denko, a leading chemical firm. He is married to Mori Mitsue, whose brother Satoru is president of Nippon Yakin, a metal manufacturing company. Another brother was the late Mori Kiyoshi, a rising member of the conservative party before his premature death in 1968. A sister is married to Miki Takeo, several times a Cabinet officer and a potential prime minister. Going back to Anzai Masao: his son is married to a daughter of Shoda Hidesaburo, president of Nisshin Seifun, a major milling company. Another of Shoda's daughters is Crown Princess Michiko, wife of Crown Prince Akihito, heir to Emperor Hirohito's throne. The examples go on almost without end. Nor are they limited entirely to the conservative sector of Japanese political life. Kosaka Zentaro, influential member of the conservative party, member of the Diet and one-time foreign minister, is married to the sister of the wife of Okazaki Shinichi, chairman of Dowa Fire and Marine Insurance Company. But Kosaka's sister married Tokyo Governor Minobe Ryokichi—the first socialist elected to that office. Minobe is the son of Minobe Tatsukichi, famous prewar scholar.

School ties are important both within the small groups and across the Establishment. Tokyo University is the main supplier of bureaucrats; Keio sends many of its graduates to business; Waseda men go into journalism and politics. The powerful Finance Ministry is filled with men from Tokyo University Law School. About seventy major companies have at least a hundred Keio men each on their payrolls. But all of the universities have people in politics, the bureaucracy, and the business world, giving members of the Establishment old school ties with other members.

A major element in the stability, even rigidity, of the system is the Japanese custom of lifetime employment. When a young man graduates from the university, he takes an examination and undergoes other screening for employment in a corporation or government agency. He enters that organization for the entirety of his career and will not change jobs even if he thinks he could do better elsewhere. He pledges his fealty to that organization in much the way a *samurai* pledged his loyalty to his *daimyo*. In turn, the organization pledges its paternal obligations to the employee. He will not be fired except for criminal malfeasance or gross scandal. He and the men who enter the organization at the same time will be promoted at the same time, as will their classmates in other companies or government ministries. Thus men of the same age and who have gotten to know each other in the early days of their careers rise to the top together. As they reach the upper rungs of the ladder, some weeding out will take place, and the less gifted or those who have not made the right connections at the very top will be retired early or shunted aside. The more fortunate will continue up, so that they and their friends and classmates all across the bureaucracy, business, and politics enter the Establishment at the same time. The twenty-five to thirty years of personal relationships behind them makes the Establishment an interlocking web.

To keep the top from clogging up, custom dictates formal retirement at the age of fifty-five. This does not apply to directors or vice-presidents of companies as it does to most bureaucrats and businessmen. This talent is not wasted but is used to enhance the cohesion and effectiveness of the Establishment. Businessmen are often retained as counselors to their firms or move to associated companies as senior advisers. They have been particularly useful in Japan's postwar economic spurt, in view of all the new industries and companies that have been started. Bureaucrats often move to senior positions in quasi-governmental corporations such as the tobacco monopoly. A 1967 survey showed that nearly four hundred retired bureaucrats were in these lucrative posts. Others are retained as advisers in business firms to keep close contact with their former subordinates who have moved into their jobs. Businessmen and bureaucrats who go into politics retain their contacts with their colleagues in their former companies or ministries.

The Establishment, in theory, is a harmonious upper level of the national family, the well-knit elite of a co-operative clan. In reality, it is a humanly imperfect organism within which people and groups constantly struggle for power, position, and prestige. The individual Japanese leader, though motivated by Confucian ethics and other ideals that derive from the Japanese tradition, is no more or less susceptible to the temptations and frictions of this world than the individual American leader who may profess the purest Jeffersonian democracy. The locus of power is continually shifting by small degrees among people within groups and among small groups within the larger groups of the entire Establishment. The confrontations are rarely direct, but are usually subtle and circuitous. Nonetheless, they are there, and the competition is often fierce. If an outsider poses a threat to the Establishment or to Japanese national interests, the struggle for power momentarily diminishes and the differences over methods for dealing with the outsider are quickly resolved. But the struggle resumes once the threat has passed.

In recent years, the power of the bureaucracy has slipped somewhat as industrialization has put more power in the hands of the business community. But the bureaucracy will remain a force by law, custom, and expertise. The politicians have been trying to reduce the authority of the bureaucracy and replace it with their own but, with a few specific exceptions, have not succeeded. The politically appointed Cabinet officer who heads a government ministry may try to get his subordinates to follow his instructions, but more often finds himself the tool of the bureaucrats. I once had a long, on-the-record news interview with a Japanese foreign minister. After the session, the direct quotes that would be attributed to the minister were submitted, as previously agreed, to the ministry's press officer to check for accuracy. He broke them apart by subject matter and took each quote around to the appropriate bureaucrat for approval before releasing them for print. The foreign minister did not see them. He thus could not speak with authority on Japan's foreign policy without first having his words cleared with his supposed underlings in the bureaucracy.

Within each major Establishment group are both formal and informal ties that make them cohesive units, despite the power struggles. The bureaucracy has its ministries, bureaus, and sections set out on an organizational chart that would not baffle the Westerner. But the inner workings are more mysterious and Japanese in flavor. Each bureaucrat feels a common bond with others in his agency and, to a lesser extent, with other bureaucrats in other agencies that arises from the mystique of the bureaucracy itself. The bureaucrats work together much more on a personal basis than according to a manual of procedure. A Foreign Ministry man who must deal with someone in the Finance Ministry whom he does not know goes first to his classmate there, even though that friend is not concerned with the question at hand. Through the friend, the

Foreign Ministry man is introduced to the official who is responsible for the matter. Then, as they discuss the problem, a new personal relationship develops and adds another strand to the web. These multiply over the years to form a tight weave.

Foreign correspondents in Japan have learned to use the same technique to have their questions answered. Calling up an export section official in the Ministry of International Trade and Industry to ask for an appointment means going through long explanations of who the correspondent is, how long he has been in Japan and what he knows about Japan, what publication he represents and why it is interested, and a dozen other items. Even then, the appointment might be delayed for weeks or never even be arranged on one pretext or another. But if the correspondent has made a friend in the ministry, and it doesn't make much difference in which section he works, a call to him and a simple explanation of the subject of interest usually results in an appointment with the proper official within a short time. The friend has made the introduction and implicitly vouched for the correspondent. And with this sort of introduction, the correspondent usually finds the new contact cordial and candid.

The business community has the usual organizational arrangements but is laced together with an additional set of crisscrossed ties that make it considerably more unified than business communities in the West, especially in America. Most obvious are the great combines such as Mitsubishi and Mitsui that continue the traditions of the *zaibatsu*. The *zaibatsu* are enormous economic clans, each with steel, chemical, oil, and other industrial corporations; each with a bank, insurance, and similar financial institutions; and each with a large trading company, real estate, and other commercial concerns. They are held together by interlocking shareholding and mutual business interest, and by history. The major change since the war is a shift from family ownership and management to more public owner-ship and professional management. The loyalties between company and company within the combine and between executive and executive are as strong as ever.

Trade associations sit astride every major line of busi-ness in Japan. The Iron and Steel Federation, the Tokyo Bankers Association, the Japan Foreign Trade Council, and dozens of others like them pull companies together into a consolidated industry. A company in a *zaibatsu* also be-longs to the trade association in its industry, providing another crisscrossed link. Mitsubishi Chemical, Mitsui Chemical, and Sumitomo Chemical are members of the Japan Chemical Industry Association as well as of their own respective combines. The trade associations serve as channels through which Establishment executives regulate and coordinate the activity of member companies. They are also the main channels for communication and negotia-tion with the bureaucracy, particularly with the Ministry of International Trade and Industry, which has a strong say in all industrial and commercial operations.

Atop the business and trade associations are several federations, which add another set of links. The most powerful are the Federation of Economic Organizations, or Keidanren, to which the associations belong, and the Joint Committee for Economic Development, or Keizai Doyukai, to which prominent businessmen belong as indi-viduals. Others are the Japan Chamber of Commerce, or Nissho, and the Federation of Employers' Associations, or Nikkeiren. These organizations are meeting grounds where senior executives discuss both national economic policy and specific problems. The organizations are also platforms for the business world to have its say in Japan's major political and international decisions.

In the political circle, the Liberal Democratic Party is organized on paper much like parliamentary political parties in the West. In reality it is not a party but a coalition of political clans or factions known as *habatsu*. The factions have a basic ideological consensus, but are banded together much more by a common interest of getting into office, staying in office, and increasing their power while in office. The party organization itself has three main elements, a secretariat led by the secretary-general, who is the chief administrative officer of the party, a policy board that determines over-all policy, and a research council with sections that parallel the bureaucracy's ministries. Diet committees are also set up in direct parallel to the ministries, often with overlapping membership between the party and the Diet committee. This party-bureaucracy parallel is strikingly similar to the organization of the Communist Party and the Soviet government in Russia.

The Establishment makes decisions at all levels, sometimes involving the entire body, other times involving only the pertinent sectors. Decisions on trade policy with Communist China are made by the whole Establishment because political as well as economic policy must be considered. Raising the central bank rate comes under the purview of the entire Establishment because it affects every phase of economic activity. At a lower level, export goals for steel are decided by the steel industry, the trading companies, the Ministry of International Trade and Industry, the Finance Ministry, and the Foreign Ministry. Political moves by the conservative party against the opposition parties involve all factions of the party and their financial backers in the business community.

No matter what the decision, nor whether it be at the national or the household level, the intricate process is the same and reveals much about Japanese values. The Japanese prefer to avoid decisions, if they can, letting nature take its course so long as the course is acceptable. Making a decision means resolving a conflict, and conflict in itself is a serious breach of virtue. But when a conflict arises and a decision must be made to resolve it, the Establishment undertakes a long, searching, and cumbersome inquiry to reach a decision. Many problems in Japan are solved by talking them to death.

Decisions in Japan are never made by individuals, always by groups. The process begins in a small group and moves through an ever-widening circle of groups. The individual never accepts responsibility for a decision and tries to spread responsibility as widely as possible. Within a group, and ultimately within the entire Establishment, decisions are made by an adjustment of views until agreement is reached. The concept of choosing one alternative by majority vote is alien to the Japanese and is rarely used except in a Western format, such as the Diet, and then only after the agreement has been reached by consensus. When the late Prime Minister Ikeda Hayato became ill and had to resign in 1964, an open struggle threatened to break out in naming a successor. Ikeda, from his hospital bed, asked Miki Takeo, a senior party leader, to prevent an open fight by consulting with other party leaders to choose a new prime minister. Miki spent the better part of a week consulting with the party and businessmen, reporting back to Ikeda daily. As it gradually became apparent that Sato Eisaku had more support than Kono Ichiro, Miki persuaded those favoring Kono to drop their opposition to Sato. Miki succeeded in getting a full consensus and took the result to Ikeda, who took ink brush and rice paper and wrote Sato's name to indicate the choice. A formal election was held later, but Sato in reality became prime minister without ever having submitted to a vote. A similar selection occurred in the opposition Japan Socialist Party in 1967 after Chairman Sasaki Kozo resigned. To prevent an open fight in a convention, several days of negotiating led to a session that went on until the wee hours of one morning and resumed several hours after sunup. The result was a compromise on Katsumata Seiichi. No meaningful vote was ever taken.

The Japanese method for reaching consensus within a small group is called *matomari*, or adjustment. A typical decision-making meeting opens with a statement of the problem by the group's senior member. Each member then exposes a slight portion of his thinking, never coming out with a full-blown, thoroughly persuasive presentation. After this, he sits back to listen to the same sort of exposition from the others. The Japanese, who has a tremendously sensitive ego, does not wish to put himself in a position where he is holding a minority or, worse, an isolated view. Nor does he wish to risk offending an associate by coming out bluntly with a proposal that might run contrary to his colleague's thoughts. The discussion goes on at great length, each person slowly and carefully presenting his opinion, gradually sensing out the feelings of other people, making a pitch subtly, following it without pressing if he finds it acceptable, quietly backing off and adjusting his views to those of the others if he finds himself not in tune with the evolving consensus. When the leader of the group believes that all are in basic agreement with a minimally acceptable decision, he sums up the thinking of the group, asks whether all are agreed, and looks around to receive their consenting nods. Nothing is crammed down anyone's throat. If, by chance, a consensus does not emerge and a deadlock seems likely, the group leader does not press for a decision, does not ask for a vote, does not rule that no consensus seems possible and thus embarrass people. Instead, he suggests that perhaps more time is needed to think about the problem, and sets a date for another meeting. The people involved can then meet informally to adjust views or, if there are positions that are wide apart, mediators will go back and forth between the people holding the opposing positions and attempt to narrow down the differences. By the time the next meeting is called, the differences most likely will have been straightened out and the process can move forward to a final decision. In all of this, the most important principle is not to stand on principle but to reach agreement. All else is subordinate to this point.

The system, like all human endeavors, is not perfect and can break down occasionally when someone fails to adjust or slips out of the consensus. If this happens, the counter-pressures are immediate. The Japanese work hard not only to reach agreement but to preserve the process itself. The flaw is corrected in much the same way the original agreement was reached, through consensus. A series of negotiations with the offender brings him back into line, but without his losing face, and a new equilibrium ensues. Several years ago, a major oil company, Idemitsu Kosan, broke an agreement on refinery output quotas that had been set by the petroleum association. The company, led by crusty old Idemitsu Sazo, was hurting because its new and unpaid-for refinery was operating far below capacity and was a drain on the company's finances. When Idemitsu ordered higher runs than the quota allowed, other oil company executives, plus a prominent outside intermediary, went into a series of consultations, brought marketing and financial pressures to bear on Idemitsu, and persuaded him to return to harmony. To avoid humiliating him, the petroleum association called a new meeting to revise the quotas, and Idemitsu was allotted a bigger run. The refinery wasn't allowed to operate at capacity, but Idemitsu got enough to make it economical, which was all he was after in the first place.

No decision or agreement is ever an absolute commitment to the Japanese. They believe that an agreement is valid only so long as the conditions under which it was made continue to obtain. When the situation changes, agreements must be changed to fit the new conditions. The Japanese avoid precedents as much as possible for this reason. They want to be free to make a new decision that is more sensible and profitable as the conditions affecting it bring about a new situation. The Japanese do not think in terms of general principles but in terms of what is expedient at the moment, making their decisions on a "case-by-case" basis. They will go to great pains, especially when dealing with foreigners, to make sure that today's agreement is not binding on future decisions. In contrast, the Western legalistic concept holds that once an agreement is reached, it must be honored throughout its lifetime, come what may. Many Westerners contend that the Japanese are devious because they refuse to be pinned down. But the Japanese see no sense in holding to an agreement when a new situation arises and requires new adjustments in the agreement.

In the process of making a decision, middle-level people are often highly influential. As the discussion of a major issue fans out and down from the top into the middle reaches of the Establishment, the bureaucracy's bureau chiefs and the business company department heads have their staffs pull together detailed information pertinent to the question. This assembled, each bureau sorts out the alternatives, drops those that they find unacceptable, consults with its counterparts in other agencies and companies, and reaches a semiconsensus that percolates its way to the top. This precludes the senior men from considering the eliminated alternatives. They cannot risk offending their juniors by overturning a carefully prepared recommendation because this would seriously disrupt the ties of vertical obligation and responsibility. Moreover, the senior men have not put the time and energy into the study that their juniors have and are somewhat at the mercy of those who have done the real work. The top men may modify a proposal, but they cannot override it completely. The possibility of a clash, however, is small because communications are continually going up and down while the middle-level people are working on the problem. Everybody involved has his antennae tuned most sensitively to readings that are coming from everywhere. Consensus is reached not in an isolation booth but in the midst of a six-ring circus.

The men at the ministry-bureau and company-department-head level use the same technique to initiate policy. The top men approve it, persuade the public to accept it, and are in the public eye; but much of the genuine policy making goes on at the next level down. If the bureaucrats in the Foreign Ministry think trade policies governing exports to the United States should be modified, for whatever reason, they first find a consensus among themselves on what ought to be done. This is communicated within the ministry to others involved in economic affairs and to those concerned with trade in the Finance Ministry and the Ministry of International Trade and Industry. At the same time, the idea is sent to the appropriate industry associations and major companies. Political leaders are informed that discussion has started. Within each sphere, committees work over the proposal and reach a consensus. That accomplished, representatives of each group meet to find a wider consensus. This may take weeks, as the representatives must check back with their own groups. Considerable informal negotiation and adjustment of views goes on outside the formal meetings. Intermediaries from the Cabinet, if it is a major policy decision, inform the bureaucrats and businessmen of the political thinking and take back to the politicians reports of developments. Thus, through a complex of intertwined, simultaneous, formal and informal discussions, a general consensus begins to emerge. By the time it has been worked over and over and has reached the top levels of the Establishment for final agreement, all but the last differences have been resolved. The senior men have only to smooth it off and proclaim it as a decision.

The informal channels of communication within the Establishment's decision-making mechanism are more important than the formal committee and consultative groups.

Members of the Establishment at every level meet each other daily. Most occupy offices within an area of two square miles and are, literally in some cases, within sight of each other. From the front of the Diet building, home of the politicians, one can look down the hill at Kasumi-gaseki, where the bureaucracy's ministries are situated, and, in another direction, past the Emperor's palace to Marunouchi, headquarters district for the big business combines. The telephone is in constant use, but the Japanese prefer face-to-face discussion when they have something serious on their minds. It is but a short walk or car ride from one office to another in this tight little area. In addition, a good part of the adjustment of views takes place in the evening in bars, restaurants, and geisha houses. Because the Japanese do not approach problems directly or confront each other with blunt proposals, the convivial atmosphere generated over a cup of *sake* or a Scotch highball helps the nuance-laden conversation to flow around all sides of the problem at hand. The same is true of the golf course, the fairways of which are populated by large numbers of the Establishment on the weekends.

When a problem is sticky, the intermediary becomes a major channel of negotiation. A Japanese does not want to offend another's ego by confronting him directly with a proposed solution that he is not likely to favor. Nor does he himself wish to risk being affronted by a sharp rejection of his proposal. The intermediary carries messages back and forth, divines the true intentions of all parties, and suggests courses that will lead to consensus. This is not done openly, by any means. The intermediary may not even receive an outright invitation to intercede but may only have hints dropped in front of him. If his involvement is open and his intercession fails, he will have been humiliated—a risk no one wants to take. Once the intermediary takes the hint and circuituously sounds out the first party, he begins a cautious and seemingly innocent approach to the others involved, broaching the subject in a gentle manner until the recipient realizes that a pitch is coming his way. There follows more sounding out all around the circle, a sifting of intent and proposals by the intermediary, a round of vague suggestions for resolution of the problem, a collection of the reactions, another series of conversations for adjustments of view. When the intermediary feels the parties are close enough to agreement that they can meet face to face to put on the finishing touches, he feigns boldness to suggest his solution. It is received by all concerned with gratified surprise and amid exclamations that they never realized the problem had come up or that he had been interested but that of course they would be happy to meet with the others. An informal session, perhaps in a geisha restaurant, follows, and at long last a formal meeting is held to put the final blessing on the agreement.

To facilitate making decisions on difficult problems, the Japanese often set up an ad hoc committee of representatives from different parts of the Establishment, plus specialists from the academic world and other intellectuals. It operates in the same fashion as a permanent group, arrives at a consensus that is accepted by the formal authorities, and is dissolved. The relationships formed during the life of the committee, however, add one more thread to the web that holds the Establishment together. In recent years, consultative or deliberative bodies have formulated national policies on the use of coal, oil, and atomic energy, reversion of Okinawa to Japanese rule, revision of the electoral system, educational reform, and consumer price inflation. While such organs usually come up with serious recommendations, they can be used, as committees are everywhere, to evade responsibility and avoid reaching what might be a painful conclusion.

The Japanese decision-making process is time-consuming to the point of frustration and can be carried to nearly ludicrous extremes. Prefectural authorities in Yamanashi-ken some time ago applied to the Ministry of Agriculture and Forestry for a one-hundred-million *yen* subsidy (about $277,778). Before it was approved, twenty-four applications had to be submitted along with forty-six supporting documents. More than ten conferences were held to discuss it. A total of 509 *hanko* ("seals," the equivalent of signatures) were required from the participating bureaucrats.

But this cumbersome system is one in which the Japanese are comfortable and one that they show no signs of altering. It is evidence of an innate Japanese preference for prudence and caution. The Japanese will walk around a problem ten times before they start edging into it. The process gives Japanese life a share of stability when it works and makes for sudden, unpredictable instability when it doesn't. Before World War II, decision making by consensus got out of kilter and the Japanese followed the militarists down the path to destruction. Since then, it has occasionally broken down and allowed Japan to drift into trouble, but subtle pressures have soon steered the nation back onto the course the Establishment thought best.

Curiously, the whole concept of the Establishment and the decision-making process is not well understood by the Japanese themselves. Because it is so thoroughly ingrained in them, very few are able to analyze and explain it. During a long series of interviews with members of the Establishment about the decision-making mechanism, I found only one who grasped immediately the point of the inquiry. This gentleman, a prominent banker, grabbed a pencil and sheet of paper and said, "Let me explain it this way. This is me," he said, drawing a small circle in the center of the paper. "And these are my connections, either as president of the bank or through personal relations," he continued, drawing a number of other small circles in a ring around himself. "I represent the bank in the bankers association and in Keidanren. I am a member of Keizai Doyukai. I have known the Finance Minister for many years and the Governor of the Bank of Japan was a schoolmate at Tokyo University. My wife is ————," and he went on through a list of relatives, friends from school or business or in politics, and how he had come to know them. "I am in touch with some of them every day," he said, "and others every week or month or so. These are the people I approach to express my ideas about the Japanese economy or about politics or even Japan's diplomacy, or they come to me informally to discuss the same problems." He described the places and circumstances in which he frequently met them. It was clear that he knew where he fit into the system and where each of the others fit in relation to himself and to each other. But most Japanese, even those at the highest levels, understand the process with their instincts, not their minds.

Chapter *5*

The
DUALITY of
POLITICS

Japanese politics are a first-rate case of Western image and Japanese reality. The Japanese political system looks like a democracy with its constitution, parliament, political parties, and elections. But democracy, which is a Western and not a worldwide political ideology, has not penetrated far into the spirit of Japanese politics. The theory and practice of Japanese politics today are far more the consequence of the Japanese heritage than of Western influence. The theory is derived from the *kokutai*, or national essence, and the *tenno-sei*, or imperial system, not from the somewhat impotent constitution imposed by the American Occupation. The practice revolves around the *habatsu*, or factions, that are the basic operative units in politics and the successors to the feudal clans of the last century. The Diet is their political battleground and the Cabinet is the executive committee of the ruling factional coalition. The public remains largely apathetic and only marginally involved in politics.

The contrast between the ideas of Anglo-American democracy and Japanese political belief is marked at least, and can often be formidable. Political sovereignty in the Anglo-American heritage lies with the people and works from the bottom up. Political sovereignty in Japan lies with the rulers and trickles from the top down. The American or English citizen can be an active participant in the processes of government, and public opinion is a recognizable political force. The Japanese citizenry is politically passive and usually consents to the leadership of the Establishment. The Westerner inherently distrusts, or at least is skeptical of, government authority and strives to restrain the exercise of political power. The Japanese basically trusts government authority and accepts the applications of its power, though this varies with his status, occupation, and education. Political decisions in the Western democracies are made by the majority for the greatest good of the greatest number, without infringing on the basic rights of the minority or the individual. Japanese political decisions are made by consensus or compromise for the greatest good of the nation-family. A fundamental ideal of Western democracy is human fulfillment of the individual. A basic objective in Japan is subordination of the individual to attain harmony within the group. Men in the West are believed to be created equal, even if they are not always treated so. The Japanese consider men to be inherently unequal and each to have his station in a hierarchy. The Western democrat ideally is tolerant and accepts diversity in society. The Japanese is intolerant and strives for conformity. The Westerner believes that as a free man he has certain inalienable rights. The Japanese believes that as a member of the national family he has certain duties and obligations. The role of the state in a Western democracy is to protect and enhance individual rights. The role of the Japanese state is to preserve a benevolent social order. Western democracies are founded on the rule of law, to which all men are equally subject. Japanese politics are based on the rule of men, who are supposed to govern for the common good but who do so with different standards for superiors and inferiors. The disparities are so great that the Japanese have no word in their language that truly means "democracy." There was no word at all before the modern era, and since then at least seven have been coined or adapted from the West, none of them fitting exactly because the concept is alien. These contrasts are offered without moral judgment and only to show that Japanese and Westerners conceive political ideas differently.

In defining the form of the Japanese state in Western terms, to say what it is not is easier than to say what it is. It is neither a democratic republic, like the United States, nor a socialist republic, like the Soviet Union. It is not a constitutional monarchy, like Great Britain, though it has some exterior resemblance to the British monarchy, nor an absolutist monarchy, like France in the days of Louis XIV. It is certainly not a dictatorship, either of the right, like Franco's Spain, or of the left, like Mao's China. Nor is it really like any other form of government in the world. The Japanese *tenno-sei* might best be described in Western terms as an imperial patriarchy with theocratic overtones. The earliest word for government in Japanese was *matsurigoto*, which means religious rituals and alludes to the unity of government and religion. This was not a clear-cut, formal union of organized religion and government but a concept that reverence for the national gods, the maintenance of moral standards, and the ethical principles of government were inseparable. The words for emperor, *tenno heika*, mean literally "under the steps to the throne of the heavenly sovereign," signifying that the emperor is the supplicant for the Japanese people to their gods.

The emperor, however, is not considered "divine," in the Judaeo-Christian sense. The ultranationalists of the 1930's distorted the sacred nature of the emperor for their internal propaganda purposes, but few believed it. Emperor Hirohito, at the bidding of the Occupation, renounced this warped notion in his January 1, 1946, repudiation of false concepts. He said: "The ties between Us and Our people have always stood upon mutual trust and affection. They do not depend on mere legends and myths. They are not predicated on the false conception that the Emperor is divine, and that the Japanese people are superior to other races and fated to rule the world." The divinity of the Emperor was perhaps the most notable of the prewar distortions swept away by the Occupation. This allowed the Emperor to resume his traditional role, in which the Japanese consider his person sacred and worthy of reverence and awe but not the possessor of supernatural spiritual powers.

Emperor Hirohito today lives a rather quiet life, still behind the great gray stone walls of the Imperial Palace that was once the Tokugawa shogun's fortress. The prewar parades on the white horse and the other militaristic trappings are long gone. He is a rather shy man, ill at ease in public but reported to be conscientious about his duties and concerned about how his people are getting on. He spends part of each day putting his seal on government documents, usually with a question or two to the chamberlain in attendance. Much of his time is taken in ritual and ceremony. He goes to the Imperial Shrines at Ise to report on the state of the nation to Amaterasu-o-mi-kami, the Sun Goddess, and to the imperial ancestors. Each spring, he plants the first rice seedlings as an offering to the gods of the fields for a good crop. He opens each session of the Diet with a short proclamation read from the red-velveted niche in which a gilt throne sits on one side of the dark-paneled, Victorian chamber of the upper house. The prime minister and his new Cabinets appear before him for attestation, a sort of swearing-in ceremony that gives them legitimate authority to govern. The Emperor presents Japanese ambassadors with their credentials before they leave for overseas posts and receives foreign ambassadors when they come to Tokyo. Each year, he and the immediate members of the Imperial Family write short poems that set the tone for the imperial contest to which anyone may contribute an entry. The Imperial Family occasionally hears lectures given by prestigious scholars who come to the palace for the event. On August 15, the anniversary of the war's end, the Emperor goes to the Budokan, or Hall of Martial Arts, to lead memorial ceremonies for all who died in the war.

Emperor Hirohito's private life, what little is known about it, is taken up with his family, to which he is reportedly devoted, and with his avocation of marine biology. Those Japanese who know him, and they are relatively few, say they have been struck by his warmth and kindness. One young man, describing his meeting with the Emperor, said later: "It must be wonderful to have a man like the Emperor for one's own father." The Emperor pursues his avocation in a small laboratory within the Imperial Palace grounds and on vacation trips to various seacoasts. He has earned himself a good reputation in the scientific community, is credited with several original discoveries, and has published at least eight books, though not until recently was he allowed to use his own name as author. The comings and goings of the Imperial Family are somberly reported in the Japanese press without much detail or excitement. He meets the Japanese press for a few minutes twice a year, but never receives foreign newsmen. People in Tokyo are generally indifferent to the activities of the Emperor, caught up as they are in the hustle of daily life. Those from rural areas show more interest. Volunteers come in each day, some from long distances, to tidy up the vast palace grounds. They pay their own way and work for nothing, yet there often is a six-months' backlog of applicants.

The Emperor is, to all intents, a prisoner. His every move is subject to the direction of the Kunaicho, the Imperial Household Agency. Whenever the Emperor appears in public, a Kunaicho official hovers about, showing him where to walk, telling him where to sit, whom to speak to, whom not to speak to. The Kunaicho is a palace guard that dictates what the Emperor will do, whom he will see, where he will go. It is staffed by what some Japanese commentators call stubborn, old-fashioned, stuffy bureaucrats and headed by retired officials and diplomats. Younger men shun the assignment if they can because of the sterile atmosphere of the agency. A major objective of the Kunaicho is to keep the Emperor as far from the public as possible. He has visited factories and hospitals in recent years, but the trips have become less frequent. The Kunaicho, after much deliberation, permitted the Emperor in 1967 to ride on the high-speed Tokaido train from Tokyo to Osaka. This was the first time that he was allowed on a train that also carried ordinary Japanese; the Emperor usually goes by special train in the imperial coach. The Kunaicho, however, reserved five of the train's twelve cars, closed them off, and made sure that he was preserved from any contact with the citizenry. Crown Princess Michiko, wife of Crown Prince Akihito, several years ago tried to let some fresh air into the court and increase the Imperial Family's daily involvement with the Japanese people in somewhat the way the British and European constitutional monarchs get out and around. But her efforts were firmly circumscribed by the Kunaicho and she lost her fight. Whether the Crown Prince, when he ascends the throne, will make any changes remains to be seen. He broke one tradition by marrying a commoner, though from a very prestigious family. A sister left the Imperial Family to marry a young man from the Shimazu family of the Satsuma clan. A brother who married last, however, returned to tradition and had chosen for him a bride from the Tokugawa family, descendents of the last shogun.

The political theory underlying Japan's imperial patriarchy is the *kokutai*, two ideographs that mean "national" and "body" but usually translated "national essence" or "national polity." It is a vaguely defined ideology, rooted in Shinto beliefs and overlaid with Confucian philosophy. It is an expression of ideals in which loyalty, filial piety, benevolence, a sense of unity between rulers and ruled, harmony, mutual respect, duty to family and emperor, and submission to authority are prime virtues. *Kokutai* became the basis for political thought in the Meiji era, particularly in the constitution and the Imperial Rescript on Education. In this century, scholars who considered themselves liberals were among its foremost proponents. Yoshino Sakuzo, Minobe Tatsukichi, and Ozaki Yukio defended Japan's *kokutai* as unique and as the foundation on which the new political order should be built. The prewar militarists twisted *kokutai* and gave it a highly militaristic and totalitarian coloration, which the Occupation eliminated.

Since then, the word *kokutai* has been discredited along with almost everything else connected with the bitter days of the militarists. This has left a void that the Japanese today are groping about to fill. Tanaka Kotaro, a postwar chief justice of the Supreme Court, a recognized authority on the postwar constitution, and a Christian, described it thus: "The only thing that has lent any ethical character at all to our political life has been the consciousness of our *kokutai* and a sense of reverence for the Emperor; but in recent times not only did these attitudes lead to superstition and a loss of sanity, but they developed into a form of ultranationalism which recognized no ethical restraints upon the nation and justified immoral practices of imperialistic aggression." Tanaka went on to point out the lack of conviction and the ethical indifference of the postwar era and to urge that Japan preserve its own legacies, moral convictions, and fine social traditions.

The postwar constitution, known as the Showa Constitution and sometimes as the MacArthur Constitution, was intended to fill the void in Japan's political theory and to be the base for a new democratic Japanese state. It appears at first glance to be a model constitution, packed with every conceivable democratic ideal, right, and procedure. But this turns out to be an illusion compounded of the fuzziness of recent Japanese political thinking and the hazy image of Japanese politics seen by the Occupation authorities. The Showa Constitution bears little relation to Japanese political realities, which are gradually eroding it. The present constitution is a marked contrast to the Meiji Constitution, which was a successful adaptation of a Western political instrument to Japanese political thought and was a genuinely Japanese document. The Showa Constitution, however, is a hodgepodge of poorly constructed ideas thrown together hurriedly under the supervision of American military authorities who had scant knowledge of Japanese history, culture, or politics. A draft of the constitution was handed to the Cabinet, which in turn presented it to the Diet. There were lengthy interpellations and debates and several amendments, but the draft passed fundamentally intact, as it had come from the Occupation authorities. No Japanese constitutional jurists were consulted, no representative convention was held, no vote by the Japanese people was taken. In sum, the constitution was dictated by the Occupation and proclaimed by the Emperor.

Some of the constitution's lofty principles, expressed in rather turgid language, are simply unreal or run counter to Japanese basic political beliefs. The Preamble opens: "We, the Japanese people . . . do proclaim that sovereign power resides with the people and do firmly establish this Constitution." Besides being a poor imitation of the language in the American Constitution, the statement is not true. Moreover, few Japanese, including liberal scholars at that time, believed that sovereignty resided with the people. All but the Communists had been anxious to preserve the prerogatives of the Imperial House. The Preamble further contends that popular sovereignty "is a universal principle of mankind." This is a nice wish for those who believe in democracy but is simply not true in the real world. Again: "We believe that no nation is responsible to itself alone, but that the laws of political morality are universal." If a nation is not responsible to itself, to whom is it responsible? The authors of the document did not say. That political morality is universal is patently not so, either in the ideal or the reality.

The two most controversial articles in the constitution are Article I, defining the status of the emperor, and Article IX, the famous "no-war" clause. Article I states that "the Emperor shall be the symbol of the state and of the unity of the people, deriving his position from the will of the people with whom resides sovereign power." Its first phrase is reasonably close to reality, the emperor having always been, among many things, the symbol of Japan and its national unity. Its second phrase, as in the Preamble, has no basis in Japanese philosophic, moral, political, or legal thought.

There is also an immediate contradiction in the constitution that is buttressed by the Imperial House Law, another product of the Occupation. If the emperor derives his position from the will of the people, it would logically follow that the people may depose an emperor or name whomever they choose when the emperor dies. Article II of the constitution states however: "The Imperial Throne shall be dynastic and succeeded to in accordance with the Imperial House Law passed by the Diet." The Imperial House Law says: "The Imperial Throne shall be succeeded to by a male offspring in the male line belonging to the Imperial Lineage." It goes on to spell out the line of succession and the circumstances under which succession is accomplished. It is difficult to reconcile the position of an emperor based on the will of the people with a clearcut dynastic succession.

Article IX, which General MacArthur personally ordered included in the constitution, has Japan renouncing
forever "war as a sovereign right of the nation and the
threat or use of force as means of settling international
disputes." It states explicitly that "land, sea, and air forces,
as well as other war potential, will never be maintained."
Both points have since died quiet deaths. Most Japanese
legal scholars, political leaders, and even the Japan Communist Party agree that every nation has the right to go
to war in self-defense. National policy and sentiment, not
the constitution, are the bulwarks against offensive action.
Further, Japan has about 250,000 men under arms in
modest but reasonably modern army, navy, and air forces
that are euphemistically called Self-Defense Forces. No
court has ever ruled on the constitutionality of these issues
nor has the constitution been amended. The Establishment
has merely gone ahead with what it deemed necessary,
which may be a comment on the over-all indifference
with which all but a vocal minority regard the constitution.

The constitution has other contradictory or meaningless provisions. "Fundamental human rights" are guaranteed, but just what they are is not specified. "All of the
people shall be respected as individuals." But individualism
—*kojin shugi*—in Japan has the connotation of egotism
and selfishness and is not considered a virtue. The state is
ordered to refrain from religious activity. Yet the very
nature of the state is religious and the names of several
state organs have religious import. The Kunaicho, or
Imperial Household Agency, translates as "Court Within
the Shrine." One constitutional article states: "All people
shall have the right and the obligation to work." Must the
government provide jobs for the unemployed? Does the
rich or retired man who doesn't need work have to work?
The authors of the constitution did not say. Article XXIX
states: "The right to own or to hold property is inviolable." The same article also says: "Private property may

be taken for public use upon just compensation therefor." Is private property inviolable or isn't it? The unending squabbles over eminent domain for the nation's expanding rapid-transit system is evidence that the issue is clearly unclear.

It seems doubtful, therefore, that the Showa Constitution will ever be truly assimilated into Japanese political thought. Rumbles for its revision started almost the day after it was promulgated. Some Japanese during the Occupation conceived of the constitution as a gesture of acquiescence they were forced to make to the American authorities and something to be done away with as soon as the Americans had gone. Their views did not prevail, however. More responsible Japanese leaders and scholars have undertaken several studies on constitutional revision, but their findings so far have been inconclusive. A major obstacle is the lack of a national consensus on revision. The left wing that developed after the war is loudly against revision, which it contends would open the way for a return of militarism and ultranationalism. Claiming wide public support for the constitution, it uses the issue as much for political as ideological reasons to attack the Establishment.

Nonetheless, flickering signs indicate that the movement for revision is alive. It is part of the resurgence of nationalism that is among the strongest motivations in Japanese life today: the belief that Japan is a unique nation whose institutions must be fitted to its own circumstances. Scholars are delving into the theoretical bases of *kokutai* and the imperial institution. Conservative leaders privately talk about revising the constitution to make it reflect the realities of Japanese politics. Some occasionally make public statements, but in guarded terms so as not to arouse the political opposition. A Cabinet minister in 1968, however, slipped and publicly criticized the constitution as "silly" because it puts Japan's security at the mercy of other nations. He was forced to resign in the uproar that followed, not because he had criticized the constitution but because he had suggested that Japan follow a course that could lead to the acquisition of nuclear weapons. That suggestion left him open to attack from the left, and the opposition leapt to it. An earlier report from the Ministry of Education alluded to Japan's political system, particularly the role of the emperor. "The Image of the Ideal Japanese," drawn up by a commission of scholars and prominent establishmentarians for the ministry in 1967, was not an Imperial Rescript on Education, but it had some of the same and breadth of the 1890 rescript. It nodded toward democratic norms of individual respect and responsibility, but most of its emphasis was on traditional virtues and ethics. It exhorted the Japanese to have patriotism and used the word *aikokushin*, a three-ideograph word meaning "love," "country," and "heart," which had fallen into disrepute because the militarists abused it before and during the war. The core of patriotism, the document said, is love and respect for the emperor, the symbol of the unity of the nation. In a typically Japanese subtlety, the report quoted fully from the constitution in its first reference to the emperor, including the clause about sovereignty resting with the people. But it dropped that clause in further references and focused on his symbolic, unifying position. The report did not specifically refer to constitutional revision. But it was another thrust in that direction.

It is entirely conceivable that the Japanese will one day scrap the Showa Constitution and start from scratch, as Ito Hirobumi and other men of Meiji did, to write a truly Japanese constitution. The renewed pride and confidence in recent years and the urge to remove all traces of the defeat and Occupation, plus the postwar re-examination of historical and cultural beliefs, may lead to this. A council of the most learned men in the nation might delve deep into Japanese history, culture, political thought, philosophy, and psychology and come up with a constitution that genuinely reflects the aspirations of the Japanese and provides them with a realistic instrument with which to organize and exercise political power. It seems fairly certain that if this is done, the central role of the emperor would once more become explicit as well as implicit and that the best principles of the *kokutai* will be reasserted, even as they are already being carried forward. A new constitution, if it achieves the high standard of Ito's Meiji Constitution, would mark the culmination of the adaptation of a Western political format to Japanese political substance.

In looking at Japanese politics, it is essential not to confuse political theory with practical politics. Among the oldest of Japanese traditions is duality in government: the separation of the imperial institution, the source of idealism and legitimacy, from the actual rulers of the country, who are eminently political and pragmatic. The tradition first flowered in the Heian period (794–1185), when men from the powerful Fujiwara family were named kampaku, or chancellor. They and their successors, the shoguns of the Kamakura, Ashikaga, and Tokugawa periods, ruled in the name of the emperor. Occasionally a strong emperor competed for power but rarely did he succeed. Once, in the thirteenth century, there were an abdicated emperor, a titular emperor, and a titular shogun from the Minamoto family, but it was a regent from the Hojo family who really had the power. Even the American Occupation fit into the pattern. The Emperor retained his symbolic place, the reviving bureaucracy and politicians appeared to run the country, but real power rested with the authorities in the MacArthur "shogunate."

The duality continues today, though the exterior forms have changed. In modern times, the Meiji oligarchy, then the militarists, and now the political parties, Diet, and

Cabinet within the Establishment are the wielders of political power in a line that goes all the way back to the Fujiwara era. Another tradition, that of the clan as the basic political unit, also persists. Fitting clan politics into Western forms of parliamentary government has been a major cause of political disruption, especially in the postwar period when politicians have become full members of the ruling elite.

Today, the *habatsu*, or faction, is the operative unit of Japanese politics. The *habatsu* are the political descendants of the *han*, or domains, that were ruled by *daimyo*, whose retainers were the *samurai*. The *habatsu* has a chief, the modern equivalent of a *daimyo*, and followers, who are his "*samurai*." A *habatsu* is formed by a politician in the Diet who has the leadership abilities, political skill, access to money in the business community, and the ambition to become prime minister. He draws other politicians around him because he has patronage and favors to bestow and the capacity to help them further their own political careers. Ideology enters the equation only insofar as the members of a *habatsu* hold generally similar beliefs. More important are the personal relations that develop over the years. Loyalty is built up vertically between the leader and his followers and horizontally among all members of the group. It is this personal loyalty, more than anything else, that gives a *habatsu* its cohesion.

Where the sword was the instrument of power for the *daimyo* and *samurai*, money is the instrument of power for members of a *habatsu*. The member does not use this money to line his pockets or to live luxuriously, though there are a few who do, but to build an organization and to do favors that preserve or enhance his political position. Every politician's constituency is his political base and he must maintain it through political workers and associations. Like the *samurai*, who drew his income in rice from his *daimyo,* the politician gets most of his funds from the leader of his *habatsu,* smaller portions coming from the party or from his own private sources.

Each *habatsu* has some degree of permanence. Rarely do members drop from one and join another. As leaders either die or retire, the leadership passes to men they have picked within the *habatsu,* and the group continues intact. When former Prime Minister Ikeda Hayato died in 1964, his *habatsu* held together under Maeo Shigesaburo, who was a prime-ministerial candidate in the November 1968 election. Sometimes, however, a *habatsu* splits and re-forms around new men who look like promising contenders for the prime minister's chair. Kono Ichiro's *habatsu* split after his death several years ago and formed two new *habatsu* under the leadership of Nakasone Yasuhiro and Mori Kiyoshi, two bright and ambitious politicians. When Mori died unexpectedly in 1968, his followers began drifting back to Nakasone's *habatsu.*

Ozaki Yukio, considered among Japan's foremost progressive political thinkers and a long-time member of the Diet, wrote perhaps the best Japanese critique of the *habatsu,* of which he did not approve. He wrote it in 1918, just as party politicians were making their move for power. It is still applicable today, when the politicians have picked up the reins that were knocked from their hands by the prewar militarists. Ozaki wrote:

> Here in the Orient we have had the conception of a faction; but none of a public party. A political party is an association of people having for its exclusive object the discussion of public affairs of state and the enforcement of their views thereon. But when political parties are transplanted in the East, they at once partake of the nature of factions, pursuing private and personal interests instead of the interests of the state—as witnessed by the fact of their joining hands with the clan cliques or using the construction of railways, ports and harbors, schools, etc., as

means for extending party influence. Besides, the customs and usages of feudal times are so deeply impressed upon the minds of men here that even the idea of political parties, as soon as it enters the brains of our countrymen, germinates and grows according to feudal notions. Such being the case, even political parties, which should be based and dissolved solely on principle and political views, are really affairs of personal connections and sentiments, the relations between the leader and the members of a party being similar to those which subsisted between a feudal lord and his liegemen, or to those between a "boss" of gamblers and his followers in this country. A politician scrupulous enough to join or desert a party for the sake of principle is denounced as a political traitor or renegade. That political faith should be kept not *vis-à-vis* its leader or its officers but *vis-à-vis* its principles and views is not understood. They foolishly think that the proverb "a faithful servant never serves two masters: a chaste wife never sees two husbands" is equally applicable to the members of a political party. In their erroneous opinion, it is a loyal act on the part of a member of a party to change his principles and views in accordance with orders from headquarters, while in the event of headquarters changing their views it is unlawful to desert them.

The *habatsu* today are formed into coalitions that have the outward appearances and trappings of political parties. The *habatsu* in a party have a common ideology, but the party is more an alliance held together by expedience to retain power or attempt to get into power. Basic loyalties are to the *habatsu*, not to the party. Japanese political parties are relatively small, elite parties of registered, dues-paying members. The Japanese voter does not belong to a party nor does he consider himself an informal member, as an American considers himself a Republican or a Democrat. He does not participate in party activities, but is limited to voting for it at the polls. The parties have permanent organizations with membership composed largely of Diet members, their immediate followers and party workers, local party officials and organizers, and members of identifiable political-support groups.

The ideological spectrum of Japanese parties ranges from the far right to the far left, the fulcrum being well to the right of center. On the extreme right are several small groups, such as Akao Bin's Greater Japan Patriotic Party, that mouth the slogans of an ultranationalist yesteryear but attract little attention.

The major party is the Liberal Democratic Party, an amalgam of *habatsu* descended from two major prewar conservative parties. The LDP, however, is neither liberal nor democratic nor a party but is a conservative, authoritarian alliance of *habatsu*. The conservatives have been in power since the end of the war except for a brief spell in 1947–8 when a left-center coalition had a disastrous fling at governing. The LDP, with 65,000 members, has about a dozen factions ranging from Prime Minister Sato's *habatsu* of more than fifty Diet members to former Prime Minister Kishi's four or five. The LDP *habatsu* are aligned in three "streams," the mainstream, or Old Right, being the more conservative and the one in control of the party leadership organs. The anti-mainstream, or New Right, is slightly to the left. Its struggles with the Old Right are due more to competition for party control than to major policy differences. In between is a non-mainstream that is supposedly neutral but uses its balancing position for political leverage. Scattered through this maze are a few mavericks who have risen because they are wealthy or come from prestigious families or simply enjoy bucking the system a bit. The lineup is not static but is a set of alliances that shifts as each *habatsu* unceasingly struggles to better its power position.

To the left of the LDP, but still well right of center, is the new Komeito, or Clean Government Party. It is the political arm of the nationalistic, militant Soka Gakkai Buddhist sect, one of Japan's "new religions." Komeito, better known by its Japanese than its English name, has had a spectacular rise due to its tight organization and its skill in assessing people from which it can gain support. Unlike the older parties, it is more of a mass party, with 200,000 registered members and all adherents of the Soka Gakkai counted as informal members. Komeito is a *habatsu* in itself and so far has not been much affected by internal struggles for power. It will be interesting to see whether the party, which prides itself on being purely Japanese, develops separate *habatsu* as it becomes more settled in daily political affairs.

Just left of center, in Western political terms, is the Democratic Socialist Party, also a *habatsu* in itself. It splintered off the Japan Socialist Party in 1960 as a consequence of both policy and factional differences. Nishio Suehiro, an old-time socialist politician, felt he was being shoved around too much by later arrivals and took his *habatsu* out of the party. Nishio and his followers are non-Marxist socialists roughly equivalent to the British Labour Party and the European Christian Socialists. Feelings between the DSP and the JSP are bitter. JSP leaders, especially on its far left, often refer to DSP as a "second conservative party." In socialist terminology, nothing is dirtier. The DSP, which claims 40,000 members, gets most of its support from Domei, the more moderate of Japan's two main labor federations.

The major opposition party is the Japan Socialist Party, with 51,000 members and support from the larger, more militant Sohyo labor federation. The JSP's *habatsu* are divided into two streams, with a greater ideological content in their differences than in those of the conservative party. The anti-mainstream is the more moderate, advocating Marxist socialism at home and neutrality in foreign policy. The mainstream is radically Marxist and pro-Communist Chinese in foreign outlook. The Marxism of its leader, Sasaki Kozo, is even further to the left than the orthodoxy of the Japan Communist Party. Sasaki's doctrinaire approach to politics and his lack of pragmatism in today's increasingly prosperous Japanese economy has thrown the JSP so out of touch with reality that it has begun to lose at the polls, after a steady upswing from the end of the war. Both streams of the JSP are officially anti-American, which is ironic, as the party and its supporting labor unions owe their very existence to the American Occupation. They had been suppressed by the prewar militarists and were encouraged by the Occupation as a democratizing influence and counterbalance to a possible resurgence of ultranationalism.

On the far left of the political spectrum is the Japan Communist Party, which also exists because the Occupation decreed that it could come up from underground. The JCP claims to be a mass party of 300,000 members but it, too, is more Japanese than Communist, having *habatsu*, personal power struggles, and splinter groups. Until the time of the Sino-Soviet split in the early 1960's, the JCP had pro-Moscow and pro-Peking *habatsu*. In the fashion of communist parties it could not abide both under one roof after the split. The pro-Moscow group has gained control of the party and purged the pro-Peking group.

Several currents running through Japanese politics may lead to a marked realignment of political forces in coming years. The LDP is stagnating from being in power so long under bland leaders. Younger, more imaginative politicians are restless under their constraint. They also have policy differences, particularly in the role they would like Japan to play in Asia. The older leaders prefer to continue more cautious, restrained policies under the shield of American protection. The younger want to be more assertive, independent, even Gaullist in outlook. On the other side, the JSP is in danger of losing its viability as a political force. It has been too doctrinaire, has little appeal outside labor, and is losing labor support as standards of living rise. Younger socialists want a more pragmatic approach that attracts voters, while remaining inside a moderate socialist framework. A realignment might see the conservatives split as the New Right *habatsu* look for an "opening to the left" and drift toward some form of centrist coalition with the DSP and the moderate JSP *habatsu*. Komeito has vowed that it will not join a coalition, but the temptation to participate in a government may be too strong to resist if it becomes a live possibility. Several New Right *habatsu* leaders toyed with the idea before the general elections of January 1967, but the Old Right crushed it with a solid win at the ballot box. Nonetheless, the idea has not died. DSP leaders have been active in promoting it, with their party as the bridge between the others. If such a realignment comes about, the major political forces would then be two alliances between the conservative rightist *habatsu* and the moderate centrist *habatsu*. Political trends in Japan today appear to preclude any drastic swing to the left.

The political maneuvering ground for the *habatsu* is the Diet, which is less a legislature than a battleground for the parties and *habatsu*. The Diet is the public forum in which the government party sets out policy, goes through the public phases of adjusting views, and informs the public of what it intends to do. The opposition parties and the anti-mainstream *habatsu* of the ruling party use it to attack the government leadership. Far more time is spent in interpellations of Cabinet ministers and top bureaucrats, both in plenary session and in committee, than in open debate. These interpellations are perhaps the most important function of the Diet, because the ruling party must define and defend its policies every day the Diet is in session. Prime ministers and Cabinet officers, who must be in attendance most of the time, have complained that too much of their working day is taken up with answering questions in the Diet. But the practice is something of a guarantee against arbitrary action and against the revival of totalitarian rule because the government is subject to public scrutiny by the opposition and by skeptical members of its own party. The interpellations, too, are a vital element in the making of a national consensus on political matters. The press publishes more about remarks and speeches in the Diet than any other political pronouncements. Particular attention is paid to the lower House of Representatives, which is by far the more powerful of the Diet's two chambers. Before the war the upper House of Peers, composed of nobles and other high-ranking personalities, was predominant. But the postwar constitution left it only secondary functions, something like those of the British House of Lords, and made the lower house the locus of power.

As a legislature, the Diet is a rubber-stamp body. The bureaucracy, in conjunction with ruling party leaders, draws up bills that are presented to the Diet, subjected to desultory debate, and passed with votes almost strictly along party lines. A more important function for members of the Diet is to serve as ambassadors from their local constituencies to the bureaucracy. Local government in Japan is weak, and most of the money and power is in the national government. Dietmen are lobbyists who try to persuade the Finance Ministry to include funds in the next budget for a new bridge or school building back home, then go to the Construction, Transport, or Education Ministries to see that it is built. Through behind-the-scenes persuading and cajoling, adjusting, and compromising, the Dietman tries to do the best he can for his constituency. Consequently, Diet members of the ruling party do not vote against the bureaucracy's recommendations. The one who does quickly discovers that the funds for his local projects have somehow got tied up in "administrative difficulties" and will not be available. He will be politely requested to "understand" and wait till next year.

A major difference between the Japanese Diet and the British and American parliaments on which it is modeled is how decisions are made. In the British House of Commons and the American Congress, a bill is debated and a vote taken. If 201 are for and 199 are against, it passes and everybody accepts the decision as fair and proper. In the Diet, the majority may be able to muster a 67 percent vote but still cannot have 100 per cent of its own way. It must concede and compromise enough to give the minority at least a one-third say in the final outcome. This is a major point of friction in the adaptation of the Western parliamentary concept that says majority rules to the Japanese practice that says consensus must prevail. It works a good part of the time because informal adjustments are made before a vote comes up. But ruptures occur and often result in physical violence on the Diet floor when the minority thinks its views have not been sufficiently considered. The minority then claims that it is being oppressed by a "tyranny of the majority." Ruptures also occur when the minority refuses to accept only the proportion of the compromise to which its relative power entitles it. It may boycott Diet sessions and play on the majority's reluctance to ram bills through. The minority opposition may blockade the chamber so that majority members may not enter, trap majority leaders in their offices so that they cannot get to the floor to call the house into session, and disrupt the balloting proceedings on the floor by out-shouting the speaker or refusing to allow majority members to approach the rostrum.

The turmoil that attracted most attention occurred during the 1960 deliberations over ratification of the Mutual Security Treaty with the United States. Prime Minister Kishi had to resort to a midnight subterfuge to get it through, which set off rioting in the streets and the cancellation of President Eisenhower's scheduled state visit. This was but the most prominent of similar incidents that take place frequently and will continue until Japanese politicians find some way to mesh the Western parliamentary mechanism with Japanese ideas of what is politically proper.

The Cabinet is the supreme executive organ of the Japanese government and, like other groups in Japanese society, collectively responsible for its policy decisions. The prime minister, while the most powerful minister, is the first among equals. He is picked, technically, from the Diet by majority vote. In practice, the prime minister is the man chosen as president of the ruling party. He is elected president by majority vote of accredited members of the party convention; in the case of the ruling LDP these are the members of both houses of the Diet. Votes are usually along *habatsu* lines. The prime minister names the Cabinet, the main criterion being to reflect the power balance among the *habatsu*. Since this constantly shifts, cabinets are shuffled about once a year either to reflect changes or in an effort by the prime minister to bring about an alignment more favorable to him. Thus, he may give a fence-sitting *habatsu* an extra place in the Cabinet in return for its support. The political or administrative competence of the prospective Cabinet members has little to do with the choice. The tale may be apocryphal, but it is said that once, shortly after a new foreign minister was named, he was asked by a news reporter what his first move would be. "Well," he said, pausing, "I think I'll find out where the Foreign Ministry is." He had never been in the building. This, in addition to the latent power of the bureaucracy, puts the minister at the mercy of his principal subordinates, particularly the experienced vice-minister at the peak of his bureaucratic career.

Habatsu leaders are not necessarily, nor even regularly, selected for the Cabinet. The prime minister consults with his own closest associates to determine how many from each *habatsu* will be in the Cabinet. He then consults with each *habatsu* leader for recommendations. The portfolios are distributed to senior men by their leader to reward them for loyalty and long service, which gives each a turn in the Cabinet to enhance his prestige with his own political organization and to make his re-election to the Diet easier. A clue to a prime minister's intentions is given by the ministries to which he assigns his own immediate followers. He usually puts his most trusted men in the areas in which he plans to make difficult or controversial moves. The lineups also give clues as to whose star is on the rise, and particularly, as to which man the current prime minister favors to succeed him. Prime Minister Sato shuffled his Cabinet in November 1968, naming Fukuda Takeo as Finance Minister. Fukuda has been a long-time associate of Sato's, had been in earlier Cabinets, and, for the two years immediately preceding the shuffle, had been Secretary General of the LDP. By naming Fukuda to the powerful Finance Ministry post, Sato clearly signaled that he had become a leading candidate for the prime minister's chair.

The Cabinet makes its decisions, as do other groups, by consensus. It meets regularly twice a week, more often when emergencies arise. The prime minister presides, presents subjects for discussion, guides the deliberation, and announces a consensus when it is reached. No votes are taken, and if consensus is not reached, no decision is made until views have been adjusted. No records are kept so that individual ministers may speak more freely and not fear that their views may one day be made public and find them out of step with the final consensus.

The role of the public in Japanese politics is negligible. In their history, the Japanese people have never demanded a voice in government. There have been peasant uprisings, mostly rice rebellions, for economic reasons, but never any mass movement—to say nothing of revolution—for political expression. Nishio Suehiro, former chairman of the DSP and for fifty years an advocate of democracy for Japan, in a news interview shortly after his 1967 retirement lamented that Japan had never had a "democratic revolution." He said that the American Occupation had tried to foster such a movement, but it had not taken hold because it came from the outside and not from the Japanese themselves.

In a decade of association with the Japanese, I have never heard a Japanese assert: "I know my rights" or any similar expression that Western democrats use to reaffirm their political prerogatives. It may seem paradoxical that the turnout at the polls for an election is relatively high, by any standard. The Japanese concept of a vote may explain this. The vote to a Westerner is a right, to a Japanese a duty or an obligation. The Japanese votes for his candidate on the basis of loyalty to him and to the political organization that has cultivated his vote through personal favors. The Japanese votes his habits; issues have little to do with his choice.

The political unimportance of the vote can be seen in Japanese election campaigns, which are dull, listless exercises. A candidate for the Diet hires a station wagon with a public-address speaker fastened atop and cruises through his electoral district every day for three weeks (or has his proxy do it, if he is a big name), blaring: "This is Suzuki Saburo of the Liberal Democratic Party, Suzuki Saburo of the Liberal Democratic Party, asking for your vote. Please (using the extremely honorific form) favor me with your good wishes." That's all. Occasionally he stops and addresses the people on the streets or those at home in a residential area, but rarely does he draw a crowd. I once accompanied an obscure candidate from a minority party and watched him spend ten chilly minutes speaking through a megaphone to passers-by on a shopping street. Only two people listened—his campaign manager and I. Another time, a very prominent and popular politician drew all of a dozen people in the center of a small town. The candidates also address a few public meetings during the campaign. Each candidate is allotted twenty minutes to speak, one after the other, with an election official watching an alarm clock on the rostrum. No crowds gather, just a few people who drift into a school auditorium to see the candidate for whom they already have decided to vote. The speeches are monotonous recitations of known records and positions; no fireworks, no mudslinging, no urgent cries either for a new Japan or a return to the good old days. A politician, once asked why he bothered to go through the barren, futile motions, replied: "Ah, but you don't understand. We must do this to show our sincerity. If we didn't, the people who have voted for us before will think that we are insincere and vote for somebody else."

One method of popular expression developed in the postwar period is the *demo,* or demonstration. But these have limited effect as they are usually parades organized by a few of the politically articulate whose supporters show up out of loyalty to them. A *demo* is most often a protest, usually from the left or labor, occasionally from the right. Rarely does anyone supporting something demonstrate. Most *demo* are orderly and attract attention only from the drivers they foul up in traffic. Once in a while, a *demo* turns into a riot and is put down by well-trained and efficient riot police with as much restraint as possible. A *demo* is considered a good political safety valve. Orderly or violent, *demo* have gained little support from outside the groups that stage them. Rarely have they forced the Establishment to change a decision, although the most obvious was the cancellation of President Eisenhower's 1960 visit. Except for those put on by students, most of the *demo* are full of sound, sometimes of fury, but signify practically nothing.

The university-student movement in Japan is a political

force of unmeasured strength. Part of it is unorganized. Students have rebelled all over the nation in recent years to protest tuition increases, mismanagement of dormitories, cramped living quarters, lack of room for student activities, overcrowding of classrooms, archaic examinations and curricula, and indifferent professors who are too busy consulting or dabbling in politics to teach. A second part is organized and more political. About half of Japan's 1,400,-000 university students belong to the leftist Zengakuren, the federation of student organizations. Of these, 380,000 are under the wing of the Japan Communist Party and another 300,000 belong to an anti-JCP Trotskyite group. Within the Trotskyites, about 10,000 members of the Sampa Rengo, or Three Faction Alliance, are the hard core that has increasingly stirred up turmoil. Their favorite tactic is the anti-American *demo* near the American bases permitted under the U.S.-Japan Mutual Security Treaty. But leaders say they will use any issue that can be turned against the Establishment to attract public attention. They are particularly interested in *demo* that can get them time on television. A Sampa Rengo leader once explained why they had used a formation like a Roman phalanx rather than guerrilla tactics in unsuccessful attempts to break through police ranks outside a U.S. naval base. "If we had used hit-and-run tactics," he said, "we could easily have gotten inside the base. But the TV cameras couldn't have stayed with us."

The students protesting inadequacies in university curricula and facilities and those primarily interested in political action joined forces in 1968 and early 1969 to bring Tokyo University to a standstill. Early in 1968, medical students in the university began class boycotts and picketing in protest against what they considered a feudalistic examination and intern system. The protest spread to other departments, partly in sympathy for the medical students, partly because students there were stimulated to protest against shortcomings they saw in their own faculties. Late in 1968, the Sampa Rengo and other militants inserted themselves into the situation to take advantage of the unrest and to stir it up into a major incident. They finally captured key buildings and areas of the campus, barricaded themselves in, refused to negotiate with university authorities, and forced the university to stop almost all academic life. In stopping Tokyo University from functioning, the students struck at the head of the Japanese educational system. They showed that they could be a negative force, at least so long as the authorities were unwilling to use the police to dislodge them. The police were eventually called, and after several pitched battles with staves, fire hoses, and tear gas, the students were either routed or arrested. They had proved that they could disrupt the university, as they have other universities for the last few years, but whether they will become a positive force for change remained unclear.

Indeed, the students may have generated a reaction among the authorities, the press, and the public that will isolate them in the future. University officials have become less reluctant to call in the police when students become violent, overcoming a restraint born of memories of the prewar secret police who ferreted into most facets of Japanese life. The police, sensing this, have become less cautious in the methods they use to put down a student riot, although undue rough stuff brings an immediate cry of protest from the press. The press, however, has become noticeably more critical of student unrest. During the Tokyo University crisis, one major newspaper editorialized that where "a violent student minority has reduced the campus to anarchy, we believe that a first step must be to call in police whenever this is essential to preserve law and order." The paper said: "If the autonomy of universities in this country is being destroyed, it is student irresponsibility that is destroying it." Still another reaction has been the establishment of the first postwar national organization of conservative students. Founded in mid-1968, the Japan Student League's objectives are to increase national consciousness, to revive reverence for the emperor, and to counteract the Zengakuren and student anarchy. Moreover, the big business companies have become more careful in screening out graduates with undesirable political backgrounds. This probably hurts as much as anything, because the students usually drop out of political activity in their last two years of school to prepare for jobs with the companies, even though they earlier believed the *zaibatsu* concerns to be the essence of reaction.

In 1968, a young man named Akiyama Katsuyuki was chairman of Sampa Rengo. He had been enrolled in Yokohama National University since 1960 but said he had lost interest in everything but revolution. "Like Lenin," he said, "being a professional revolutionary has a strong attraction for me." Akiyama sat in the cluttered second-floor office of a small print shop one day discussing his movement and its aims. Surrounded by other leaders, his "cabinet," he called them, he said they were trying to overthrow the government, not to make it more responsive to public opinion. "As long as the present government exists," he said, "vice will survive. The easiest thing to do is overthrow the government." The short, slight, quiet-spoken Akiyama, looking not at all like the stereotyped wild-eyed radical, said they had been striking the police at their strongest points but were thinking of hitting where they were weak, and without the fanfare of earlier demonstrations. He said that they were thinking of advancing from their stave-bearing, rock-throwing tactics to setting fires. But he ruled out, for the present, throwing bombs. "Killing [Prime Minister] Sato would be easy," he said, "but that wouldn't attain our objective." Akiyama had little but scorn for the Red Guards of Communist China, whom he considered rightist revisionists. "Our movement is from below," he said, "theirs was from the top. They believed in reverence for Mao [Communist Party Chairman Mao Tse-tung] and the government organized their demonstrations. Our movement is aimed at throwing out established society and setting up a new government." Akiyama spoke of the "international revolution," but the specifics of his conversation showed him to be concerned solely with Japan and to be nationalistic in his emotions.

Everything he said was strangely reminiscent of descriptions of the fanatics of the 1920's and the aggressive young officers of the 1930's. It had all of the alienation from the existing order, the willingness to resort to violence, the nationalism combined with radicalism. Kita Ikki, young prewar leader of the radical ultranationalists, and Akiyama Katsuyuki might have had much to say to each other. Political scientists have pointed out that the political spectrum is not in a straight line but is bent in a circle. It is but a short step from the far left to the far right.

Chapter 6

The ECONOMIC

MENTALITY

There is nothing in the world a Japanese would rather talk about than economics. Every speech by a Japanese politician or businessman refers to the recovery of the economy after the war and the "economic miracle" since then. Talk with a bureaucrat, and sooner or later he will mention that Japan's growth rate was a certain per cent last year and is expected to be so much this year, that exports to Country A have jumped 10 per cent but the market in Country B is the one to watch. Newspapers pay more attention to turns in the economy than probably any press in the world. A taxi driver, the neighborhood rice store proprietor, and housewives can carry on well-informed conversations about the economic state of the nation. The Japanese are justifiably proud of the stupendous job they have done during the last century in building the first industrial economy outside the bounds of Western civilization, and especially in the advances they have made in the past twenty-five years. Japan's gross national product is now third largest in the world, behind the American and Russian superpowers but ahead of West Germany, Britain, France, and other major powers. The swift progress of the economy is the single most important factor in the restoration of Japanese confidence in themselves that has taken place in recent years.

Economic statistics, which spew from every ministry and business office to attest to the economic thrust, are but a small part of the evidence of Japan's great leap forward. The gleaming oil refineries along Tokyo Bay, clicking electronics factories all over the country, shipyards beside the Inland Sea that daily drop tankers and freighters into the water, quiet camera and precise optical plants in Tokyo, thundering steel mills in central Honshu and northern Kyushu, clattering automobile assembly plants near Yokohama and Nagoya, heavy machine factories in Kawasaki and Hiroshima, hissing chemical and purring plastic plants, humming textile mills—all attest to the industrial advance. Ships of all nations docked or at anchor at Yokohama and Kobe are signs of Japan's immense foreign trade: the imports of raw materials for a resource-poor nation, the exports of a country whose human resources are its wealth. An integrated airline and railway network runs with dispatch. From Tokyo's International Airport at Haneda, jets climb into the skies bound for all points of the world. Between Tokyo, Kyoto, and Osaka, the high-speed Tokaido line, on which run perhaps the world's finest trains, follows the same route over which the Emperor Meiji was carried in a man-borne palanquin a century ago. Japanese railroads are so efficient that if your train is scheduled to depart at 12:47 and you board one at 12:47 and 10 seconds, you are on the wrong train.

Japanese consumers, for the first time in their history, are enjoying a taste of the Affluent Society. Few in Japan are rich—but few are poor either. The Japanese are by far the best fed, best clothed, and healthiest people in Asia. A solid and growing middle class patronizes department stores and specialty shops along the Ginza that could compete in variety and class with those in New York, London, and Paris—and outdo them all in service. The forests of television antennae across the countryside, the transistor radios, the electric irons and rice pots, the sewing and washing machines, the refrigerators and fans, and the electric or gas stoves that have replaced the attractive but fire-prone charcoal *hibachi* cooking vessels evince the material well-being of the average Japanese. Leisure, too, has become an ordinary part of life. Beaches swarm with bathers in summer, and ski slopes in winter are crowded with the world's most avid and, it must be said, most reckless skiers. Mountain resorts are full all year long, and travel tours for the world's most dedicated sightseers are booked months in advance. Golf is the rage of the executive, bowling for the white-collar "salaryman." Theatres and concerts are always packed. Books sell by the ton. Nor is saving neglected among a people for whom thrift has always been a virtue. The average family's savings account is a tidy sum, and safety-deposit boxes have become popular, especially as hiding places for *hesokuri* ("to put in the navel"), the secret savings that husbands, and, more often, wives, set aside.

The economic miracle, however, is neither complete nor perfect. Rapid expansion has caused all manner of imbalances. The financial underpinnings of the economy are shaky and held together with baling wire. Foreign exchange reserves are a constant source of concern and corporate debt is more than enough to give orthodox economists the shivers. Many enterprises are inefficient, waste labor, and suffer from archaic management. Some technology barely meets modern industrial standards. Consumer price inflation has risen unchecked since 1960 and eaten away a good part of the workingman's gain. Wages are rising, but the Japanese works long hours for his modest income. Education and medical facilities have not come close to keeping up with industrial development. Roads are being improved but are nowhere near sufficient to handle the automotive population explosion. Harbor facilities are inadequate. Water supply is so poor in places that Tokyo Governor Minobe Ryokichi once remarked that some of his citizens could buy a Coca-Cola but couldn't get a drink of fresh water.

Westerners have evidence of Japan's industrialization all about them. MADE IN JAPAN is stamped on radios, television sets, steel, clothing, machine tools, motorcycles, baseball gloves, and a cornucopia of other things. The label once meant cheap junk; it now means the product of a sophisticated industrial complex. Westerners, seeing this, may assume that because the products of the Japanese economy are like the products of a Western economy, the system that produces them may also be like their own. But behind the Western façade of corporations and factories is an economic structure and mode of operation that is different. It defies Western labels of capitalism, or socialism, or state capitalism, or communism. The Japanese have absorbed deep injections of technology, methods of trade, financial concepts, and corporate organization from the West while they developed their own ways of operating and controlling their economic machine. Japan's economy today is probably the world's most deftly guided economy, governed by a set of controls more refined than Karl Marx, V. I. Lenin, or Josef Stalin ever dreamed of.

The centralized control of the modern Japanese economy began during the Meiji period, when the oligarchs welded a strong alliance of themselves, the bureaucracy, and the new industrialists to foster economic development. Businessmen, politicians, bureaucrats, and militarists struggled for control of the economy in the 1920's and 1930's, the militarists bringing it under their domination. The Occupation started to break up these controls but relented when the advent of the Cold War made an economically strong Japan an asset against possible encroachments by the Soviet Union or Communist China. After Japan regained its sovereignty in 1952, the controls that had been dismantled were among the first to be reassembled. They have become even stronger as the economy recovered and moved into its tremendous expansion. The Japanese, a deliberate people, are reluctant to leave anything to chance, and regulate the economy to bring all its components into harmony. They intensely dislike competition. The Japanese are personally competitive for power and prestige but fear that if this is not controlled, what they consider excessive competition will cause economic chaos. Japan has limited space for agriculture and industry, limited natural resources, limited capital. The margins for error are small, and the Japanese believe that laissez-faire, uncoordinated decision making, and the play of market forces are luxuries they cannot afford.

Concerted Japanese action in foreign trade is even stronger than in the domestic market. They believe they are dependent on the rest of the world for markets and that it matters less that an export product was made by a given company than that it was made in Japan. In international competition, it is Japan against the world, Japanese steel against American steel, Japanese cameras against German cameras, Japanese textiles against British textiles. To achieve this regulation, the Japanese have made a way of life of investment, production, and trade targets; of cartels, quotas, and fixed prices; and of combining the influences of the bureaucracy, the political world, and the business community in economic decision making.

There is no single economic control agency in Japan, but a meshing of information from business companies and the bureaucracy's ministries into guidelines and targets set down by the Establishment. The Economic Planning Agency, whose director is a Cabinet member, is responsible for accumulating facts, analyses, and projections, and for publishing general economic objectives. EPA relies on the prestige of its director and the quality of its staff work to persuade, exhort, and warn the business community.

Economists in research institutes, commercial firms, and banks also have considerable influence and regularly exchange and adjust views with government economists.

The single most influential agency in economic policy making is undoubtedly the Ministry of Finance, most powerful of the bureaucracies. It makes its influence felt primarily by monetary policy, then by fiscal policy and its control over other ministries, and lastly by the personal, intangible pressures of its able staff.

The Finance Ministry's most direct impact on the economy is its regulation of monetary and credit policy. The minister appoints and has supervisory authority over the governor of the Bank of Japan, the central bank. The bank is also the depository of the government's funds, which are controlled by the Finance Ministry. The Bank of Japan, in turn, directly regulates the commercial banks by setting the central-bank interest rates that determine interest rates charged by the commercial banks. The Bank of Japan further applies what the Japanese call "window guidance": controlling the amounts, lengths of time, and terms of loans made by commercial banks to industrial and commercial firms. This has great impact because a public money market has not yet developed in Japan. Industrialization has run well ahead of capital accumulation, and the mass of private investors still prefer to put their savings into bank accounts or government savings, which pay high interest, rather than risk them in the securities market.

Japanese firms are heavily dependent on banks for investment capital and operating funds, unlike their Western counterparts, who can raise money independently on the public money market. The sensitivity of industrial and commercial firms to bank influence has been accentuated because they have borrowed so much to finance the roaring expansion of the last decade. Nearly all Japanese companies are deeply in debt, the average firm having less than 25 per cent of its capitalization in its own equity and more than 75 per cent in bank debt. This debt-equity ratio is almost exactly the opposite of what is considered acceptable in the United States or Western Europe. This dependence on borrowed money makes the regulations imposed by the Finance Ministry through the Bank of Japan and the commercial banks quickly felt by industry and commerce. The Finance Ministry has its hand on a valve that it can open or close ever so slightly to generate a rapidly stimulating or retarding effect on the economy.

Japan does not rely much on fiscal policy. Postwar economic growth has been so fast that tax revenues have been higher than government expenditures, which has resulted in a series of tax cuts. The national budget is usually balanced and national debt is tiny. Keynesian principles of increasing government spending to stimulate economic growth have not been applied. To some extent, the opposite has been true. The government has refrained from spending to keep from adding inflationary pressures to the economy. A major reason for the conservative fiscal measures is that Japan has had to spend little for defense. That has been provided by the United States and has allowed Japan to put its resources into productive investment rather than arms.

Nevertheless, government spending, which runs about 20 per cent of gross national product, has considerable effect on the economy. This, too, is largely controlled by the Finance Ministry, which draws up the government budget. The ministry has a budget section for every other ministry and agency that each year receives budget requests and considers recommendations from Diet members and others in the Establishment. The requests often are three times the amount a ministry expects to get, and the negotiations between Finance Ministry bureaucrats and other bureaucrats almost preclude other work during the budget season. After the Finance Ministry pares each request down and assembles the budget, it is sent to the

Diet. Minor alterations may be made, but the Diet does not tamper with the main features, and approves it intact. The Finance Ministry's word is the next thing to law. The ministry further controls the disbursement of funds. The Ministry of Construction, for example, must have its proposed budget approved by the Finance Ministry and then get its funds from the same place.

The Finance Ministry's control over the budget and disbursements gives it influence even beyond the economy. The Foreign Ministry and the Finance Ministry have been arguing about Japanese foreign aid for several years, with the Finance Ministry having the last word and therefore a major say in Japan's foreign policy. The Japanese government in 1965, on recommendation of the Foreign Ministry, pledged to the Development Assistance Committee (DAC) of the Organization of Economic Cooperation and Development (OECD) that Japan would contribute one per cent of its national income in economic aid to developing countries. Japan's foreign aid was to rise to the one-percent figure by 1970. In 1967, however, the Finance Ministry made quite clear, after much contentious negotiation, that it had no intention of fulfilling the commitment. It contended that Japan did not have the financial resources, that chronic weakness in the balance of international payments would not support the outflow, that Japan's per capita income must first be raised. The Foreign Ministry argued and cajoled, and may still be arguing and cajoling, but so long as the Finance Ministry says no, the funds will not be forthcoming. The Finance Ministry, moreover, doesn't hesitate to say no, even to the prime minister. In 1967, Prime Minister Sato went on an extensive journey through Southeast Asia. Before leaving, he let it be known that he intended to take along about $100,000,000 worth of credits as tokens of Japan's good will and as an earnest of Japan's intention to help with economic development. But Sato did not pass out a single *yen*. The Finance Ministry said quite firmly that current problems in the balance of international payments made the timing inopportune.

Ministries other than Finance have direct controls over the economy through "administrative guidance," a power they have acquired from custom and law. Foremost is the Ministry of International Trade and Industry, better known as MITI. It has offices for most industries—steel, oil, chemicals, heavy industry, light industry, small business, mining. No major decision is taken by an industry without MITI's cognizance. Japan's antitrust laws are anemic, and nonexistent if MITI approves a cartel, a price-fixing arrangement, or production and export quotas. Much of MITI's day-to-day influence is felt through the trade associations to which the companies belong. Major investments and mergers are subject to MITI approval, and MITI urges industries to move along certain lines. The automobile industry, which has a profusion of companies, has been under steady pressure to merge into larger, more productive, and internationally competitive companies. MITI pays particular attention to the oil industry because the nation is entirely dependent on outside petroleum supplies. Oil is one of the few Japanese industries in which foreign management has extensive influence through equity ownership, joint ventures, loan agreements, and long-term supply contracts. MITI does its best, cooperating with Japanese oil companies, to restrain foreign access to Japan's oil market, the fastest growing in the world. Other industries are under the purview of the ministries of Agriculture and Forestry, Transport, and Construction, and of special agencies such as the Science and Technics Agency. Various agencies undertake basic and applied research, the results of which are turned over to industry, particularly the small and medium-sized industries that cannot afford research facilities. Fees are nominal, the government providing the service in the national economic interest.

In Japan are found perhaps the greatest concentrations of economic power among the industrial nations outside the Communist bloc. The Japanese business community is centered around the *zaibatsu,* a form of business organization that is unique to Japan. *Zaibatsu* is sometimes translated "financial clique," or "propertied class," or "plutocracy," but in today's terms "business combine" or "conglomerate" might be better. The *zaibatsu* business clans are part of the Establishment and each has connections with political leaders and their *habatsu.* (The ideograph for *batsu* in each word is the same and means "group.") The combines are, by their nature, key elements in the economic decision-making mechanism. The four major *zaibatsu* that began in the Meiji days eventually acquired or started enterprises throughout industry, commerce, and finance; but each has tended to be stronger in one in particular. Mitsubishi is known for its heavy industry. Mitsui is strong in trade and commerce. Sumitomo is an exploiter of natural resources. Yasuda has focused on banking and finance. Each also has its own characteristics that can be traced back to its origins, although these features have blurred as each has expanded and diversified.

Mitsubishi, founded by *samurai* Iwasaki Yataro in 1870, added new ventures so that by 1928 it had sixty-five firms under its aegis. Responding to demands from the militarists in the 1930's, it combined its shipbuilding and aircraft industries into Mitsubishi Heavy Industries, Japan's foremost builder of warships and the famed Zero fighter plane. It had holdings not only in Japan but in Korea and Manchuria, and was involved in the Greater East Asia Co-Prosperity Sphere. The Occupation began to break Mitsubishi apart, purged a number of leaders, and stripped away its overseas holdings. But the combine quickly formed again after the Occupation, executives who had been purged returned, and the companies resumed the Mitsubishi name and trademark. Formal and informal ties were re-established by the mid-1950's, the only major change having been the assumption of control by professional managers in place of the Iwasaki family. Today, Mitsubishi Heavy Industries, Mitsubishi Electric, Mitsubishi Oil, Mitsubishi Chemical, Asahi Glass, and Nippon Kogaku (maker of Nikon cameras) are among the top five national firms in each of their industries. Mitsubishi Bank, Meiji Life Insurance, and Tokyo Marine and Fire Insurance are the combine's financial backers. Mitsubishi Shoji is a leading trading company and Nippon Yusen Kaisha (NYK) is the foremost shipping line. In all, about sixty companies belong to the main Mitsubishi group, each with more subsidiaries and affiliates that spread throughout the economy.

The Mitsubishi *zaibatsu* has no formal policy board to direct the business clan's affairs, but company presidents and senior directors maintain close personal contact. The presidents meet regularly once a month as the Kinyo-kai, or Friday Club, where they hear reports and discuss common problems. The Kinyo-kai rarely makes policy decisions as these are worked out on a case-by-case basis. If a Mitsubishi company wants to invest in a new plant, its top executives get together with officials from the Mitsubishi Bank, the Mitsubishi Shoji trading company, and others from sister industrial companies to decide where the funds will come from, whether the market will absorb the projected plant's output, and whether the bureaucracy will approve. When the combine wants to strike out into a new field, as it has in atomic power, cement, petrochemicals, and plastics in recent years, the senior executives and financial specialists of more than twenty companies may be involved in making the decision and implementing it. On a day-to-day basis, middle-management executives are constantly conferring, arranging for Mitsubishi machinery stored in a Mitsubishi warehouse to be transported by NYK to a Mitsubishi chemical plant. The collective leadership at the top and in the middle may appear unwieldy, but it works. Mitsubishi today has a standing in the Japanese economy roughly equivalent to that a conglomerate of General Electric, General Motors, du Pont, Kodak, and perhaps twenty more major firms would have in the American economy.

Japan's second largest *zaibatsu,* the house of Mitsui, goes back to 1673, when the Mitsui family opened dry goods stores in Osaka, Kyoto, and Edo. Mitsui has expanded along the same lines as Mitsubishi, but has subtle differences in approach, reflecting more of its mercantile than *samurai* founders. Before the war, Mitsui had a falling out with the militarists and several members of the family were forced to resign. Today, it tends to be more flexible, adaptable to changes in business techniques, and gives its middle-management executives more individual responsibility. Mitsubishi, which claims its men are "*samurai* in spirit, merchants in talent," tends to be more rigid, highly disciplined, and intensively group-oriented. But these are only two slightly divergent paths toward the same objective. Mitsui has about fifty companies, including giants like Ishikawajima-Harima Heavy Industries, Toshiba Electric, Mitsui Chemical, Japan Steel Works, Mitsui Shipbuilding and Engineering, Toyo Rayon, and so on across the economic face of Japan.

Japan has a number of large companies that are not part of a *zaibatsu* but are the center of a cluster of smaller concerns. Hitachi is one such and is a leading maker of industrial and consumer electrical products. Another type of combine is the descendant of the prewar *shin-zaibatsu,* or new combines. They built their empires largely in Japan's conquered territories. The Nissan Company, today a major automobile producer, was started in prewar days by Aikawa Yoshisuke in Manchuria. All Japanese companies have close relations with the government, but some work in particularly close cooperation.

Yawata Iron and Steel was part of the quasi-governmental prewar Japan Iron and Steel Company, which was split into Yawata and Fuji Iron and Steel by the Occupation. Yawata and Fuji are rejoining forces, however, to form the New Japan Iron and Steel Company, which will be the world's second largest steelmaker behind U.S. Steel. Senior Yawata executives consider themselves more industrial statesmen than ordinary businessmen.

A peculiar feature of Japan is what the Japanese call their "dual economy," the existence of thousands of small components makers alongside the industrial giants. Every industrial area is dotted with cramped shops in which a few men turn out parts or tools for their larger neighbors. Many large enterprises are not fully integrated but rely on these five- to fifty-man shops to supply them with items made to their specifications. The small operators survive, some handily, because of the family instinct in Japanese life. A father is the owner, his brothers the engineers, their sons the foremen. Those outside the immediate family who work there are treated as part of the family. The shops can compete in a day of mass production because they have little overhead, they drive their machinery well past the point a large enterprise would consider safe or efficient, they specialize in a few items, and everybody works very hard.

Most have longstanding ties with the large companies and keep costs down because they don't need a sales force, can obtain low-cost loans from their patrons for new machines, and get technical advice for nothing. The big companies don't buy them up because the little ones can supply them faster and cheaper than they can do it for themselves. For paternal, emotional reasons, it is just not right for the big man to put the little man out of business. The small shops can also fill special, one-time orders the bigger company would find uneconomical. The director of a major industrial research laboratory was one time asked where he got all the special equipment, tools, and components for his projects. "Come over to the window," he said. The lab stands atop a hill overlooking the industrial city of Kawasaki, just south of Tokyo. "You see that out there," he said, pointing to the thousands of homes and shops that make up the city. "All Kawasaki is my workshop. I can have anything I want made down there."

Some Westerners see signs that Japan's clannish industrial order is changing. They point to Sony, maker of transistor radios and television sets, including the "tummy television," and Honda, world's foremost producer of motorcycles. Sony was set up right after the war by Ibuka Masaru and Morita Akio in one room of a bombed-out department store. Starting with $500 in capital, they have built up a successful corporation in the best Western entrepreneurial tradition. They have done it themselves with little outside help from *zaibatsu* firms. The Sony name comes from the West, adapted from the Latin *sonus*, meaning sound. They have encouraged individual accomplishment along with the group spirit. Sony has stressed research and development of new products, including the Esaki diode invented by Dr. Leona Esaki. The company has concentrated on one line, electronic products, rather than branch out into the multitude of *zaibatsu*-style ventures. Sony first produced consumer goods, then moved into industrial products, which is opposite to the *zaibatsu* pattern. The company's advertising is in the best Madison Avenue style. Sony has looked for new markets rather than carve up established markets as the *zaibatsu* do. In all, the Western businessman would probably find himself more at home in Sony than in any other Japanese firm.

But—and here's the catch—Sony is not at all representative of the trend in Japanese business; it is the exception that proves the rule. Sony, Honda, and a very few others are mavericks. They are *ronin*, masterless *samurai*, that Japanese society, for all its conformity and rigidity, finds ways to accommodate. They have pioneered a new trail, but few are following them. The average university graduate, and even more so the above-average young man, does not aspire to explore the still perilous tracks of Ibuka and Morita but to plod the known path to a directorship in Mitsubishi or Mitsui. The young executive has no desire to get his hands greasy in the factory alongside Honda Ichiro, founder, president, and still chief mechanic of the motorcycle world. Today's young man on the rise wants to wheel and deal in the complicated maze of big business. Others like Ibuka and Morita and Honda may come along, but they will be few and they will not change the system.

Another business organization peculiar to Japan is the trading company. These companies are old-fashioned merchants that resemble the East India Company of British Empire days and the traders such as Butterfield and Swires that continue to ply the Asian trade from headquarters in Hong Kong but are unlike anything in America. The big trading companies buy and sell anything and are the purchasing agents and sales forces for industrial companies in domestic and foreign markets. They perform the classic middleman function, locating suppliers and buyers, negotiating prices, extending credit, collecting accounts. They are the *nakodo*, the go-betweens so cherished in Japanese life. Some, like Mitsubishi Shoji and Mitsui Bussan, are immense and turn over more than $5 billion worth of goods a year for a tiny .2 to .3 per cent after-tax profit. Another eight or ten companies do more than $1 billion worth a year. The larger companies handle 50 per cent of Japan's foreign trade, but the landscape is dotted with hundreds of smaller traders. The big companies handle everything from antimony to zippers, the medium-sized more limited lines, the smallest one or two products, such as electric guitars. Mitsubishi and Mitsui have offices all over Japan and in most countries in the world; about half of their business is in the domestic market, the rest importing and exporting, with a small amount of third-country trade between, say, Indonesia and Australia. A small guitar company has only one office in Tokyo, buying from Japanese makers and selling either in Japan or nearby Asian markets. But the functions are the same.

The trading companies were formed in the Meiji period and led the way into foreign trade, developing trading skills, finding markets and supplies, learning financing, and acquiring knowledge of foreign languages. They specialized in trade while others learned technology and production. Each *zaibatsu* today has its own trading company that is its central purchasing department and sales force. But the traders also handle the myriad items produced by the small companies in the dual economy. For a small company to maintain its own sales force would add 5 per cent to its costs, while the trading company can handle sales for 2 to 3 per cent, commissions being much smaller than in America. Some industrial companies have set up engineering sales forces as products have become more sophisticated. They often work in conjunction with the trading company, pooling engineering and marketing talent. A few large industrial companies maintain sales promotion offices but do the actual selling through a trading company. Yawata Steel has an office in New York to maintain customer relations and to look for new markets. But the man with the order pad comes from Mitsui Bussan or other traders.

Some Western businessmen predict the decline of the trading company, arguing that it is an anachronism and that Japanese industrial companies must turn to direct selling to cut out the middleman. These businessmen, however, overlook the strength of continuity in Japanese business methods. Moreover, a glance at a Mitsubishi Shoji balance sheet demolishes the argument. From 1963 to 1967, the company more than doubled its turnover from $2.5 billion to more than $5 billion.

A Western businessman approaching a Japanese company the first time, walking up to the front door of a building that looks much like the one he just left in New York or London, may feel he will be among his own kind and that the business practices he brought will apply in Japan. He enters the lobby, speaks to the smiling young lady at the reception desk, is taken up in the elevator, greeted by another smiling and bowing young lady, and is escorted to a reception room. She asks him to be seated, bows herself out with polite excuses, and reappears in a short time with a cup of green tea. (The procedure is the same in every Japanese business.) As the Westerner sips his tea and waits for his host, it dawns on him that he has entered another world. By the time he concludes his business and leaves Japan—most likely many weeks hence—he will be absolutely convinced that Japanese business is indeed much different from that which he does at home.

The clues begin right away. Japanese businessmen rarely greet their guests in their own offices but in private reception rooms that invariably have overstuffed chairs arranged around a low table. Only the very highest executives have private offices in Japan, and only the most important visitors ever see them. Middle-management executives sit in huge bullpens, at row on row of desks with the subsection chief's desk perpendicular at the end, his back to the window. The section chief's desk is in the corner, diagonal to the rest. The pecking order is clear.

The refreshing cup of green tea (admittedly an acquired taste) is the second clue. There are dozens, perhaps hundreds, of varieties, each with a distinct flavor. Each company has its own, sometimes picked by the president, who takes pride in finding one more delicate than his rival's. The teacups, too, are chosen to reflect discriminating taste. The visitor who has been carefully briefed will know that he should pick it up with both hands, turn it slowly, and make admiring remarks to his host.

The third clue is the *meishi*, or name card, which is presented immediately upon introduction. Calling cards in the West are a nice social amenity. In Japan, they are conveyors of essential information and to fail to exchange them is a serious breach of etiquette. It identifies not only the bearer but his affiliation and his place in his own company, important to the prestige-conscious Japanese.

A fourth clue is that the conversation takes what may seem forever even to begin approaching the business at hand. The Western visitor can expect a litany that varies little: "When did you come to Japan?" (meaning "Do you know anything about Japan?"), "Where are you staying?" ("Does this guy know which are the 'right' hotels?"), "Do you know Mr. Smith of XYZ Company, whom I met in New York last year?" ("What kind of contacts does he have?"), and the inevitable "How do you like Japan?" ("Let's see if he comes up with a good answer"). The visitor can expect to be drawn out in detail about his company and its history and his own personal career. The Japanese will gradually unfold the same on his side. In Japanese business, a sound personal relationship is a prerequisite to further business dealings, and the Japanese wants to know a good bit about the people with whom he might do business.

A managing director of Mitsubishi Shoji once said to a Western visitor: "If you want to understand Mitsubishi, you must first understand the Japanese mentality." He referred to the concepts and atmosphere in which Japanese business is done. A corporation, to a Westerner, is an impersonal organization for which he works and from which he receives an income. Ideally, he feels some loyalty to the company and takes more of an interest in his work than just putting in time each day. The company, in turn, treats the employee as something more than a chattel. But neither feels any emotional ties. The employer is free to fire the man if he thinks it necessary; the employee is free to find himself a better job. A Japanese company, in marked contrast, is a family. The word *kaisha*, or company, is a two-ideograph word that has clear social and religious overtones. The same two ideographs in reverse order, *shakai*, means "society" or "social." This may help explain the paternalism, the lifetime employment system, the deep personal involvement of the employee with his firm.

The man who goes to work for a Japanese company does not "get a job," he "enters the company" and pledges it a lifetime of service. The company undertakes to look after the well-being of the employee for the length of his career. Thus, the lives of the company and the employee become inextricably intertwined. The employee takes pride in his association with the group and acquires prestige from the company's reputation that he would not have as an individual, no matter how talented. The company shares the joys of its employees and comforts them in their sorrows. When a young man takes a bride, the place of honor at the wedding goes to his employer, hopefully the president of the company, not to his or his bride's parents. The company will keep a sick employee on the payroll no matter how long he is absent, and will see that he is promoted along with his contemporaries. If an employee turns out to be incompetent, something will be found for him to do where he will not cause harm. But he will not be dismissed, and neither will he leave to find a better job.

Once in the company, the employee is steered into a planned career development in which he is promoted by seniority up through the middle reaches of the company, where merit begins to take over. It is a rigid system but, in one of those paradoxes of Japanese life, has hidden flexibilities. Most Japanese companies avoid organizational charts and specific assignments of responsibility so that a department head can pick one of his subordinates for a particular job even if his seniority does not entitle him to it. When the department head wishes to reach down into the ranks to pick out a junior man, he must do so obliquely and delicately so that those senior to his choice are not offended. The chosen man may not be promoted or have his salary raised, but he is rewarded by the recognition he receives from his superiors and perhaps by material rewards that are quietly slipped his way. In companies where a premium is put upon technical, engineering, or scientific skill, men with special training are sometimes selected over their seniors to take on a job for which they are particularly qualified. Yet the man selected in such situations must watch his step and not make mention of his out-of-turn rise, or else he will be subtly cut down by his contemporaries. A young, eminently able diplomat, early in his career was chosen to serve in two prestigious embassies abroad, then in a prominent Tokyo position, all in succession. When it came time for him to be transferred again, he asked for a place in a less important embassy. Much to his embarrassment, he was sent to another very important embassy—and with a promotion. Where an ambitious Westerner would have been delighted, the Japanese was fearful that his contemporaries would think ill of him.

At the very top levels, executives sometimes change from one company to another. Usually this is within a *zaibatsu* or among a group of associated companies, where one company gets into trouble and needs fresh executive approaches to straighten it out. The senior men in the group may decide that Yamaguchi-san, who is among their best managing directors, is the man for the job and will ask him to take it on. But Yamaguchi would not think, of his own accord, of leaving his company and looking for another position. In the fast-growing Japanese economy, where new companies are often being formed, the same procedure is used to staff the top echelons of the new venture. Sometimes the moves are made after consultation throughout the top levels of the business community. Some years ago, a major Japanese oil company was about to go under due to mismanagement and a near-failing financial condition. An American company wanted to step in, buy an interest in the company, and bring in its own managers. Its main objective was to establish a new channel for selling oil in the Japanese market. This was the last thing the Japanese oil industry wanted. Executives from a wide range of companies got together, selected from among themselves top managerial people for the oil company, and arranged loans to see it through. But neither the ailing company nor an ambitious executive made the approaches. The changes were made by the Establishment.

Despite the security of the lifetime employment system, a Japanese businessman works hard. He is motivated partly because he wants to reach the top ranks, which are awarded for merit. He is motivated more by a sense of loyalty and obligation to the company—the same sense of duty he feels to his family and country. Obligations are ingrained in the Japanese ethic, and the businessman's performance is more for the good of the company than for himself. Moreover, the Japanese regard work and accomplishment as ends in themselves. A favorite adjective for a good worker is that he is *kimben,* or diligent. It means that he spends long hours on the job, pays great attention to detail, is responsive to the slightest wish of his superiors, and can be relied upon.

Money is not a large part of Japanese motivation because everyone at the same level is paid about the same wage. Lack of mobility means one cannot go to another company for a better salary. Further, base pay is only part of each man's income. A large part is the bonus paid twice a year, three to six months' pay in each bonus being commonplace. The bonus originally reinforced a man's loyalty to the company because their fortunes were linked. But bonuses have become more standardized and do not fluctuate much. The bonus is a form of enforced saving and accounts for the semi-annual consumer splurges on major appliances and other costly items. Bonuses have also retarded the growth of consumer credit because a man can pay cash for a television set twice a year but cannot afford the monthly payments the rest of the time. Many Japanese companies also furnish housing at nominal cost, pay employees' transportation to work, provide low-cost meals in cafeterias, pay major medical expenses, provide recreation and vacation facilities at nominal cost, and arrange a variety of extracurricular activities like judo lessons and learning to play the *shaku-hachi*, a Japanese flute.

For the senior executive, salary is still very low by Western standards. But the extras make for a good life. He is furnished a nice house at little cost, a servant or two, a car with chauffeur, membership in a plush golf club, a nearly unlimited expense account for entertaining in geisha houses, and vacation trips paid by the company. Occasionally these include trips abroad, ostensibly for business but really for fun. It is truly amazing how many Japanese businessmen turn up in Las Vegas or on the Riviera looking for machine-tool markets.

Paternalism is not limited to the white-collar "salaryman" but applies equally to labor. Once a laborer becomes a permanent employee, he may not be fired. If business goes bad, he may not be laid off. In the steel industry, where production fluctuates, a decline means that hearths and rolling mills are shut down but that workers go to other crews in the plant, attend retraining courses, or perform maintenance. Even if business is slack during the hiring season after high school graduation, the company will hire about the same number of men as when business is good. Otherwise it will not be able to get them when things turn up, because there is no floating labor supply. Moreover, irregular hiring would throw seniority promotion out of kilter.

The paternalistic employment system puts the burden of social security on companies rather than on the government. Unemployment is low, and measures such as unemployment compensation are unnecessary. The government provides some medical insurance to cover small businesses and the self-employed, but retirement pensions are primarily a company responsibility. Most are paid in large lump sums that are calculated on length of service and position at retirement.

Paternalism also accounts for the lack of a strong labor movement, compared with those in America and some European countries. Most unions are company unions that include all workers from one company rather than the industry or craft unions that are common in the United States. These company unions feel little need for a struggle with management. As the economy has prospered, labor has negotiated for higher wages and bonuses, better benefits, and safer working conditions, but probably would have gotten them anyway from paternalistic employers. Although almost every year the labor unions mount their "spring offensive" for higher wages and better working conditions, strikes of more than a few hours are rare and a prolonged labor dispute almost unheard of. The major labor federations, Sohyo and Domei, direct their attention to politics on the theory that political changes will benefit the workingman more than labor strife.

Japan has supposedly developed a labor shortage in the last few years. Industrial expansion has dried up the excess labor supply from rural areas and the young adults who are the result of the immediate postwar baby boom. Companies complain that they can't get enough people to fill all the jobs that have opened up, causing speculation that a competitive, mobile labor market will begin. The labor shortage is an illusion, however, as it is predicated on the practice of employing ten men for three men's work. The social ethic says that everybody will be given work and the income divided so that everybody has a minimum living wage at least. The labor shortage could and may be solved by giving each employee more work to do and increasing his income. The amount of wasted labor in Japan would stagger even the best featherbedders in American labor. Every department store has a legion of pretty, polite young girls who do nothing but stand alongside escalators, whisper *"Irasshaimase"* ("Welcome") and bow to customers, give a direction or two to ladies' lingerie, and wipe the rubber handrail with a cloth. An entrepreneur could staff a sizeable new electronics factory with these girls alone. Moreover, changing the retirement age from fifty-five to sixty-five would extend careers and add 30 per cent to the labor and management force without putting on a single new person. A move to the five-day week (work weeks are of five and a half to six days presently) would cut into some of that. But the combination of a better use of labor and longer careers will most likely preserve the paternalistic employment system, which is deeply rooted in social values.

Japanese business practices and ethics today are derived from the traditions of the Tokugawa merchants and the *samurai* who went into industry during the Meiji era. The merchants contributed their economic acumen, their pragmatic outlook devoid of ideology, their experience in making decisions by expedience. The *samurai* brought with them their autocratic traits, their belief in privilege and status for those with power, their fierce loyalties and willingness to compromise with friends, their aggressiveness with its touch of ruthlessness towards rivals.

Japanese businessmen make decisions by consensus and on a "case-by-case" basis. Each company is managed by a board of directors, all from within the company, that is collectively responsible for its performance. Discussions start in a small group and widen out, just as they do in the national Establishment. Middle-management men can have a strong say by reaching a consensus among themselves and passing it upstairs for approval. Japanese businessmen avoid precedent and deprecate legal, contractual obligations because they believe an agreement valid only so long as the conditions under which it was reached continue to hold true. They view contracts with suspicion and draw them up with an eye to flexibility, in contrast to the American practice of trying to close every conceivable loophole. Few disputes between Japanese businesses ever go to court because this would be an admission that they have not been able to negotiate a compromise. Courts operate on the same theory and endeavor to mediate a compromise if a dispute comes to them in desperation. Courts are deliberately slow, not only because care is required but because the longer a court holds off, the better the chance the two parties will be forced to compromise.

The Tokyo Hilton Hotel case in 1967 was a good, if somewhat dramatic, illustration of Japanese views toward precedents and contracts. Hilton had a twenty-year contract to manage the hotel owned by the Tokyu chain. After four years, however, Tokyu decided it wanted to run the hotel itself and not pay the Hilton management fee. Tokyu executives simply walked into the hotel, installed their manager in the office while the Hilton manager was out, and prevented the Hilton man from returning. Tokyu announced that it was taking over because changes in the corporate structure of Hilton and an upcoming merger of Hilton International, a subsidiary of the Hilton parent company, with Trans-World Airlines invalidated the Tokyu contract with Hilton. In Tokyu's eyes, the conditions had changed and the agreement could be broken. Hilton, however, claimed that Tokyu had no sufficient or just reason for breaking the contract and went into a Tokyo court. The majority of Japanese and American businessmen in Tokyo were sure the court would delay ruling on the case and would eventually decide in Tokyu's favor. But the incident had implications that affected every American venture in Japan and Japanese relations with their vital customers in America. The repercussions were immediate. A Japanese about to sit down to sign a contract with an American businessman in New York was told it would be reconsidered in light of the Hilton affair. Pressures were then brought to bear in Tokyo on both Tokyu and the court, which, to the surprise of everyone, ruled that Tokyu was out of order and must abide by the management contract.

The Hilton case, although illustrative, was a rare incident because the Japanese usually do not let things get so far out of hand. It was the result of a basic cultural difference in the concept of an agreement. A blow-up of that sort between two Japanese would be almost unthinkable because of the overwhelming importance of personal relationships that have developed between them in the course of doing business. A personal relationship can often be more decisive than the usual criteria for a business transaction such as price, quality, and credit. Suzuki's widgets may sell for 20 *yen* and Yamamoto's for 25, but Tanaka will buy from Yamamoto because he is the husband of Yamamoto's second cousin's daughter. Personal relations explain much of the emphasis Japanese put on business entertainment. Japanese get to know all about each other at lavish dinner parties in geisha restaurants, Saturday and Sunday afternoons on the golf course, or a few quiet drinks in a favorite Ginza club. Elaborate gifts keep the friendship going and are normal features of business life. All this is officially condoned as the tax laws permit most business entertainment to be charged off as operating expenses. They are the lubrication that keeps the economic machine running.

In a business negotiation, the Yankee is aggressive and asks for more than he expects, then backs off slowly until he finds a common ground with his adversary. The Japanese is a counterpuncher. He offers as little as possible at the beginning and tries to entice the other fellow to show his hand first. He does not ask for more than he expects but offers less than he is ready to give. The Japanese, unlike the American, feels no compulsion to keep a conversation going. He pauses for thought, like a chess player, whenever he feels like it. The opposing businessman sits and waits for the quiet one to make up his mind. The Japanese, who have perhaps the world's keenest sensitivities to the subtleties of power, never drive their adversaries into a corner. A businessman who fails to give another an out may make his deal—but it will not last and he will never make another with that man or any of his friends. Stern talk is a serious breach of ethics and is never condoned, the toughest bargaining being muffled in utmost courtesy. If a businessman uses highly honorific, formal, and polite language, it can mean that a deal is less likely to be made because good business friends can speak more informally. Even then, the Japanese never goes to the heart of the matter but is roundabout and vague. Candor is horrible. All this makes the Japanese, as an American businessman in Tokyo once observed, "the world's best bargainer from a position of weakness."

One of the main objectives of the Japanese business community today is to keep Western influences in the Japanese economy as small as possible. The Japanese have protected their economy since the days of Meiji from imports and foreign investment except for what they thought they needed. Japan in recent years has been forced to reduce some protectionist barriers under pressure from the United States, other major trading partners, and international organizations such as the General Agreement on Tariffs and Trade (GATT) and the International Monetary Fund. But they have built a defense in depth of administrative controls, internal taxes, and foreign exchange controls. They are fighting especially hard to prevent direct private foreign investment in industry. The Japanese don't want any more Western competition than they have to accept. That Japan earns much in American and European markets and should allow Westerners into theirs is a point the Japanese concede only with great reluctance. The Japanese maintain that they would lose control of their economy to the bigger, richer, and more efficient enterprises from the West, which, they say, would come to Japan only for plunder.

More important, the protectionist wall in Japan has been erected against foreign investors because the Japanese inherently dislike and distrust foreigners. The insular Japanese do not want American and European businessmen fostering business practices they think unsuitable for Japan. They do not want Westerners upsetting the familial, paternal corporate life, the lifetime employment system, the business ethic rooted more in personal relations than in the profit motive. The one exception is a Western enterprise that has technology the Japanese want badly enough to overcome their antiforeign sentiments. International Business Machines (IBM) has done well in Japan because its technology is superior.

The last century of Japanese economic history has been a long lesson in science and technology, a replay of the Western Industrial Revolution in less than half the time the original took. The Japanese still import great amounts of technology in licensing arrangements. But they are striking out on their own. The Japanese turned their attention first to production techniques, then into researching new products and materials, now more into basic scientific research. They have come up with some first-rate production methods, original products, and occasionally a scientific first in electronics, steel, shipbuilding, cameras, and railroads. The West can look for more originality from Japan in coming years as leading corporations put more capital and staff into research and development. With the emphasis in modern industry on cooperative, group research, the Japanese should be able to hold their own. More and more innovations will go into products stamped MADE IN JAPAN—right from start.

Chapter 7

A REGULATED
PRESS

The press, especially the daily newspaper, is part of the cement that holds together a literate, industrial nation. It is modern society's fastest, most pervasive, and most influential form of communication. The press in Western democracies publishes news so that citizens may have the information they need to participate in the civic process and to run their increasingly complicated daily lives. The press, ideally, is a mirror of public opinion and a medium through which citizens make known their demands on their elected leaders. Public officials, in turn, report through the press on their stewardship to the people to whom they are responsible. For dictatorial regimes, whether of the right or left, the press is a vital channel for telling people what to think and what to do; the citizens do not take part in making national decisions, but vast numbers of people must be told quickly and simultaneously what is expected of them.

The Japanese press, like all others in the world, reflects the character of its society and fills a role peculiar to its nation. The press is part of the Establishment and a key element in the decision-making process. It originates some ideas and refines others as the nation moves toward the consensus that governs its actions. The Japanese press is not a mirror but a molder of public opinion on behalf of the Establishment. It dispenses the decisions of the Establishment and assists in persuading the public to follow. The press in Japan started as an independent force but was quickly brought under control by the nation's rulers and has remained so since. It has not developed a tradition of independence but has been subject to domination by the authorities or to their indirect influence. The enduring historical theme of the Japanese press has been the evolution of its relationship with the ruling elite.

The newspaper had no precedent in Japan. The nation had a long and rich tradition in literature, written first for the aristocracy and later for the merchant class. Street criers, somewhat like the town criers of pre-Revolutionary New England, passed gossip and bits of entertainment to townspeople. But there was no written news until the newspaper was brought in by Japanese who had been exposed to the West and by Westerners who lived in Japan. The models for the press were English and American newspapers. The press was adapted to Japanese needs and absorbed into Japanese society, developing its own style. Like so much from the West, the press has been assimilated over the years to the point that an English or American newsman today often has a hard time recognizing the connection between Japanese journalism and his own craft.

Unlike the deliberate borrowing of technology from the West, the introduction of the press to Japan happened almost by accident. In 1851, a fourteen-year-old lad named Hamada Hikozo was sailing in a small coastal vessel from Edo to his home in central Honshu. He was shipwrecked, rescued by an American whaler, and taken to California. There he learned to speak English, was converted to Christianity, and became the first Japanese to acquire naturalized American citizenship. He was probably the first and maybe the only Japanese to shake the hand of Abraham Lincoln. Hamada eventually returned to Japan with tales of life in America that fascinated his friends, especially Kishida Ginko. The latter was particularly interested in Hamada's description of American newspapers, which were then printing accounts of slavery, states' rights, and the Civil War. Hamada and Kishida started Japan's first vernacular newspaper, the *Kaigai Shimbun*, or Overseas Newspaper, which they put out in June 1864. It was not much of a success because no one really knew what a newspaper was. It folded shortly and Hamada lost interest. Kishida, however, went on to earn a place among the true founders of the Japanese press.

The next paper was founded by an Englishman, the Reverend M. Buckworth Bailey, chaplain of the British Consulate in Yokohama. Bailey, who had learned Japanese, started the *Bankoku Shimbunshi* in 1867 to break down the barriers in communication between the foreign trading community and the Japanese. By 1868, at the time of the Restoration, a dozen papers had been started by Japanese in the Tokyo-Yokohama area. Known as the Keio papers, they were printed by wooden blocks on which Japanese ideographs had been carved. They contained a few pages of concise articles written in simple rather than literary language. Perhaps the most influential of the Keio papers was Fukuchi Genichiro's *Koko Shimbun*. Fukuchi, born in Nagasaki, had studied Dutch and traveled to Europe in 1860. He criticized the men who had come to power, charging that the Meiji Restoration was but the transfer of power from one family to another. The Meiji oligarchs showed their displeasure by clapping him in jail, giving him the dubious distinction of being the first in a long line of Japanese editors to be imprisoned.

Shortly after the men of Meiji took command, they made clear that they would accept the press only on their own terms. A newspaper regulation was promulgated in

February 1869 in response to a memorial to the Emperor contending that a press was indispensable for spreading knowledge among the masses. This press law was the first major departure of the press from its Anglo-American origins. "Indiscreet" criticism of laws or "indiscreet" publication on religious matters was prohibited, and dissenting opinions on military affairs were not tolerated. More restrictions were added in 1873 and 1875. Among the prohibitions were: slander of national policy, discussion of the law, publicity for foreign laws, and attempts to obstruct the law—all provisions allowing loose and arbitrary interpretation. Editors who criticized the government could be fined or punished. Some newspapers tried to circumvent the regulations by appointing dummy or "jail" editors, usually minor employees or even janitors. When the government cracked down, the dummy editor went to prison while the real editor kept on working. But this was small relief and the papers still published in an atmosphere of subservience.

Throughout the Meiji period, the Japanese got rid of direct foreign influences as rapidly as they could. Foreign influence in the press was among the first to go. The 1875 law decreed that, to prevent subversion, foreigners were forbidden to own or edit newspapers. This appears to have been particularly aimed at an Englishman, John Black, who was the first professional journalist in Japan and a major contributor to the start of the Japanese press. Black had been editor of an English-language paper for the foreign community in Yokohama. Having learned Japanese, he started a vernacular newspaper to help overcome what he described as childlike Japanese ignorance of the outside world. Black's biggest problem was getting the Japanese to understand that a newspaper printed new and different information every day. He built his circulation slowly, mostly by explaining to nearly every customer why he should read the paper.

Almost all of Black's staff were *samurai*, the warriors who had been forced to lay down the sword in the new order. These men brought to journalism their values of personal loyalty, service, vitality, and industry. Because they were the "outs" in the new order, they tended to be critical of the "ins" until they themselves became "ins" or were brought under control by the ruling oligarchy. Black wrote that "it may be easily seen how very important a field of labour the press opened up for the old two-sworded men—the real brains of the country. But the same irrepressible boldness that they have always possessed in action has displayed itself in their utterances. They will write; and regardless of all the consequences, they refuse to avoid criticism of the government and the officials. It has never once been found that when one writer or editor has been incarcerated, there was no man of ability to step at once into his place, and run the same risks. It is true that they are more prudent than formerly, and present what they have to say in guarded language, but with all their care the censor is constantly down upon them, and it may be truly said that since the Press Law has been promulgated uneasy lies the head of him who wields an editorial pen."

About this time, most newspapers came under the control of one member or another of the ruling oligarchy. These Meiji leaders used them to propagate ideas to other members of the oligarchy and to the bureaucrats, soldiers, and the merchants who counted. Among the earliest of the men of Meiji to recognize the possibilities of using newspapers to guide the public had been Kido Koin, the young *samurai* from Choshu. He wrote to a friend who had been sent to observe the Franco-Prussian War in Europe, outlining his plans for a news office and asking for dispatches about the war. Kido wrote: "As our country's cultural standard is considerably lower than that of the countries of Europe, I hope you will make the articles as easy as possible for our people to read. As you know, our people—eight- or nine-tenths of them—are obdurate and stubborn. Thus, if this newspaper office is opened by the government, they will suspect that it is at the government's disposal, and they will pay little attention to it. Therefore, I should like to have it opened as if the government had nothing to do with it. I feel it should be permitted to discuss the government's affairs to a certain degree—and even critically, if there is anything unreasonable about them."

The Meiji Constitution of 1889 defined the role of the press that had evolved in the twenty years since the Restoration. Article XXIX read: "Japanese subjects shall, within the limits of the law, enjoy the liberty of speech, writing publication, public meetings and association." All previous regulations governing the press thus became constitutional, as would others in the future. Ito Hirobumi, author of that constitution and the foremost political leader, outlined in his *Commentaries* his views on the press. He said publications are "media through which men exercise their influence in political or social spheres." Newspapers were not, in Ito's view, organs for the expression of public opinion nor for inquiry into the performance of government or the exercise of authority. He showed his distrust of a free press: "But as every one of these edged tools can easily be misused, it is necessary for the maintenance of public order, to punish by law and to prevent by police measures delegated by law, any infringement by use thereof upon the honor or the rights of any individual, any disturbance of the peace of the country or any instigation to crime."

Still another newspaper law in 1909 further defined the subservience of the press and set regulations under which it operated until the end of World War II. The main provision of this new law gave the home minister the power to prohibit distribution of newspapers or to seize newspapers if they printed articles he deemed inimical to peace, order, or public morals. The Army and Navy ministers and the foreign minister were given authority to prohibit articles on military and diplomatic affairs. Violations were punishable by fines, imprisonment, suspension of the publication, or seizure of an edition. Application of the law vacillated according to the exigencies of internal or international politics but became increasingly severe over the years.

Postpublication censorship prevailed until World War I. Prepublication censorship started during the war, when bans on prior announcement of ship or troops movements were enforced, as they are in most nations in wartime. Additional censorship of international news was applied to items the government thought premature, misleading, or inconvenient. In 1914 alone, 453 editions of newspapers were confiscated and one newspaper was suspended. Nor were the controls eased after the war. By April 1920, a total of thirty-eight subjects were forbidden to be discussed in the press. Even in the era of party and parliamentary government of the 1920's, bureaucratic controls were much the same as during the oligarchic days. Under Hara Kei, the first prime minister who came from the party ranks, government suppression of news was so strict that in February 1921 five leading papers published a declaration condemning the government for its intolerant attitude. Prime Minister Hara and his administration ignored the protest.

Despite a history of restrictions, newspapers flourished. The Meiji oligarchy gave priority to education, and by the mid-1870's literacy was spreading rapidly. The papers then were primarily journals of opinion rather than news. Editorial writers were held in high esteem as learned men and used this as a starting point for their own thrust into politics. When political parties formed around 1890, many papers identified themselves with one or another. The commercial press also began to thrive in the 1890's. It emphasized news rather than editorial opinion and started a competition that goes on to this day. Education continued to improve, communications reached out across the country, the assimilation of technology progressed, and the economy moved ahead. More people were involved with the changes and developments in Japanese society, and the newspapers kept pace. At the turn of the century, they shifted to yellow journalism, engaging in sensationalism and muckraking, and were exceedingly loose in their regard for accuracy and truth. They appeared to have escaped suppression because no one took them seriously. Yellow journalism, however, had one lasting effect. It brought the papers within the comprehension of the people and popularized them to a level from which they have never fallen. In the period before and after World War I, the formation of national news agencies helped coalesce the press by providing the papers with an expanded flow of news. Most papers fell into one of two categories: serious or entertaining. The serious papers printed foreign, political, economic news, and interpretive articles. The others specialized in gossip about geisha, crime, sensational fiction, amusement pages, and a wide assortment of scandal.

The most direct and thorough domination of the press occurred between 1931 and 1952, from the invasion of Manchuria until the San Francisco Peace Treaty. The press was first under the supervision of the Japanese government and subsequently the American Occupation. That long experience has had singular influence on the role of the press in Japan today and on the cast of mind of Japanese journalists. The complete suppression of the press took place step by step as the militarists consolidated their power before World War II. They enforced rigid censorship, controlled transmission facilities, hired newsmen as writers of propaganda, intimidated other newsmen and editorial writers, and increased the seizures of specific editions. The two main news agencies were merged in 1936 to form Domei, which became the major producer of domestic news, the channel for foreign news coming into Japan, and a propaganda arm of the government. Because most newspapers were subscribers to Domei, the Home Ministry had a single, easy, and effective throttle on the flow of news.

The establishment of the Bureau of Information in 1940 completed the government's move from telling papers what not to print to telling them what they must print. After the attack on Pearl Harbor in December 1941, the last vestiges of autonomy were taken from publishers and assigned to the Japan Press Association, which was under the joint jurisdiction of the Home Ministry and the Bureau of Information. It ran the newspaper world and indoctrinated journalists with the "wartime spirit." The Association supervised the merger of newspapers that reduced the press to a handful of metropolitan papers and one paper for each prefecture. Newsprint shortages and financial troubles added to the decline. By the end of the war, Japan had only fifty-three papers, a 95 per cent drop in less than ten years.

The American Occupation came with the avowed intention of demilitarizing and democratizing Japan. The Occupation authorities gave priority to fostering an independent and responsible press that would stimulate democratic public opinion. But there was a basic fallacy in the presumption that the Japanese press could acquire a sense of independence and responsibility imposed from the outside. Telling a newsman that he must report the news the way he honestly and objectively sees it, when he has little in his own experience to know what that means, is a contradiction in terms. A major instrument in the attempt to foster press freedom was military censorship, another inherent contradiction. The Occupation also ordered the press to print certain kinds of articles and to discuss prescribed topics. The methods used in the press-reform program were not much different from those used by the

Japanese militarists, though the ultimate objective was the opposite.

Immediately after the surrender, the Japanese press adopted an anti-American tone but was brought up short by the Occupation authorities. In September and October 1945, the headquarters of the Supreme Commander of the Allied Powers (SCAP) issued six directives that governed the press until the end of the Occupation. The directives were enforced at first by complete prepublication censorship, every word published passing under the eyes of a military censor. Prepublication censorship was stopped in 1948, but SCAP continued to scrutinize the press and warned, reprimanded, or fined editors who did not follow directives. Another Occupation reform was the purge. Four senior Japanese news executives were named as war criminals, though none stood trial. The Occupation ordered all editors down through assistant managing editors removed if they had supported military aggression between 1937 and the attack on Pearl Harbor. Those who backed the government after that were excused on grounds of natural patriotism. The purge had less effect than the Occupation thought, since some of the purged editors remained powers behind the scene and others returned after the purge was lifted in 1948. Moreover, the large staffs on the newspapers meant that a reservoir of journalists with the same background as those purged was available to furnish replacements.

On the positive side, the Occupation tried to inculcate new ideas with a series of tutorial conferences by the Civil Information and Education (CIE) section of SCAP. Publishers and editors were called in and told they had failed to establish an independent press in accord with SCAP directives. They had failed, SCAP officers said, to explain to the public the meaning of SCAP policies, to discuss war criminals, to report foreign news adequately, or to comment on the Imperial Household. CIE demanded that these omissions be corrected. The American authorities pointedly encouraged the Japanese press to publish analyses of Occupation policies but forbade the papers from criticizing Occupation personnel, most especially General MacArthur. The Occupation was like the Bureau of Information in telling the press not only what it could not print but what it should print.

Another Occupation move similar to wartime controls was the formation of the Japan Newspaper Publishers' and Editors' Association, the Shimbun Kyokai. The initiative came partly from publishers who wanted to combat leftist unions that were struggling to seize control of several papers, notably *Yomiuri*. SCAP backed the publishers in reasserting their rights to determine editorial and business policy. Another motivation was the intrinsic Japanese tendency to organize for collective decision making. Under auspices of the Occupation and the Shimbun Kyokai, the Canons of Journalism was drawn up. They continue in force today. This document's most important injunction reflects the Japanese press philosophy acquired from its own experience and from Occupation tutelage: "The press should enjoy complete freedom in reporting news and in making editorial comments, *unless such activities interfere with public interests or are explicitly forbidden by law*, including the freedom to comment on the wisdom of any restrictive statute. The right of the press should be defended as a vital right of mankind." (Italics mine.) The exception (italicized above) makes possible enormous restrictions on freedom of the press.

The postwar constitution is more firm than the Canons of Journalism but still does not provide for clear-cut freedom of the press. Article 21 says, in part: "Freedom of . . . speech, press, and all other forms of expression are guaranteed. No censorship shall be maintained, nor shall the secrecy of any means of communication be violated." Article 12, however, says that while rights are guaranteed, the people "shall refrain from any abuse of these freedoms and rights and shall always be responsible for utilizing them for the public welfare." Demagogues and arbitrary rulers since time began have used alleged abuses and the public welfare as excuses to restrict one freedom or another. The Japanese Diet, in 1951, adopted an antisubversive activities law that the government contended was necessary to regulate organs such as *Akahata* (Red Flag), published by the Japan Communist Party. Japanese correspondents returning from Vietnam more recently have been forbidden to bring with them certain pictures of the Vietnam war. The Asian edition of *Life* magazine, published in Japan, was once censored for printing a picture of a Chinese execution by beheading that was taken during the 1930's. In both cases, the authorities ruled the pictures inimical to public interests.

The Japanese press emerged from the Occupation with its ninety years of tradition largely intact. The Occupation washed over the press, as it did over many Japanese institutions, leaving all but the surface unchanged. The press, having never known genuine independence, groped along for a few years recovering from defeat and then resumed its function as the communications instrument of the national leadership. Wartime consolidations carried over, dividing the press into a well-defined hierarchy.

The press today is dominated by the *Asahi Shimbun, Mainichi Shimbun,* and *Yomiuri Shimbun,* which have the most space, the largest staffs, and the biggest circulations. They constitute the backbone of the national press, and blanket Japan with their multiple editions printed in several cities. The three major papers not only influence their readers but the rest of the newspapers as well as other media. Below them are several smaller and more specialized papers, such as *Nihon Keizai Shimbun,* a paper similar to *The Wall Street Journal;* local metropolitan papers like *Tokyo Shimbun* and *Osaka Shimbun;* and the provincial papers such as *Hokkaido Shimbun* and *Nishi Nippon Shimbun*. Around the newspapers are a bewildering variety of political, economic, sports, ladies', and entertainment weekly and monthly magazines. The Japanese are the world's most literate people, and their consumption of reading matter is enough to stun the uninitiated. Radio and television, too, have reached into the remote hamlets of the land.

The major change in the press is that it is no longer subservient to the ruling elite but has been upgraded into membership in the Establishment. It has joined the Establishment as a result of its history, because a vacuum opened as the postwar power structure took shape and the press slipped in, and because the Establishment needed the press as its communicator and transmitter of information. Moreover, the press is considered part of the intellectual community and is obliged, in the Confucian tradition of benevolent service, to use its knowledge to serve the nation. The press also has more tangible ties with the Establishment. Owners and publishers, as businessmen, are Establishment members, and many newspapers have large loans from banks and carry an increasing amount of advertising from business. Some journalists have gone into politics and yet maintained contact with their former colleagues.

The press is thoroughly enmeshed in the Establishment's decision-making mechanism. Staffs of the big papers have trained and thoughtful specialists who have access to extensive research facilities to turn out thoroughly prepared articles on national problems. Some ideas originate with the writers and are presented for discussion and eventual action; for example, Kishida Junnosuke of the *Asahi* is a leading thinker on Japan's security questions and is widely respected for his original commentaries. Other articles seek to refine proposals under consideration. A debate in the press over reducing restrictions on foreign investments covered every thought and fact about the issue for three years. The press, by omission, assists the Establishment in avoiding questions it does not wish discussed. Japan has suffered from a roaring consumer price inflation for seven years, but the press has confined its coverage to dutiful, low-keyed reports of isolated statistics. Few hard-hitting analyses or editorial calls for relief have come out.

The press transmits information within the Establishment both publicly and privately. In the intricate process of reaching consensus, the Establishment needs a tremendous amount of information, not only about the question at hand but about the thinking and pressures coming from the different sectors of the ruling elite. The papers cover these down to the slightest nuance. When the Japanese economy runs into trouble, the finance minister, director of the Economic Planning Agency, and governor of the Bank of Japan begin holding press conferences in which they mention various economic trends. They drop, ever so gently, a hint that raising the central bank rate may be in the offing. This alerts the rest of the Establishment that trouble is at hand and opens a debate over measures to be taken, including the pros and cons of raising the bank rate and how much. It goes on for several months until the bank rate, inevitably, is raised—the warning sign having been plain for all to see since the day it was first mentioned.

The private transmission channel runs through the huge staffs that cover every facet of the Establishment. Reporters are usually on close terms with the people they cover and often act as an intelligence service for the Establishment. Information picked up by a reporter assigned to the headquarters of the Japan Socialist Party is passed to his colleague in the headquarters of the Liberal Democratic Party and from him to his contacts in the LDP. Since every paper has reporters all over the lot, the network is the nearest thing going to an organized grapevine. If a bureaucrat wants to communicate his views to certain politicians but does not want to be identified as the source, he puts the word out through his reporter friends who pass it along to their associates and to the ears of the politicians. Clever members of the Establishment use the grapevine to influence policy in a skilled and sophisticated manner. Nor is this limited to them. A Western diplomat who speaks Japanese once confessed that he used the grapevine all the time to serve his nation's interests. He said he could move an idea throughout the Establishment in a matter of hours.

The press helps the Establishment to lead the people through both its news columns and its editorial pages. The pattern of reporting and news play and the subjects and style of editorials reflect this role. Domestic news is handled gingerly, and members of the Establishment are rarely subjected to sharp questioning by reporters. The news briefing of an official is published without independent reporting to see whether he has told the truth or told all the truth; little attempt is made to put it in perspective or to give the news interpretation. Many accounts of briefings are written exactly as the official gave them, without any reorganization of the information to put it into some order of importance. If he happened to mention something of particular import toward the end of his meeting with reporters, it very likely will end up in the fourteenth instead of the first paragraph of the story.

News is covered from a preconceived point of view to fit with the consensus of the Establishment. If a consensus has not been reached, facts and interpretation are selected to influence the Establishment's decision. Foreign correspondents working alongside Japanese reporters covering a story have often been surprised by the difference in the accounts. The Japanese delegation at the initial 1966 meeting of the Asian and Pacific Council in Seoul, according to most Western reports, angered several other delegations with its obstructive and negative tactics. Japanese dispatches, however, led the reader to believe that those delegations appreciated the Japanese insistence on moderation. The main purpose of editorials and interpretive columns is to expose the thinking of the Establishment gradually to the public so that it may be eased into following the lead of the elite. The deliberate, cautious Japanese do not like surprises, nor do they care for rapid changes. Little in Japanese life turns sharp corners, but eases slowly around a wide bend. Editorials nudge these changes along by shades of nuance, not by thundering exhortation. Panel discussions, either in print or on radio and television, are akin to this editorial technique. Several prominent men get together with a press commentator to ruminate on the topic under consideration and expose to the public the thinking going on in the Establishment as it moves toward a consensus.

Japanese newspapers usually print a far larger amount of foreign news than most Western papers because they are freer to analyze and criticize this than they are domestic news. The Establishment often has no views on news from abroad or finds critical press articles helpful in its negotiations with a foreign power. Japanese correspondents in Vietnam have rather consistently filed dispatches critical of American policy that Japanese leaders have used to resist American pressures for moral and political support of the war. They contend that they cannot come out in public support of the United States because public sentiments are against it. The same is true of editorials on foreign affairs. The Establishment does not object if editorials use America as a whipping boy—so long as this does not damage Japanese exports to the United States.

The theoretically ideal role of the press is to foster harmony, but it is not always unified in its views and must make adjustments like other segments of Japanese society. The opposition of the press or a particular newspaper to a proposal in its formative stages does not mean that the press opposes the Establishment or the government. It is merely partaking in the endless discussion that is part of the process of reaching consensus. The closer to consensus the Establishment gets, the more the press falls into line. After a decision is reached, the press or a single paper may push for a revision, which is fair game, but it will not advocate turning back on the decision already reached.

Moreover, the Japanese press is sometimes viewed as pro-socialist or pro-communist, which is an error. The press, either in print or in the personal opinions of newsmen, gives few indications that it wants drastic changes in Japan's form of government or its social order. Nor does the press give much sign that it wishes the conservative government turned out of office, though there are alley-cat fights to turn particular people out. The press, rather, has become highly nationalistic and often expresses this nationalism in anti-American terms. Taking an anti-American stance often means adopting a position that comes close to that taken by the left. But these positions are advocated within the framework of the existing order in Japan, not to overthrow it.

During May and June 1960, a turbulent debate over the security treaty with the United States ended in ratification of the treaty, the last-minute cancellation of President Eisenhower's visit, and the resignation of Prime Minister Kishi Nobusuke. Many students of Japanese affairs look on the 1960 events as evidence that the Japanese press is antigovernment. But careful study of the role the press played in those days shows that it acted as part of the Establishment and not as a reflector of public will against the government.

For several years prior to 1960, the Establishment had been unhappy with the security arrangements concluded with the United States at the end of the Occupation. The Japanese considered these an unequal treaty and a reminder of Japan's defeat. The government negotiated a new treaty and presented it to the Diet for ratification in the spring of 1960. The socialists opposed the treaty because they wanted to see Japan break all military agreements with the Americans and force the United States to withdraw the military forces that remained in Japan. The socialists were supported by the communists, who wanted to break up the American defense system in the Western Pacific. Leftists in the Diet refused to deliberate the treaty, but Kishi forced a vote, which set off the turmoil. The press demanded Kishi's resignation primarily because the papers thought he had broken the rules of the game by not compromising and persuading the opposition to debate the issue. Kishi, in their view, had also ignored the demands and advice of the press in reaching a decision on the treaty, another fracture in consensus. The quarrel with Kishi was thus more of a fight within the Establishment over methods than it was a disagreement over policy.

During the two months of disruption, the press sometimes followed a course parallel to that of the leftist opposition, but for different reasons. When leftists demonstrated in the streets, the press first warned that the demonstrations should not be turned into mob violence. The newspapers then became somewhat ambivalent. They opposed the violence editorially but indirectly encouraged it by references to student uprisings earlier that year in Korea and Turkey. For one ten-day period the papers supported the demonstrations, so long as they were orderly. When President Eisenhower's press secretary, James Hagerty, who came to Japan in advance of the planned presidential visit, was mobbed near Haneda Airport and had to be rescued by helicopter, the press turned against the demonstrators and condemned their violence and the damage they had done to Japan's international prestige.

The press afterward split on the question of whether the Eisenhower visit should be canceled, some papers contending the original plan should be followed to improve Japan's international standing, others urging that it be canceled to keep the American President from becoming involved in Japanese politics. After the Kishi government decided to cancel the visit because it could not guarantee Eisenhower's personal safety, the press campaign against Kishi slacked off quickly. The papers knew he was on his way out and they had accomplished their objective in the intra-Establishment infighting. In all of this, public opinion had little to do with events, which were caused by the clash of the opposition with the government and by the efforts of Kishi's enemies, including the press, to force him to resign.

The nationalistic and anti-American expressions of the Japanese press have become more noticeable in recent years. Extremist elements of the Zengakuren student organization on two occasions in the fall of 1967 rioted near Tokyo's Haneda Airport to protest overseas trips by Prime Minister Sato to Southeast Asia and the United States. Both were violent, the students battling police with staves and rocks, the police endeavoring to control the situation with tear gas and fire hoses. In the first incident a student was accidentally killed by other students. The press generally was critical of the violence and blamed the students for it. In January 1968, however, the press changed its tune when the students attacked police outside the American naval base in Sasebo, in southern Kyushu, to protest the first port call of the nuclear-powered aircraft carrier *Enterprise*. Because this was a direct assault on an American installation, the press tended to applaud the student action and gave it wide coverage. A professor at Tokyo University, in an analytical article following the incident, was highly critical of the distorted and inaccurate reporting of the press. He pointed to several instances in which facts were changed and events made up to emphasize the anti-American tone in press coverage.

The Japanese philosophy of news and its dissemination is quite different from that in the Anglo-American press. An American newspaper determines the news it will print by considering the public's right to know, its need to know, and its anticipated interest in the information. This is not to say that any American newspaper always, or even mostly, shows flawless news judgment. But the criteria are meaningless to a Japanese editor. Two senior Japanese reporters once explained that a potentially newsworthy event in the Western sense should not necessarily be reported when it happens nor perhaps at all. The primary considerations in selecting news for print, they said, are the effects the dispatch will have on Japanese society, the political implications, and the consequences for Japan's national interests. Many Japanese reporters, for instance, knew for months that a conservative member of the Diet named Tanaka Shoji was involved in several illegal ventures. But because he was a member of the Establishment, they did not report the story until Tanaka was indicted by the public prosecutor.

The two Japanese reporters further said that information about international affairs must be measured against the probable impact on Japan's diplomacy. Accounts of Red Guard activity by Communist Chinese correspondents in Tokyo did not appear because the Japanese feared damage to their trade relations with Peking. To the Japanese press, news is not a commodity with value to the public and for the public to use as it best sees fit, but is a lever to move subsequent events in the direction the reporter, or his editors, or the Establishment, thinks they should go. There is a higher level of consideration, the two reporters said, than the immediate public interest in a newsworthy bit of information. The reporter must judge whether it is in the best interests of Japan to have it published. They acknowledged that this concept burdens them with a grave responsibility and claimed that it makes them use their judgment much more critically. They strongly maintained that the American view of news and its dissemination is not acceptable in Japan, and at no time during the long conversation did they mention the public's right to know.

The manner in which the Japanese press uses news in an attempt to influence subsequent events, and its virulent nationalistic and anti-American stance, were vividly illustrated in another incident that began in Sasebo in May 1968. A routine check by Japanese harbor officials of water from the bay during the visit of an American nuclear-powered submarine showed a slight increase in radioactivity. This was routinely reported in a local paper but immediately seized upon by the national papers and blown up into what they saw as a major international incident. By the time the furor quieted down several weeks later, extensive investigations by Japanese and American experts failed to show any increase in radioactivity and pointed, though inconclusively, to faulty measuring equipment. No scientific case was ever made that the submarine had caused the higher reading.

During the course of the affair, Japanese reporters mobbed a team of American experts flown out from Washington to investigate. The reporters surrounded the men as they came off the airplane, hounded them into a waiting room by physical force, shouted abusive words at them, harangued them during what was supposed to have been an informal press conference, and threatened to detain them until the Americans agreed that the submarine had caused the radioactive reading. Attempts by the Americans to explain that they had just arrived, had had no chance to see the evidence, and to promise that a full report would be made subsequently went unheeded. The Americans finally escaped when one forced a Japanese reporter standing in the door to step aside and permit the American delegation to reach their cars. They went under police escort into Tokyo and the American Embassy.

When the American investigators finished their work and submitted a report to the Japanese government, they held another press conference. The report was made public and the team opened the conference for questions. Instead of studying the report and asking questions, the Japanese press directed a verbal barrage of accusations and recriminations against the men who were supposed to be news sources. Very little of the report or the comments of the Americans showed up in the next day's papers. The press instead focused on its own criticisms of the Americans. Little effort went into telling the readers what actually happened. The American Embassy press office later published a transcript of the news conference and a gist of the scientific report in hopes of getting its story told, but this too was ignored by the Japanese press.

A mass circulation magazine later published a commentary on the entire affair and summed up: "The case of the abnormal radioactivity incident at Sasebo not only exposed the abnormal 'nuclear allergy' of the Japanese mass media but was also characterized by a planned and persistent anti-U.S. and antisecurity treaty campaign, using this incident as its instrument. The incident should have been treated with the utmost scientific precision and objectivity. The data-gathering attitude of the reporters, however, was extremely tendentious and emotional, sometimes even reflecting their political designs."

The Japanese press is unique in the way it operates from day to day. Its physical arrangements alone are astounding. *Asahi*, for instance, publishes forty-two editions a day, fourteen in Tokyo and the rest in other printing centers. The paper has a staff of 7,900 employees, making it four to five times the size of a comparable

American paper. The same loyalties, lifetime employment, compensation, and other aspects of Japan's paternalistic corporate life apply to newspapers as they do to other businesses. Decisions are made by consensus and newsmen, unlike their Western counterparts, work in groups, articles being the product of numerous reporters who feed information to a writer who turns out the completed story. A Japanese newspaper can smother a story with more manpower than any ten American papers. At a 1966 United States–Japan ministerial meeting in Kyoto, *Asahi* alone sent more reporters than the entire foreign press corps there.

The most distinctive feature of the Japanese press is the "press club," which is an association of reporters attached to every government agency at the national and prefectural level and often at the local level. It is also attached to political parties, business firms and industry organizations, labor unions, educational and social organizations. The press clubs are the main, and usually only, channel into which news from a source moves through the newspaper to the readers. Before World War II, they were "organs for the adjustment of news and for regulating newsgathering activities," according to the 1967 annual review of Shimbun Kyokai, the press association. The review contended that today the press clubs "maintain themselves as simple social organs with newsgathering activities left on a free and unrestricted basis." The most cursory observation will show that this is patently not the case. The press clubs are so powerful that they determine who is allowed to cover the news, what questions are asked, what information is released to the public, and generally how media conduct their news operations. An individual reporter has little say in these matters, which are decided collectively by the clubs. Enterprise or investigative reporting is pointedly discouraged. A leader of one press club explained that the main purpose of the club is to do away with "excessive competition" and "extreme enthusiasm" and to prevent "overzealous newsgathering." The press clubs are splendid examples of the Japanese preference for group action, collective responsibility, careful regulation, and conformity. They are also a subtle but effective form of censorship.

The press clubs are the main link between the Establishment and the press, and could not exist without the implicit approval of Japan's newsmakers. Some politicians contend that they go along with the press-club system only because they will be attacked in print if they fail to. But most are quite comfortable with the clubs because the system gives them tight control over the news that goes out into the public domain. Reporters assigned to cover a particular politician become so cozy with him that they rarely report anything critical about his activities—if they do, it is usually a slip-up. The politician sees that they are well informed on the understanding that they will report only what he wants to see in print, and then only in the manner that will serve him best. He keeps this arrangement alive with lavish entertainment and a constant flow of gifts, and often assigns a competent lieutenant to see that every wish of the club is met in arranging meetings, travel, and communications. The same is true with clubs covering government agencies. Because little independent reporting is done, a news report from the Foreign Ministry can be considered a policy statement or an authoritative explanation of the ministry's position even though a comprehensive set of facts might lead to another interpretation of what is really going on.

The prime minister's press club is the most important and meets with the chief Cabinet secretary three or four times a day. The latter official is the official spokesman for the prime minister and the Cabinet and is the chief source of pronouncements designed to persuade the Establishment and the public. The chief Cabinet secretary tells the press club more than appears in the public prints, making the club privy to high government policy and, in effect, an extension of the prime minister's office. The press club, however, does not always defend the prime minister and can turn out to be his severest critic within the Establishment. The press club can decide that it is time to "get" the current prime minister and force a change, as it did successfully with Prime Minister Kishi in 1960 but unsuccessfully with Prime Minister Sato at the time of the "Black Mist" political scandals of 1966–7. The attack is not direct, which would be a violation of the rules. The press waits for the opposition to criticize the prime minister and plays that criticism big, or feeds damaging information to the prime minister's political opponents inside or outside the party, giving top coverage to the news when it comes out.

Not only do the press clubs have a stranglehold on news originating from sources they cover but they have a blanket over news outside the press-club system. Consequently, little that does not come from the press club ever sees print. One-time American Ambassador to the United Nations, Arthur J. Goldberg, addressed an international audience during a visit to Tokyo, discussing ideas that had not been heard before in Japan. Because it was outside the system, little of what he said appeared. But long accounts of a routine press briefing followed his meeting with the Japanese foreign minister were given top play. Similarly, a senior official of the Japan Socialist Party gave an important on-the-record briefing to foreign correspondents, outlining plans for a trip to North Vietnam. Although Japanese reporters were not present, they had access to the news through the international news agencies. Nothing appeared, although the story received top play in the United States and Europe. In another instance, a Western correspondent fed a solid tip about a significant change in a prime minister's thinking on China policy to a Japanese colleague to see what would happen. Had it been followed up and printed it would have made front-page news. But the tip originated outside the system and nothing happened. An American reporter was also once roundly chastised by a Japanese reporter from a major paper for reporting a story that had been dug out of five or six of the leading politicians in Japan. The Japanese reporter was incensed because the story had not been first checked with the proper press club members and had their okay before it was printed.

The Japanese press also reflects deep-seated antiforeign sentiments of the Japanese people. The press considers most events in Japan the concern of the Japanese alone, and of a small number of Japanese at that, and resents information being published abroad if it thinks it does not show Japan in a good light. Much news is either ignored or diluted by the press in an attempt to prevent internal problems from being known outside Japan. Foreign correspondents in Japan, though often on cordial personal terms with Japanese officials, politicians, businessmen, and journalists, are held in noticeable suspicion and obstructed from doing their jobs, especially by the press clubs. The Japanese do not like foreigners poking around in their country except in places marked off for them. They like least of all the foreign correspondent who is curious and skeptical by nature.

Chapter 8

NEW
DIRECTIONS
ABROAD

Japan's relations with the outside world, being an extension of its internal national character, and the making of Japanese foreign policy have their own distinctive flavor. After the end of seclusion, the Japanese learned from the West how to conduct diplomacy and other international relations. But the influences that determined the Japanese approach to foreign affairs were the consequence of the particular Japanese view of the world and their own national interests. Today, the Japanese are searching for new directions in which to move in Asia and the world. Where Japan will go and what it will do are not yet clear as the present influences are conflicting. Some influences tend to restrain the Japanese from taking positive action, others urge Japan to assert itself. A rambling, ill-defined national debate has been underway for several years, with indications that some sort of consensus will take shape during the early 1970's.

For the United States and the West, the outcome of this search is critically important. Japan has again become the most powerful nation in Asia. The elements of Japanese power are impressive. One is its strategic location, off the shore of the Asian mainland and astride the sea and air lanes from Asia to North America. A second is its 100,000,000 industrious and educated people. A third is its political order, unthreatened by subversion and destined to grow stronger as the Japanese eliminate the frictions caused by the adaptation of Western political institutions. A fourth is Japan's well-known economic and technological capacity. A fifth is the nation's modest existing military force and its potential for great military strength. The manner in which the Japanese choose to exercise—or not to exercise—their power will do much to determine the stability of East Asia, the degree of Communist China's influence, and the posture of America in Asia during the 1970's.

Among the most striking features of Japan is the profound sense of isolation and insularity that pervades Japanese society. The Japanese throughout their history have had less interchange with other peoples than probably any other major nation. This fact helps explain their unique qualities and the differences not only between them and Westerners but between the Japanese and other East Asians. Before the modern period, Japan's only large-scale impact from the outside was the infusion of Chinese culture in the sixth through the eighth centuries. There were no Japanese parallels to the conquests of Alexander the Great or the Romans, no Crusades or Islamic religious wars, no mass immigrations like those that made America, no colonial empires. Thus, when Commodore Perry and Admiral Putiatin sailed into Japanese ports, they found a nation that had had little foreign intercourse not just for 250 years, but for the better part of one thousand years.

With the coming of the West, the Japanese learned four channels for relations with the outside world. One was imperialism and military aggression, which they practiced on a scale equal to that of the West. But it sent them down in flaming disaster, which was a bitter lesson that still stings in the national soul.

A second was trade. The men of Meiji early decided that their resource-poor country must have access to natural resources to build the industrial economy and military arsenal they thought necessary for national survival. To pay for imports, they learned that Japan must export, and so developed labor-intensive industries that would take advantage of the nation's most productive resource: the diligent people. Trade later became intertwined with imperialism but never lost its identity as a prime factor in Japan's external relations.

The Japanese, thirdly, learned diplomacy from the West. Japan gradually educated a skilled diplomatic corps, with many sons following their fathers because they had acquired the knowledge of foreign lands and languages while living abroad in their youth. But Japanese diplomats have rarely been, and are not today, influential in making Japanese foreign policy. They are considered a breed apart from the norm, largely because so many have lived and been educated abroad. They often do not conform to the Japanese image of themselves and are sometimes suspected of having too many foreign ideas. And like all diplomats, they have little base of power in their domestic society.

Lastly, the Japanese opened up channels of cultural exchange. Christianity came to Japan, as did Marxism, in the nineteenth century. Writers and other artists were influenced by those of Europe and America. In the Meiji period, scholar Fukuzawa Yukichi was a prolific writer on Western life, and his works sold extremely well. Later, novelist Natsume Soseki and other prominent authors were influenced by ideas and techniques from the West. But the insular mentality of the Japanese had a restraining effect. They have been interested in the outside world more for practical purposes and less for thought. Despite a century of missionary persuasion, Japanese Christians today number less than one per cent of the population. Marxism is confined to a relatively small group of intellectuals and has stagnated. Many writers have turned away from Western influence. Kawabata Yasunari, who was awarded the Nobel Prize for literature in 1968, broke with a European-oriented school of writers in the 1920's. He and Mishima Yukio, his best-known protégé, are distinctly Japanese in theme and style.

Japan's intercourse with the rest of the world since the Meiji Restoration falls into rather well-marked periods. From 1868 to 1895, the Japanese went through the heaviest part of the borrowing process and fended off incursions from the West as best they could. The wars that led to the annexation of Korea in 1910 also led Japan into the imperialistic race that picked up during World War I, hit full stride in the 1930's, and ended with defeat in 1945. During the Occupation, Japanese had little contact with the outside world except with the Americans who governed their country. When Japan regained its sovereignty in 1952, diplomatic relations and trade resumed, but Japan remained an American client state until 1960. The turmoil over the ratification of the new U.S.-Japan Mutual Security Treaty and the cancellation of President Eisenhower's state visit was something of a declaration of independence from the United States. The Japanese, however, have taken a subdued role in all international relations since then, except trade, where they have been aggressive. The Japanese have been unable to exert much influence in Asian affairs because the nation lacked the required national consensus that would give at least basic support to a positive foreign policy.

In 1965, however, there began a national debate over whether Japan should remain in what the Japanese call low posture or should move to a higher, more assertive posture. The discussion has spread and become more intense in recent years and, at the time of writing, was still going on without a conclusion in sight. The influences at work can be identified, but they are an inconsistent and contradictory lot, making a final assessment or prediction impossible. The Japanese genius for finding a widely acceptable compromise, however, should not be underestimated. The consensus necessary for national action most likely can be reached even from widely divergent factors.

Japan's isolation, more than a hundred years after the Restoration, is still strong. Except for a superficial curiosity, the Japanese are seldom deeply interested in and rarely empathetic with the world beyond their shores. The people and the Establishment, with individual exceptions, do not understand how other nations function, what others believe important, why other peoples do what they do. The Japanese view of the world is misty and seen through the haze of their parochial insularity. More and more Japanese businessmen and officials in recent years have traveled overseas and, as foreign-exchange restrictions have been relaxed, more tourists are going on visits abroad. But they usually go in groups with other Japanese, stick close together, and absorb little of the real life of the nations they visit.

Japanese scholars who spend a year or more abroad in research demonstrate an inability to synthesize their experiences into a comprehensive analysis when they return to Japan. Japanese newsmen are much the same, unable to adapt to the news-covering techniques of Americans or Europeans and transmitting dispatches that show little comprehension of the significance of events in their host nations. Japanese businessmen abroad on long-term assignment return with little understanding of the vast differences in the business methods of the countries in which they have been working. One reason for all of this is that the Japanese are not good linguists. They have an extremely complicated language, and techniques for teaching foreign languages in Japan have not been formulated to overcome this handicap.

The Japanese inability to understand how other people think was illustrated during the 1962 Cuban missile crisis. When President Kennedy announced that the Soviet Union was preparing missile-launching sites in Cuba, ninety miles from the Florida coast, Americans saw this as a potential sneak attack much like that of Japan against Pearl Harbor. An American might have thought that, with all that Americans and Japanese have gone through together in the last quarter-century as enemies and allies, the Japanese of all people would understand the serious concern Americans felt about Soviet missiles in Cuba. To the contrary, the Japanese were, for the most part, mystified. They did not see the parallel with Pearl Harbor and thought Americans unreasonable to be upset by the Soviet move. They could not understand the American point of view, which is not to say they would have agreed with it if they had.

The Japanese outlook on foreign affairs today is strongly influenced by pacifism. This, too, arises from Japanese history, in which foreign wars have been few and domestic conflicts largely limited to the 5 or 6 per cent of the population who belonged to the *samurai* class. The mass of the people did not participate in wars before the modern era, except as the unhappy victims of power clashes among the warriors. More immediately, the devastation of American fire-bombing and the horror of the Hiroshima and Nagasaki atomic bombings have left the Japanese with an abhorrence of war that must be the greatest in the world. A large majority of the Japanese want nothing to do with war for whatever reason and no matter what happens to them. Pacifism explains much of the Japanese antipathy for the Vietnam war. While there has been political and ideological opposition to American policy, at the base of it the Japanese have been afraid that the war would escalate into a direct conflict between the Americans and the Chinese and spill out beyond Vietnam to engulf Japan.

A longing for neutrality is another restraining element in Japanese thinking about international relations. The Japanese not only want to stay out of other people's quarrels but do not want to be involved even as mediators. This form of neutrality differs from the neutralism of India or of the United Arab Republic, in which a government does not align itself with the major powers but still attempts to exert influence on the course of world events. The Japanese low posture has precluded them from making any effort, other than offering platitudes, to help settle international crises. The United States encouraged the Japanese to mediate discreetly in the Indonesia-Malaysia confrontation several years ago, but Prime Minister Ikeda Hayato adamantly refused. After the Arab-Israeli six-day war of 1967, the Japanese delegation in the United Nations voted on one side in one resolution, then turned around and voted for the other side in a subsequent resolution. Japan has sat on the fence in every major international issue of the past decade, except the nuclear test-ban treaty, which it supported. The Japanese, the only people to have suffered an atomic bombing, have even been equivocal on the nuclear nonproliferation issue.

The Japanese have shown little willingness to accept responsibility in international affairs. Just as the individual Japanese shuns responsibility and functions within the group, so Japan as a nation shuns responsibility, keeps its own counsel, watches which way the winds of consensus are blowing, makes adjustments, and allows itself to be borne along. Moreover, the Japanese have lacked self-confidence on the world stage, a consequence of the wartime defeat. An amusing illustration of Japan's fear of responsibility occurred in the 1966 United Nations' consideration of the Rhodesian question. Prime Minister Ian

Smith had led his government in a break with the British to enforce Rhodesia's segregationist racial policies. The issue of sanctions against Rhodesia came up before the Security Council, on which Japan that year had a non-permanent seat. The Japanese delegate's turn to be chairman, in the monthly rotation, came just as the issue reached a critical point. This brought cries of anguish from Tokyo because he would be in the spotlight and would have to take definite responsibility for Security Council actions. To the surprise of no one at the United Nations, Ambassador Matsui Akira handled the situation in a thoroughly professional manner and brought credit to himself as a diplomat. But when his month as chairman was over, the Japanese Establishment in Tokyo let out a collective sigh of relief.

A spurt of initiative in foreign policy beginning in late 1965 seemed to indicate that Japan was moving toward exerting some regional leadership in Asia. The Japanese called a conference of Asian economic ministers to discuss development, helped form the Asian Development Bank, joined the Asian and Pacific Council, assembled creditors of Indonesia to help straighten out that nation's economy after President Sukarno had been deposed, sent Foreign Minister Miki Takeo and Prime Minister Sato Eisaku abroad on good will missions, and several times announced that it stood ready to help settle the Vietnam war. But the promise so far has proven illusory. The Japanese have wanted the prominence that went with such moves but have not been willing to get down to the hard work and exert the leadership to turn out realistic results.

The reluctance of the Japanese to assume responsibility and leadership was perhaps best seen in their attitude toward the Asian and Pacific Council (ASPAC). It was formed in 1966 under the leadership of South Korea and Thailand in an effort to pull together a loose alliance of non-Communist Asian nations for economic and cultural exchange. They hoped, and still hope, that ASPAC would evolve into a collective-security arrangement. They and the other members, including Australia and New Zealand, wanted the Japanese in because all recognized that no regional organization in Asia could be effective unless the Japanese were in it. Japan, however, opposed ASPAC because it feared this would turn into just the sort of organization the Koreans and Thais envisaged, with a hard-line stand against the Chinese. The Japanese joined ASPAC reluctantly and mainly to prevent it from becoming a working organization. Japan has continued its original policy and so far prevented ASPAC from accomplishing anything substantive, even along economic lines.

The economic cost of ASPAC and the other apparent initiatives has been a major reason for the lack of Japanese enthusiasm. The cost of any foreign-policy decision is carefully calculated and subjected to severe internal pressures to keep it down. The Japanese are concerned almost solely with their own economic development and have contributed but a pittance in economic aid to developing Asian nations. Most of that has been an open or disguised form of export promotion. Japan has extended loans or credits to several nations but at high-interest, short-length commercial terms rather than the low-interest, long-term "soft" loans extended by other economically advanced nations. At their 1965 meeting of economic ministers in Tokyo, the Japanese indicated that they were ready to assist in economic development on a large scale. But subsequent ministerial meetings in other capitals have produced little except suggestions for studies and surveys. The Japanese were enthusiastic at first about the formation of the Asian Development Bank, seeing it as an excellent export promotion mechanism. If other nations contributed funds for economic development, Japan would be the logical source of supply for equipment and other materials. But after the bank's head-quarters were situated in Manila, the Japanese considered withdrawing. They were persuaded to stay in by having a Japanese named as first president of the bank. Japan has contributed its share to the capitalization of the bank but has otherwise lost interest. Similarly, the Japanese have promised sizable loans to the Indonesians and South Koreans but have found it inconvenient, for one reason or another, to put all the committed funds on the table when the Koreans or Indonesians asked for them.

Economic costs also count heavily in Japanese think-ing on military defense. The United States has provided for the major portion of Japanese security since 1952. This has been, indirectly, a large contribution to Japanese prosperity. Japanese investment has gone into factories, railroads, golf courses, and ski resorts instead of guns and aircraft. Japan has spent only about 1.3 per cent of its gross national product and only about 7 per cent of the national budget on defense each year compared with about 10 per cent of gross national product and over 50 per cent of the national budget in the United States. Japa-nese defense spending has risen in absolute amounts, but not much relative to over-all economic capacity. The Establishment and their economists are well aware of this and are loath to give it up.

Among the more important considerations in the Japa-nese outlook on foreign policy is trade. The first question that comes into the mind of the Establishment when it is confronted with a question of foreign policy is what effect it will have on trade. Most nations, even the smallest, are customers or suppliers, or both. Since any international quarrel is likely to involve two or more trading partners, the immediate Japanese reaction is to look for a position that can offend no one. If that cannot be found, the Japa-nese prefer to take no position at all and to issue a plati-tudinous statement hoping that a peaceful and fair solution can be reached. Japan has taken no position on either side of conflicts between India and China, India and Pakistan, Malaysia and Indonesia, Russia and Czechoslovakia, Israel and the Arab nations, South Africa and black African nations, the United States and Cuba—all of which are trading partners. Sometimes nothing stands in the way of trade. Scores of Japanese businessmen attending trade fairs or negotiating sessions in China during the Cultural Revolution submitted to Chinese political indoctrination just to get export orders.

These are all powerful restraints that militate against taking a foreign policy stance that requires action, leadership, money, and risk. Yet in recent years there have appeared other forces, some perhaps equally powerful, that urge Japan to assert itself and to exert that power in Asia of which it is capable.

Foremost among these is the resurgence of nationalism. Renewed national pride is coursing through every segment of Japanese society and may well be the strongest force in the determination of foreign policy in the coming decade. The Japanese are becoming more self-confident through an awareness of their economic accomplishments and their political stability. They have become tougher and more demanding in external negotiations on trade and investment and the nuclear nonproliferation treaty, where they sought relentlessly to insure that Japan's views were incorporated in the final version of the treaty and its implementation. More and more Japanese leaders and intellectuals are speaking out to demand that Japan assume, and the world recognize, what they consider to be their nation's rightful place in the sun. The simple pride that a Japanese has in being Japanese has become more evident with each passing month.

This, in turn, is leading to a rising desire for international prestige. In Japanese life, prestige and position are more important than money and comfort. This is equally true in the international arena. It is important to all Japanese that other people think well of them, recognize their achievements, and accord them the respect they believe is their due. Although the Japanese have shown no desire to take international responsibility, they have worked assiduously to make sure that they are included in the leading international organizations along with other advanced industrial nations. The Japanese have recently been quietly lobbying for a change in the United Nations Charter that would give them a permanent seat on the Security Council along with the United States, the Soviet Union, and other major powers. The Japanese contend that the council should be restructured to reflect the changes in relative power that have come about since the end of World War II.

Japanese concepts of the applications of power are likely to become an especially strong determinant in the nation's foreign policy. As in their daily domestic affairs, the Japanese apply their highly refined sensitivity to the subtleties of power to their relations with other nations. They are guided not by principle but by what is possible. They are pragmatic and expedient. Ideology, political commitment, and precedent have little to do with foreign policy decisions, any more than they have to do with internal decisions. The Japanese are collectors of great amounts of information, are deliberate and calculating analysts of that information and prudent formulators of policy based on it. In any negotiation, they strive to know exactly their own strengths and weaknesses, and the same for their adversary. They look at problems in international relations on a case-by-case basis, assessing the balances of power in a given situation and acting accordingly. As new power balances emerge in Asia during the coming decade, the Japanese may find that they have the power to further their national interests and decide to apply it.

This sensitivity to power and willingness to use it

makes treaties and other agreements with the Japanese weak or even useless unless the other party has some form of political, economic, or military power—and the will to use it—to enforce the pact. Japan's international agreements, as with internal agreements, are subject to constant modification as the conditions bearing on them change. Japan has a Treaty of Friendship, Commerce, and Navigation with the United States that is a standard commercial agreement between nations. It contains a provision that allows the citizens of one nation to invest in commercial enterprises in the other nation on a basis equal to that of the citizens of the host nation. The Japanese, however, for years have refused to allow Americans to invest in Japan on the same basis as Japanese. American Cabinet officers, prominent businessmen, and diplomats have tried repeatedly to have the Japanese abide by the treaty, but to no avail. The Japanese have either ignored the protests or have blandly informed the Americans that they have no intention of abiding by the treaty provisions. In reply to further American protest, the Japanese have said the United States could take the issue to the World Court, where it would be fought out over perhaps ten years to an uncertain conclusion. The only realistic course left to the Americans has been economic retaliation. But the Japanese have figured, so far quite rightly, that the Americans would not resort to this because it would damage their own considerable export trade with Japan and would harm the entire American drive toward freer world trade.

Japanese attitudes toward their military security are, obviously, a prime factor in the making of their foreign policy. Since the end of World War II, the mass of the people have either opposed moves toward rearmament or have been apathetic about questions of national defense. They have been preoccupied with economic recovery and then prosperity, while the psychological aftermath of the war caused them to put military security out of their minds. Further, few Japanese have felt that their nation faced an external threat from either the Soviet Union or Communist China. Perhaps most important, they have had the United States to take the major responsibility for defending them, a reliance most of the Japanese have taken very much for granted.

Even so, Japan has built up without fanfare a modest but modern military force. Some 250,000 Japanese are under arms and fully equipped. The Japanese navy has new submarines, destroyers, and antisubmarine aircraft carriers, with more on the way. The air force has first-class fighters, transports, and naval patrol planes. Considering the military machine the Japanese were able to build before and during World War II, it takes little imagination to see the military might they could assemble with the incomparably greater industrial complex and population of today. The ultimate in military power is nuclear weapons. Most experts agree that the Japanese could make nuclear arms within two years of a decision to do so, faster if they undertook a crash program. They could also put a nuclear warhead atop an intermediate-range ballistic missile as soon as the warhead is built. Japan's rocketry and missile research and the nation's space program have moved ahead steadily without much public notice.

Beginning in 1965, some influential members of the Establishment, including several intellectuals, started talking publicly about the need for revising Japan's defense posture. The discussions took no particular direction but ranged over the entire issue. Even nuclear arms came into the debate. Before that, even to mention the subject publicly evoked the same reaction that an off-color story would have at a Sunday school picnic. The unmentionable and unthinkable has slowly become mentionable and thinkable as the Japanese have ever so gradually begun to shed the "nuclear allergy" that resulted from the Hiroshima and Nagasaki atomic bombings. A small but powerful number of leaders have come to feel that a nuclear-armed and belligerent China is a potential threat to Japan, though the Chinese so far have given them no overt reason to think so. The Russian invasion of Czechoslovakia in 1968 has reinforced the thought that no nation today is immune from nuclear, conventional, or subversive attack. Increasing tensions along the demilitarized zone that divides North and South Korea have brought the possibility closer to home.

Further, Japan's increasingly nationalistic leaders have started to feel that reliance on another nation, the United States, for military security is humiliating for a sovereign nation. This reliance is also potentially dangerous, many believe, because they have come to realize that the United States would defend Japan only in its own national interests, not for an altruistic interest in Japan. Signs of neo-isolationism and the demands for a complete withdrawal of American forces from Asia following the end of the Vietnam war that have come from an increasingly wide range of Americans have made Japanese leaders nervous. Thus in 1967, Prime Minister Sato launched Japan into a public reassessment of the nation's attitudes on military security, hoping to evolve a national consensus that would permit Japan to take over responsibility for its local, conventional defense while leaving nuclear defense to the American umbrella. The opposition socialists, playing on public apathy and antipathy for war, have vigorously protested, charging that the Prime Minister would lead Japan into militarism again. This deep division and lack of consensus, at the time of this writing, was far from resolved. The manner in which it is resolved and the final consensus at which the Japanese arrive will have a marked impact on the future of Japanese foreign policy, especially with regard to its role in East Asia.

Japan's attitudes toward its neighbors and their attitudes toward Japan are still another factor, one that can be either a restraint or an assertive element, in the making of Japan's future foreign policy. The Japanese tend to look down on the less developed peoples of Asia because they have failed to accomplish what the Japanese have accomplished. The Japanese have little racial affinity with other Asians and tend to make their judgments more along nationalistic lines. Their attitudes toward the Koreans, the Nationalist Chinese on Taiwan and the Taiwanese, the Filipinos, and the Indonesians are semicolonial, the Japanese vaguely considering them peoples who must be guided, if not ruled, by a major power.

In return, those other peoples who were victims of Japanese aggression before and during World War II have mixed emotions toward the Japanese. Memories of harsh Japanese conquest and rule are still vivid for many. They fear Japanese economic domination and look askance at any Japanese move that has the slightest military implications. Yet they know that they need Japanese help and would like to have Japan do more to assist them economically and, except for the Indonesians, would like Japan to be cooperative in mutual defense. The Japanese are aware of these fears and tend to govern themselves accordingly. Those who would have Japan take an active role in Asian regional affairs know that if Japan is ever to have the influence of which it is capable as a major power, it must find ways to overcome the latent hostility and distrust of many of its neighbors and to persuade them of Japanese good will and honorable intentions. If the Japanese overcome their reluctance to extending constructive economic aid, this may do much to abate the ill feeling among other Asians and consequently make Japan economically and politically influential throughout the region.

Similarly, Japanese sentiments toward America work both ways. Despite the benevolence of the Occupation and the generally good relations between Japan and America since then, many Japanese still feel a deep resentment toward their conquerors. Moreover, the presence of American military forces on Japanese soil for a quarter-century has caused friction and has been a living reminder of humiliating submission. No people in history has ever welcomed for long the presence of foreign troops on its soil, no matter how good the reason nor how friendly the relations. Further, Japan has lived in America's shadow politically and internationally since the war's end and has had to stand by idly or follow meekly the American lead in Asia and world councils—which causes resentment.

Yet the Japanese today have respect and even admiration for America, its ideals, its political leadership, its economic and technological achievements, and its military power. Most Japanese know that they need America, especially its markets, to sustain their prosperity. Many Japanese are curious about America and would like to visit the United States, even if they are not especially eager to understand the way Americans live and think. Japanese are personally cordial to Americans who visit or live in Japan. They only wish that Americans, personally and officially, were as much concerned about Japan as they are about America. Japanese often say that the two peoples see each other through the opposite ends of a telescope. The Americans loom large in the Japanese eye, but the Japanese are small in the American view. In all, the Japanese emotional involvement with America is something of a love-hate sentiment. On one side, the Japanese want to be equal partners with the Americans in the affairs of the world; on the other, they wish the Americans would go away and leave them in peace to pursue their own national interests in the manner they best see fit.

Japan's foreign policy, like that of any nation, is directly a function of geography. The world, seen from Tokyo, divides itself into five areas of major importance: nearby neighbors Korea and Taiwan, the Soviet Union, China, Southeast Asia and Australia, and the United States.

Beyond the Pacific Basin, Western and Eastern Europe are significant but secondary trading partners. The Middle East is a vital source of oil supply and a small market, but the Japanese are not otherwise interested in problems there. Latin America and Africa are modest trading partners, but are considered marginal elements in the balance of world power.

Korea and Taiwan are important markets for Japanese exports, but the major concern is that the Korean peninsula and the island of Taiwan, which sit on the military flanks of Japan, do not come under the control of a hostile power. The Japanese Establishment has been uneasy with North Korea under Communist domination but has felt that Japan is secure so long as American and South Korean forces prevent the North Koreans from taking over the entire country. As the regime of Prime Minister Kim Il-sung, the North Korean Stalinist leader, has become more belligerent in recent years, thoughtful members of the Establishment have become disturbed, though they have said little publicly. As for Taiwan, the Japanese have tried to stay out of the complicated question of the island's eventual fate. The Communist Chinese on the mainland say it belongs to them, the Nationalist Chinese under President Chiang Kai-shek on Taiwan say it is but a refuge from which they will one day return to the mainland to retake control of China, and the Taiwanese themselves say it is their land and wish that all Chinese would go away and leave them alone. While the Japanese have been equivocal publicly, members of the Establishment privately have made clear their opposition to any move that would permit Taiwan to come under Communist Chinese control.

Japanese attitudes toward the Soviet Union are marked by the antagonisms that reach back to the days of imperialistic competition and the Russo-Japanese War of 1905. More recently, clashes between Russian and Japanese troops along the Manchurian border broke out intermittently during World War II, although Russia did not enter the war against the Japanese until its last nine days. Thousands of Japanese were taken prisoner and shipped from Manchuria and Korea to Siberia, there to die or remain for many years in concentration camps. The fate of some is still unknown. Territorial disputes over several small islands just north of Hokkaido remain as unsettled vestiges of World War II. The Japanese have not concluded a peace treaty with the Soviet Union, although there was a declaration of peace in 1956. On the other hand, the Japanese wish to increase trade with the Soviet Union and see possibilities for participating in the economic development of Siberia. They see lucrative markets there for machinery, plants, and equipment for agriculture and mineral exploitation. The Russians have been quietly cultivating the Japanese as a counterbalance to China, and the Japanese have cautiously accepted the Russian approaches in hopes of increasing trade.

The Japanese have profound respect for historical China and for Chinese civilization. Some Japanese, who are very race-conscious, see in themselves a racial affinity with the Chinese. But the emotional ties about which these Japanese speak are a myth for the majority. There is little evidence that the Japanese feel any particular attachment for the Chinese or show any special understanding of modern China. Few Japanese study the Chinese language today, which worries the Foreign Ministry and the trading companies that someday may need linguists to maintain diplomatic and trade relations. Some Japanese "China hands" from prewar days say they have guilty feelings about the misery Japan caused China then. But this does not spill over into the rest of Japanese society. Curiously, these same Japanese profess no special guilt for Japanese aggression in Korea, the Philippines, or elsewhere. Japan's main concern with China today is to find a mode of peaceful coexistence with its giant and sometimes belligerent neighbor. Japanese businessmen are anxious to increase their exports to China, where they see an immense market of 750,000,000 people now and perhaps 1,000,000,000 by the turn of the next century. Trade between the two has been a good barometer of political relations, which exist even if diplomatic relations do not. When Sino-Japanese political relations improve, trade goes up. When they deteriorate, trade drops. The Japanese expound a policy of separation of economics and politics when dealing with the Chinese. This is another myth; no Communist government, and certainly not the Chinese government, separates economics from politics. But the Japanese policy serves to placate their American allies, who oppose Japan's trade with China.

Southeast Asia and Australia are major markets for Japanese exports and are suppliers of raw materials and food. Japanese trade and some investment has gone a long way to establishing an economic hegemony in Southeast Asia that Japanese soldiers failed to establish with the Greater East Asia Co-Prosperity Sphere. The Japanese worry about political stability in Southeast Asia primarily for economic reasons. But they also fear that a hostile power might dominate the region and control the Straits of Malacca, between Singapore and Indonesia, and thus have a lock on the sea lanes between Japan and India, Africa, the Middle East, and Europe. Japan and Australia have become major trading partners within the last few years and show promise of becoming even more closely tied. Japanese and Australian interests in Southeast Asian political stability are parallel and may lead to some form of political cooperation between them.

None of these areas is so important to Japan's interests as the United States. About 30 per cent of Japan's two-way trade is with America, Japan's financial resources are almost completely tied to the dollar, the United States is Japan's strongest political ally, and the Japanese so far have depended on America for their defense. The focal point of Japan's relations with America in the immediate future lies in two interrelated issues, the continuation of the Treaty of Mutual Cooperation and Security and the reversion of Okinawa. The security treaty is the basis for the Japanese political and military alliance with the United States. Its two main articles provide that the United States will defend Japan in the event of an attack and that Japan permits the United States to station land, sea, and air forces in Japan for the defense of Japan and other nations in the Far East. The treaty also states that in 1970 either party may notify the other of its intention to terminate the treaty on one year's notice. Almost from the day it was ratified, in 1960, the Japanese have been debating over whether they should continue it in force, negotiate a revision, or abrogate it when it becomes possible to do so.

Okinawa, in the island chain south of Japan, was captured from Japan toward the end of the war and was retained under American control when the peace treaty was signed in 1952. The United States has since agreed that Japan retains residual sovereignty over Okinawa and that the island, along with the other Ryukyu Islands, would be returned to Japan when the international situation in Asia stabilized. The United States has spent billions of dollars constructing an immense complex of military bases on the island, making it into what the Pentagon calls the "Keystone of the Pacific" for its role in military operations from Korea to Vietnam. But the Japanese, regardless of the security situation, now want it back. Okinawa has little economic value to Japan, and the Okinawan people are considered inferior by the Japanese. Even so, nationalistic sentiments in Japan have become so strong that they demand that this stigma and symbol of defeat be erased by having Okinawa revert to Japanese political control.

The issue turns on the military bases. The United States has the right to station troops, aircraft, and ships on

Okinawa and to deploy them from there without consulting the Japanese government, as it must for movements in and out of Japan proper. The Americans also have the right to emplace and to launch nuclear weapons from Okinawa, a right they do not have in Japan itself. American military authorities are reluctant to give up those rights, contending that they are essential for national security and military operations in the Pacific. The Japanese, at the time of writing, appear willing to have the Americans retain their bases on Okinawa but want their status to be the same as those in Japan proper, where the prior consultation and nuclear prohibition policies apply.

The Japanese debate over the security treaty and Okinawa is encompassed within the over-all reassessment of their foreign policy and military posture. Although there is no political or diplomatic reason for any change in June 1970, when the treaty can be abrogated, the date has become something of a psychological deadline for the Japanese, a people given to setting deadlines for themselves. The treaty issue has become the catalyst that is stimulating movement toward a decision on the larger question of what the Japanese wish their nation to do and to be as the leading power in East Asia. Whether the Japanese will reach their consensus in the summer of 1970 or at some time thereafter is unpredictable. But all the evidence points to the setting of new directions abroad in the early 1970's.

As the Japanese sort out all of the factors that go into the making of foreign policy, they have several alternatives from which to choose. Some can be ruled out from the start: Japan will not go communist nor will it try to arrange a working alliance with the Chinese or Russians. The fundamentally conservative Japanese will not accept communism and neither the Japan Communist Party nor the pro-Peking wing of the Japan Socialist Party have much chance of taking control of the Japanese government. In a practical sense, Japan's economic ties to the

West are far more valuable than anything the Chinese and Russians can offer. Similarly, it is doubtful that Japan will turn to the unarmed neutrality that some Japanese leftists advocate; they are not likely to gain enough domestic power in the foreseeable future to lead Japan in that direction.

A return to the imperialism and aggression of the 1930's and 1940's is impossible. The Japanese, quite simply, want no more war and are not likely to undertake anything that risks it except in self-defense and at the gravest provocation; Japan would also be opposed by the Russians, the Chinese, and the Asian nations that have bilateral alliances with the United States. Lastly, the days of Japan as a client state of America appear to have drawn to a close. Nationalism in Japan and the uncertainty many Japanese sense in America's future policies in Asia make this status no longer possible. Leftists also oppose it, though for their own political and ideological reasons. Some Japanese appear willing to see Japan remain passively under American protection because the economic costs of any other policies are certain to be large. But they are a dwindling minority.

This leaves three live possibilities: some form of armed neutrality, a full working alliance with the United States, or an independent course resembling that taken by former French President Charles de Gaulle.

A neutral course has widespread appeal among Japan's moderate conservatives, the centrists, and the moderate left. Such neutrality could be along nineteenth-century lines, or the modern Swiss-Swedish variety, with no commitments or entanglements with other nations. It could also take the form of the nonaligned neutralism of India or the United Arab Republic in which Japan would join with other nations in the "third force" in their attempts to influence world events. In either case, Japan would acquire enough military strength to provide for its own defense but have no commitments to send troops to other nations. Either would mean the abrogation of the security treaty with the United States, the withdrawal of American forces from Japan, and the reversion of Okinawa, with the American bases there dismantled or turned over to Japanese forces. The Japanese might try to retain a loose agreement with the Americans for nuclear protection, obtaining such an arrangement on grounds that Japan would then not feel it necessary to acquire nuclear weapons itself. American policy has been and will be, if present trends continue, to discourage the proliferation of nuclear arms beyond the nations that now have them.

A large group of conservatives and Establishment members advocates a full-fledged alliance with the United States in which Japan would become a partner on the order of Great Britain. The Japanese would become responsible for their own conventional defense while continuing to rely on the United States for nuclear protection. The Americans would continue to post forces in Japan and Okinawa, perhaps on a more limited level than has been true in recent years. The Japanese would undertake political and economic initiatives in Asia in coordination with those of America. The sharing of the political burden and the economic costs would be in proportion to the relative power of the two partners. The alliance would require the Japanese to make major efforts toward Asian stability and the United States to put full confidence in Japanese leaders and to consult with them with the same frequency and candor that Americans have with the British and other European allies. To arrive at such an alliance would mean many changes in past Japanese attitudes, but those who advocate such a policy may have the position and prestige to bring about a consensus to support it.

The last and latest possibility is an independent Japan that would adopt a Gaullist international course. This would entail loosening the ties with the United States, perhaps severing them completely. Japan would assert its own political and economic policies in Asia and attempt to become the dominant power in Southeast Asia. Advocates of Japanese Gaullism believe that the United States, the Soviet Union, and Communist China will not permit one of the others to dominate Southeast Asia, and that this might lead to a stalemate and the withdrawal of all. That would leave a power vacuum into which a major power must move if that Balkanized region is to have stability. Because Southeast Asia is vital to Japan's trade and security interests, Japan would be the power to move in. Japanese Gaullists do not foresee a major military role for Japan in Southeast Asia but rather an influential political and economic role. The number of Japanese Gaullists is small but growing, both among intellectuals and politicians. They are feeding on nationalism, the ambivalent emotions toward America, the belief that Japan must look to itself for security, and the desire to see Japan exert its power for its own national interests. Japan would increase its armaments to the point where its own security would be assured, possibly even developing the Japanese equivalent of a *force de frappe*, a nuclear arsenal along the lines of French nuclear development. Gaullism would also require a great change in Japanese attitudes, but it may have a wider appeal, given the surge in nationalism, than neutrality or an alliance with the United States.

Japan's choice will have a great impact on the American defense posture in the Western reaches of the Pacific during the 1970's. It will probably be the single most important factor in determining what America must do to maintain its security west of Hawaii. This is not merely a question of whether the United States will be able to retain bases in Japan and Okinawa but is a far broader question of whether Japan will use its power in conjunction with that of the United States or go off in a direction that will have adverse effects on American security.

Japan's importance to America is predicated on three fundamental assumptions. The first is that a continued American presence in Asia is considered essential to the national security. Japan will be vital if America intends to remain as deeply involved in Asia as it has been from World War II through the Korean and Vietnam wars. Japan's role will become even more pivotal if the United States decides, as an increasing number of thoughtful leaders suggest, to reduce its military commitments and pull back from the defense chain that runs from Korea through Japan, Okinawa, Taiwan, and the Philippines to Australia. This does not mean a pullout but a reduction of forces in the far Pacific and a pullback to a mid-Pacific defense line. This would put the emphasis on political and economic efforts to reach stability in East Asia, an under-taking that would require full-scale Japanese participation. If the United States decides to withdraw completely from Asia and return to fortress America, Japan and other na-tions will be important only if they become adversaries or ally themselves with adversaries.

A second assumption is that the plodding steps toward an uneasy détente with the Soviet Union will continue. Kremlinologists think that the Russians, faced with the balance of nuclear terror, hold détente to be in their na-tional interests and will keep on moving toward it with the United States. But few foresee any lessening of political competition with the United States anywhere, including Asia. This means both will be competing for allies to main-tain a balance of power.

The third assumption is that China will continue its hostile attitude toward the United States. As the leadership generation of Chairman Mao Tse-tung passes, less aggres-sive revolutionaries may rise to take their places. They may slowly lessen the tensions by directing their efforts to the internal construction job that China must undertake to become a power worthy of its potential. But no Chinese leader on the horizon has given any overt indication of a change in China's basic attitude toward America. Some prominent Japanese and Americans see Japan's role as a bridge between America and China. The chances of this coming to pass are not good until the Chinese show some desire to let their end of the bridge rest on anything but quicksand.

In the complex turbulence of Asia today, only four nations are capable of exercising power: the United States, the Soviet Union, China, and Japan. The Europeans are no longer on the scene. The Dutch are gone from Indonesia, the French from Indochina. The British have left from all but Hong Kong, their trading post, and Singapore, their major base east of Suez. They are now withdrawing their power from that last bastion. Industrial Australia lacks the necessary people and resources to be a major power, naturally rich and populous Indonesia is generations away from pulling itself together. India is too weak internally, as is Pakistan. The smaller Asian nations can, at best, exert only marginal influence in their localities.

The United States does not need an alliance with Japan to deter Soviet or Chinese nuclear threats as American nuclear power alone is sufficient for that. The lessons of the Korean and Vietnam wars, however, indicate that America alone cannot deter conventional or subversive military aggression but must have Asian allies for logistic and combat support bases, for troops, and for political support in the world arena. Such allies will undoubtedly be even more important in the future than they have been in the past.

A greater need lies in alliances to counter the expansion of Russian and Chinese political and economic influence. The United States, alone or in alliance, cannot contain this sort of expansion. But it can be countered with a balance of power similar to the nineteenth-century balance of power in Europe, in which no single nation was predominant and alliances maintained an equilibrium that precluded major war from the fall of Napoleon until World War I. The United States alone might be able to maintain such a balance against Russia and China, but only at an extremely high cost in military expenditure, economic aid, and political time and effort. Moreover, the resentment and the active or passive resistance of Asian nations to an American policeman could easily be enough to upset the balance. The only alternative is collective security, which can take a number of multilateral or bilateral forms. Japan is the only Asian nation that can provide the necessary weight to the non-communist side of the scales to keep the balance of power in equilibrium.

Since the United States became totally involved in the Vietnam war, few Americans among the public, in the press, or in political life have given much thought to the longer-range problems of the American presence in Asia. This is especially true of America's relations with Japan, which should receive top priority if the United States wishes to contribute to stability in the Pacific region and thus to its own security. For America to continue to ignore its relationship with Japan is to do so at its peril.

PART THREE

The PEOPLE and THEIR FUTURE

Chapter 9

WE JAPANESE

My name is Watanabe Taro, which is something like John Smith or John Doe, and I would like to tell you about myself and the Japanese people. You may think I am presumptuous to say that I am typical of all Japanese because there are an infinite variety of people in Japan, just like any country. But we Japanese are a very unified people and we live in a closely knit society in our small island country. We Japanese have the same basic beliefs and traits and language whether we live in the city or the countryside, or in northern Honshu or southern Kyushu. It can be said, in my opinion, that we Japanese have a definite national character. Conformity is important to us, and we Japanese soon hammer down the nail that sticks up.

I am a rather average middle-class Japanese. I was born here in Tokyo and have spent most of my life here, except for two years when I was a boy during the war. My two younger brothers and my younger sister and I were sent to live with my uncle, who has a small business in a mountain town north of here. My father, who is now retired from the bureaucracy, had to stay in Tokyo, and my mother stayed with him, though she came to visit us when she could. After the war, I went to high school here and to Keio University, where I studied economics. Then I entered a large trading company, where I work in the accounting department. I have been promoted along with those who entered the company with me, and I think someday I will be made department head.

About three years after I entered the company, I married a girl my parents selected for me. Akiko is the daughter of a close friend of my father's in the ministry where they worked. I did not have to marry her and actually denied my parents' requests to marry two other girls they picked before Akiko. I agreed to marry her because she is from a good family and is healthy and well brought-up. She is a good wife, and after we had been married for a year or so I became very fond of her. Our marriage is somewhat different from my parents'. Before the war, it was the custom for parents to arrange marriages without consulting the two people to be married. Fortunately, my grandparents selected well, as my parents have had a happy marriage. It is not always so.

Akiko and I have two children, both boys, and plan not to have any more. Families nowadays are not so large as before the war because birth control is so easy and cheap. Most Japanese, especially in the cities, would rather spend money on television sets and vacations and other things that make a good life than on children. We must also think of their education. But it is still important to have children to carry on our family name and to take care of us when we get old. I must admit that I take much joy in my sons. It is said that we Japanese are very affectionate with children and, from my own case, I think that must be true.

I have studied English and have read some American and European history and have been to America twice and to France and Britain once on short business trips, so I know a little about the West. I also have some foreign friends here in Tokyo whom I have met through business.

We meet sometimes in the evening when I take them to a geisha teahouse or they invite me to dinner or a nightclub. (Akiko and their wives don't go, as it is not our custom to take them with us when we go out in the evening.) We often discuss the differences between Japanese and foreigners and we talk frankly because we have known each other for quite a long time. From my trips abroad, I have learned that most foreigners think we Japanese are like Westerners. But my foreign friends in Tokyo tell me— though not directly, as they are too polite—that we Japanese are devious, inscrutable Orientals.

I don't think either picture is the true one. Just because we Japanese wear Western clothing and ride on trains and work in office buildings and things like that doesn't mean we are Western. When I go home at night from the office, the first thing I do is take off my Western clothes and put on a kimono and sit down on the *tatami* mats of my house and, if it is a nice evening, look out the sliding doors at my small garden, while I drink the green tea Akiko has waiting for me. I am very Japanese in my home. I agree with my foreign friends here that we Japanese are difficult to understand, but that is because we are so different from foreigners and not many of them learn enough of our language and customs to tell what we are thinking and doing. Actually, we Japanese behave in a rather clear manner. We use certain expressions in certain situations and we are consistent in the way we react to most things. We may be an indirect people, but we have ways and signs that we use to communicate with each other and we find it easy to know what another Japanese is thinking very quickly. In many ways, we Japanese are an eminently predictable people, once you have discerned what we are like.

We Japanese are very egotistic, it must be said. Especially we Japanese men. We are self-centered and introspective and concerned with our own inner feelings. We are extremely sensitive to anything that reflects on us personally, good or bad. We are a subtle people, and all Japanese are keenly aware of the nuances of anything that is said about us or happens around us.

One day in the office, a man who works near me went to the desk of the section chief and talked to him for a long time. I could not hear what they were saying, but I noticed that the section chief looked in my direction several times. After they finished talking, the man went back to his desk without saying anything to me. But the next day, when we met in the washroom (I think he deliberately followed me in there) we discussed our work and he made a slight reference to one of my accounts, saying he hoped it was as accurate as the last time the auditors looked at it. Right away, I was sure he had seen something wrong, and I was not surprised when the section chief called me over. He discussed something else but mentioned briefly that particular account and said he knew the auditors would find it in order whenever they checked it. That night I stayed late in the office to go over the account and found a bad mistake, which I corrected. Nothing else was ever said about it.

We Japanese are anxious to have prestige and to have recognition of our status by other people. Status is more important to us than money or comfort. One of the reasons we Japanese work hard is to achieve status. I don't get much personal, inner satisfaction from my work, but I am as diligent as possible so that the section chief and the higher executives will praise my efforts. I also strive for good results because I know it will help my company and improve its reputation. As I am known by my association with the company, this will increase my prestige in the eyes of people who are important to me. Of course, I must work hard to stay alive and to care for my family. Our economy has done very well, but there are many Japanese, and our per capita income is still low. We know

now that we can have happy lives but we must work for them.

Our strong egos make us somewhat exhibitionistic, I think. We Japanese men, particularly, like to show off a bit, though we try to do it without being too obvious. You can see it when we are skiing or at the beach. A skier will try to show how good he is, but he pretends that he is doing fancy turns only for his own enjoyment. I am amused at the beach sometimes when I see a young man doing exercises with an expression on his face that says he wants people to believe he is just taking care of his health. But what he really wants is people to admire his muscles. At a geisha party, we Japanese all take turns being the center of attention. Each of us has a favorite song or dance, and we like to perform for those attending the party. We Japanese even do it on a national scale. We all worked hard to make the Olympics a success because we wanted to show foreigners how well we can do things.

We Japanese are an emotional people and are moved more by our emotion than by our intellect. We respond to a great many sentiments, like the delicate beauty of the cherry blossoms in the spring moonlight or the majesty of Mt. Fuji when it is covered with snow. Everybody knows about these, but we Japanese also have secret favorites. There is a craggy peak in the mountains that you can see from the train that goes toward Niigata and a valley north of the city of Yamagata that bring up deep emotions in me. We Japanese can be volatile and can become angry or even infuriated by insults that touch our emotions. Sometimes the insults are real, but other times I think maybe we are so sensitive that we are offended when there really wasn't any offense even remotely intended. When we discuss things, my Japanese friends and I, we don't think logic and rational persuasion so important as personal feelings. I become sympathetic to my friend's opinion when he expresses himself with human warmth and understanding. I sometimes have a hard time understanding my foreign friends because they put so much emphasis on logic, which I think is cold and sterile and impersonal. I think they lack feeling and humanity. Even on a national scale, we Japanese are affected much more by an intangible and nebulous mood that drifts across our society than we are by straight facts and clear issues. It is almost always difficult to define a particular mood, but we Japanese know that it's there because we can feel it. It can be a serious mood, perhaps a political mood or sentiment about an international question such as the reversion of Okinawa, or it can be a frivolous mood about a fad of some kind. One of my American friends likes to talk about public opinion in his country, and I think our Japanese mood may be something like that. We have public opinion polls here, but they do not register our real feelings, which can be seen only by listening to what many prominent people say and by reading many newspaper and magazine articles and listening to many television discussion programs and things like that. To know what our mood is, you have to immerse yourself in it and try to sense it with your emotions rather than your mind. If you do, you will have some idea of what we feel about something and what we are likely to do about it.

We Japanese are very conscious of our bodies and our health. One of the joys of life is our hot bath, which I take every night in a round wooden tub in my home. Even better is the chance to get up to the hot spring resorts in the mountains, where the steaming water is piped right out of the ground into the *ryokan,* a Japanese-style inn. You scrub yourself off outside the bath and when you are clean you ease yourself into the hot water to soak. (I took one of my foreign friends one time and he almost scalded himself.) The soaking restores warmth and relaxes the muscles and, even nicer, soothes the mind and takes away all my tensions. We Japanese are also fond of massage. When I come home from the company, Akiko often pounds my back and kneads my arms and legs to relax me. In our barber shops, a massage of the head, neck, arms, and back are included with the haircut, shave, and shampoo.

We Japanese are very keen on sports, both those we have learned from the West like baseball and soccer and our traditional martial arts like *judo* and *kendo*. I belong to the company *dojo*, a sort of a gymnasium, and go there once a week early in the morning to practice *kendo*, fencing with long sticks. Both Akiko and I like to ski, and my sons are old enough now to enjoy it, so we all go to the mountains in the winter, where we ski all day and then soak in the hot bath together. In my office, and in many offices and factories, we stop twice a day to stand up and do stretching exercises and light calisthenics. A physical training teacher instructs us over the loudspeaker system. We Japanese are careful to keep in good health, and as soon as anyone in our family is even slightly ill, we go to the doctor. We take vitamins every day and special tonics in the summer and winter and often various kinds of pills. Drugstores in Japan are really drug stores, not like the soda fountains I saw in America, and are a thriving business. One of my foreign friends jokes that we Japanese are a nation of hypochondriacs. It may be so.

We Japanese feel not so much shame in our bodies as the Americans. We like sex, just like anybody else, but we don't see much exciting in nudes. After all, there are only two kinds of human beings, men and women, and once you have seen one male and one female you have seen them all. We are fortunate enough to have a bath in our house, but many Japanese do not and must go to the neighborhood public bath, where men and women bathe together in a big pool. Nobody thinks anything about it. Many Japanese men take off their outer garments in a hot train in the summer time and sit in their underwear, which you must admit is a lot cooler. (I don't, because I learned in America and Europe it is considered bad taste.) There was a funny incident right after the new Tokyo Airport building was completed. It has a wide balcony where you can watch the planes land and take off. As soon as it was opened, people went down on Sunday afternoon in the summer with their families. Then men would take off their clothes and stand in their underwear to get cooler. But it seemed to shock the foreign visitors arriving, and the government made the men stop because the officials didn't want the tourists to have a bad impression of Japan. During the Occupation, we Japanese learned about the striptease, and you can find nude shows in Tokyo and the resort areas. But we Japanese don't think they are so sexy. It is said that a Japanese striptease is all "strip" and no "tease."

Despite all our emphasis on health, we Japanese are somewhat indifferent to what Westerners might think is discomfort. Living conditions in our crowded country are difficult, but we rather ignore them. Akiko and I could spend a little more on our comfort, but we think it more important to live frugally and save for our sons' education and our old age. We have a small house, four rooms including: a kitchen with the bath off of it, a four-mat room where our sons sleep (we Japanese measure by the number of *tatami* mats, which are about three by six feet), a six-mat room for Akiko and me, and an eight-mat room where we take our meals and which we use as a living room. We don't have the furniture that Westerners have as we sleep on mattresses and quilts that can be folded up and put away in the day time and we sit on the mats around a low table. But we have a television, a transistor radio, a waist-high refrigerator, a small washing machine, and other appliances like that. Fortunately, my parents have their own house so that they don't live with us, which gives us more room in our house than many families have.

Even though we are egotistic and emotional, we Japa-

nese are a disciplined people. I suppose we have to be or
we would not have order in our society. Our morality
comes from outside the individual, not from the inside.
We Japanese are not religious in the sense of the Judaeo-
Christian heritage. I don't believe there exists the kind of
god the Christians have, but I vaguely believe in the
teachings of Buddhism and that our Shinto spirits have
some influence over our crops and steel mills. I don't think
about it much, and we don't have things like services on
Sunday. But I do have some religion and I always make it
a point to go to the shrine the first thing on New Year's
Day, like most Japanese. Akiko and I were married in a
Shinto shrine, and when her mother died we had a Buddhist memorial service for her. I think there might be some
kind of afterlife but I don't know, and what happens to
me in this life is much more important. I honor my ancestors and I teach my sons that they must remember Akiko
and me after we die. But religion doesn't much affect the
way I live and what I think is right or wrong.

We Japanese have strong social ethics that tell us how
we should live and what is expected of us. I don't feel
these are something inside me, but more like rules from
our society outside me. I have talked with my foreign
friends about sin and guilt, but I don't really understand
what they mean. We Japanese think in terms of what is
proper and improper and what is acceptable or unacceptable to the people around us. We follow a Japanese version
of the Confucian teachings, though only those who have
studied the classics realize it, I suppose. Our fundamental
view of mankind comes from the Confucian teaching that
five relationships determine much of the social order: superior and inferior, father and son, elder brother and
younger brother, husband and wife, and friend and friend.
We Japanese don't believe, despite the democratic teachings since the war, that men are created equal but that
men are really unequal and some are superior to others.

These personal relationships are possibly the most important ethical guides we Japanese have.

When I was a little child, I had a great deal of freedom. My parents allowed me to do almost anything I wanted, especially since I was the eldest son. I suppose this explains why we Japanese are so self-centered. Child psychologists say that a person's basic personality is formed during the first four years of life, and that is when we Japanese are the most permissive with our children. I can remember, just before I reached school age, that my parents began telling me for the first time that I couldn't do certain things. They didn't tell me that it was right or wrong, but that I mustn't do it because of what other people would think. All through my childhood after that, my parents would remind me that I must conduct myself so that other people would think well of me and of our family. My father, who was very strict, taught that I must respect his authority immediately and without question. I think this is why we Japanese have such deep respect for older people and for authority. We have a saying: "There are four things in life to be feared—earthquake, thunder, fire, and the wrath of an angry father."

As I grew up, my father taught me to bow when I passed on the street men in our neighborhood who were important. He was particularly insistent that I respect his friends. I remember one summer we went to the beach at Hayama, not far from Tokyo, for a few days' holiday. I was with my father early one evening at an outdoor food stand where they sold noodles and beer and *sembei* (rice cookies) and things like that. My father unexpectedly met an old friend, and when he introduced me to him I forgot to bow enough. My father immediately put his hand behind my neck and pushed my head forward firmly to bow properly. He wasn't rough, but I have never forgotten it. We Japanese add more and more people to whom we have personal ties and obligations as we get older. The big steps came when I entered the company, when I married, and when my father retired. Now I have heavy responsibilities to fulfill my obligations to the company, to care for Akiko, to raise and educate my sons so that they are good Japanese, and to care for my parents. They don't need much financial help because my father has a good pension from the ministry. But we must see that they are not lonely and that they feel respected. We visit them with our sons almost every week, and sometimes I go over alone in the evening to see them. Akiko calls my mother on the telephone three or four times a week. It is important that she show respect for her mother-in-law.

As I grew up, my parents taught me to keep my own thoughts to myself if I did not agree with other people. It is very important, they said, that my actions and thoughts be in harmony with the actions and thoughts of other people with whom I have a personal relationship, and to subordinate myself to our family and the school and my company. We Japanese don't like individuality, and even the word *kojin*, which means "individual" in our language, has a rather bad meaning. If we Japanese say a man is *kojin-teki*, or individualistic, we mean that he is egotistic and wants to do things his own way rather than getting along with his group. My foreign friends sometimes tease me, "Why don't you stand up for your rights?" They don't understand that we Japanese don't think much about rights.

Obligation is the thing that is important to us. We Japanese have many words that are translated "obligation," but each has a different nuance for us and applies to a particular situation. *Gimu* means an obligation or duty outside ourselves, like following custom, educating ourselves, fulfilling our responsibilities to our parents, our family, our company, our country, and to *Tenno Heika*, His Majesty the Emperor. *Giri* is more of a personal obligation to repay a favor or kindness that someone has done for us. If my classmate from Keio who works for one of my company's customers tells somebody in my company that I have done an especially good job in connection with our business and that good word reaches the managing director who supervises my department, then I have received an *on*, or "credit," from my friend and it is my *giri* to repay the favor someday. We Japanese often speak of the *giri ninjo*, which means "human obligations," that we have with many, many people.

We Japanese feel a strong sense of *chugi*, or loyalty to the Emperor and our country. We have many other loyalties to the family and the company and other groups. We Japanese base our loyalties much more on personal relationships than on principle. Loyalty to an abstract idea such as democracy is cold to us, like logic. Loyalty to people and to the groups to which we belong is much warmer. We Japanese feel a different sense of loyalty to different people and groups, depending on how close they are to us. Most of the time, each of us knows rather clearly which loyalties take precedence, and we are able to achieve harmony among the different loyalties we have.

But sometimes our loyalties conflict and cause tension. My father once asked me to take him to see a particular play at the Kabuki-za, which is our national theatre. My mother was away visiting her relatives and my father didn't want to go alone. It was a good chance for us to do something together, and he looked forward to the occasion. Of course, I agreed right away and went out in my lunch hour to buy the tickets. I even spent more money for good seats because I knew it would please my father. Then, the day before we were to go, the managing director of my department called me in and said that he would be entertaining some important business guests in a geisha house the next evening and he would like me to attend. I was really caught in a predicament. If I canceled the theatre appointment with my father, he would think I was not showing respect and loyalty to him. If I did not do as the managing director wished, he would think I lacked sincerity and loyalty to the company. I thought about it all afternoon and finally decided that I must obey the managing director for the good of the company. I went to see my father that night and was very apologetic in excusing myself from the theatre the next evening and explained to him why and gave him the tickets, suggesting that one of his friends might like to go with him. My father was very stiff and said he understood but I could see that he was disappointed. I stayed and drank tea with him for a little while, but it was a cold and uncomfortable visit and I left as soon as I could without insulting him. I found out later that he didn't go to the play at all.

I think it may be said correctly that we Japanese are an honest people. Japan, of course, has its share of professional thieves, just like any other country, and especially in the big cities, which are more impersonal than the small towns in the countryside. But most Japanese take pride in being scrupulously honest about money, property, and service. I have left money in the pocket of my trousers at the dry cleaners and have always gotten it back. I never look at a bill in a restaurant or count my change because I know that it is correct and that I have been given the right change. (We Japanese are also good at arithmetic, so you don't have to check that either.) I once forgot my camera and left it on my desk in the office where any of the visitors coming through could have picked it up or the cleaning women at night could have taken it. But nobody touched it except to pick it up when the desk was wiped off. I am sure that when I took my television set to be repaired the repairman did exactly what was required and didn't make me pay for parts that he hadn't put in. I think all Japanese subconsciously feel some obligation to one another. I know the dry cleaning store proprietor and the television repairman only slightly, but they are Japanese and I am Japanese and just that gives us some human bond. Of course, I am their customer and they want my business. But I would never know if they cheated me.

Our education, from our parents and in our schools, teaches us to be honest. Ever since the Meiji period, our schools have stressed ethics. Even though that type of teaching was ordered eliminated by the Occupation authorities, the ethical kind of thinking carried over into our lives today. The Ministry of Education is trying to revive the ethical teaching, and I think I support it. I would not like to see Japan go back to the militaristic kind of teaching, but I worry about my sons and would like to have them learn in school about the things that we Japanese think are proper and valuable. Anyway, another reason we Japanese are honest, it must be said, is that we are afraid of getting caught. Not so much because we would feel guilt, but for the great shame it would bring on the thief and his family and all the other people around him. The fear of disgrace is a much stronger deterrent than the fear of going to prison. You must have heard how we Japanese work hard to save face. Getting caught stealing or doing other things wrong is about the most terrible way to lose face.

In our personal relations with people outside our families, we Japanese follow somewhat the same pattern as inside our families. We have what is called the *oyabun-kobun*, which is father-son relations, all through our business world, in the political *habatsu* (factions), the bureaucracy, and in labor. The *oya* is the senior, the *ko* is the junior. My *oya* is the head of my department, who went to Keio University many years before I did and who has taken an interest in me ever since I entered the company. Three of my classmates entered at the same time, and we have all become his *ko*. As our *oya*, he looks after our general welfare in all sorts of things. When I have personal problems or financial difficulties I always seek his advice. One time Akiko and I had a bad disagreement, which was surprising as she usually does as I ask her, and I went to my *oya* for his advice. He was very busy that day but listened to me for an hour and suggested what I should do. Then he called up Akiko on some pretext and talked with her. He didn't say anything about the disagreement, but told her how well I was doing in the company and that he knew she was a great help to me in making a happy home so that I could concentrate on my work and things like that. Anyway, we soon resolved the argument. He also arranged for my son to get into a particularly good school. The boy had passed the examination but we were afraid that others with better connections would fill all the places. My *oya*, however, knows the headmaster and was able to persuade him. I, of course, pay great respect to my *oya* and listen to him carefully and do as he says diligently. I do anything I can to increase his prestige by my good performance and attitude.

The *oyabun-kobun* relationship doesn't break even if I am transferred to another department. Several years ago, I was shifted from accounting into the economic research department for a year to help them and to gain wider experience, which is useful for the company. But I retained my ties to my *oya* in the accounting department, too. I would find a reason to visit his office every week or ten days to tell him what I was doing and to listen to his advice.

The *oyabun-kobun* goes all the way up and down. My *oya* is *ko* to the president of the company, who is a close friend of my *oya*'s father. I am not so senior yet, but about a year ago some new men came into our department and two young Keio graduates were assigned to me as assistants. I have become their *oya* and am beginning to help them as best I can. I spend a lot of time making sure that I fulfill my *oyabun-kobun* obligations. But I feel very secure in the system. I think, too, all these *oyabun-kobun* relationships, which overlap, help to make our company stronger in personal relations and therefore to work better.

We Japanese like to be secure. We don't like to be in strange situations where our social ethics don't tell us what to do. When I receive an invitation to a geisha dinner party from one of our customers, he always lets me know why the party is being given and who else will be there. If I don't know some of them, he will tell me, discreetly of course, who they are and why they have been invited. I go to the party confident that I will behave properly because I know who is senior to me and who is junior. We Japanese always make a great fuss over trying to make other people sit in the more honored seats so that we can show humility, but we always end up in the proper rank of seniors and juniors. My foreign friends say we are the best Alphonses and Gastons in the world, but I don't know what they mean.

I feel uncomfortable sometimes when my foreign friends invite me, because I never know who's going to be there. I have a close Japanese friend who works for one of them, and I call him to ask about the party and the people who will be there. Then I know what their status is and how much respect to pay them. But sometimes I can't find out ahead of time. So when I get to the party I hesitate in the door until my host comes and I ask him as discreetly as I can who the other people are. He tells me which companies they are with and what they do, which helps me to know whether they are senior or junior to me. My foreign friends are funny. I have watched them walk right into a cocktail party, say hello to the host, and they start drifting around shaking hands and introducing themselves without even knowing who the other people are. I could never do that.

We Japanese are intensely competitive outside our families and small groups. We strive very hard for prestige and position, power and money, and even for space in our

crowded country. But we are aware that excessive competition can be dangerous and could cause much harm in
politics and business or daily life, if we did not control it.
We have many ways of making sure that competition does
not become too strong. My foreign friends, particularly
one who is an aggressive American businessman, says we
control competition so much that we have none at all.

It is true that we Japanese try diligently to prevent any
situation from becoming what we call *tairitsu,* a confrontation, whether in our personal lives or in business or politics.
Sometimes confrontations are inevitable, but that can't be
helped. As much as we Japanese are deliberate and try to
regulate things, we know it is an imperfect world. I think
we must have a streak of fatalism as one of our favorite
words is *shikataganai* ("It can't be helped"). Anyway, a
confrontation means what you would call a showdown.
Someone must give way, and the one who gives way will
lose face and have his ego hurt. No Japanese wants to
suffer this, and we try not to put anybody else in the same
position. We always try to leave room for compromise.
We also know that if we are not ready to compromise, we
will accomplish nothing with other people because they
won't have anything to do with us. We Japanese have a
strong feeling of revenge, too, so that if one gets the
better of another without a compromise, the other will
wait and plan for his revenge for the rest of his life, if he
has to.

A little incident in my neighborhood one time shows
how we avoid confrontation. The son of a neighbor is a
university student named Akira, a good boy, very polite,
and a good student. Our street is narrow, with just enough
room for one car to pass. A stranger got in the habit of
parking his car just across from their garage so that they
couldn't get their car out. Akira's father was angry about
this but didn't know what to do about it. If he asked the
stranger not to park his car there, he might refuse and

there would be a confrontation. So one night, Akira went out quietly and let the air out of two tires. When the owner returned, Akira told me later, and saw the two flat tires, he couldn't move the car. He couldn't get help as our neighborhood gasoline stand was closed for the night. So he took a taxi and went home and came back in the morning. Akira saw him and went out to help him take off the tires and carry them down to the gasoline stand to be pumped up. It must have taken an hour to get them back on so that the car could be driven. The stranger went away and never parked his car there again. He had gotten the point (one flat tire might have been an accident, but not two) even though no one had said anything to him and Akira had shown his good intentions by helping him. So a confrontation was avoided.

Our Japanese language tells much about what kind of people we Japanese are and how we think. Linguists say that it is among the world's most complex languages. It may be so, because it takes even us Japanese longer to learn our own language in school than it does for American children to learn English. Japanese is rather imprecise, and we use it more to create a mood than to define exact meanings. We Japanese converse around the main point of a subject and never go directly to it, and we often leave out many specifics. We prefer to leave that to the listener to pick out for himself.

Our language is poetic and full of flowery expressions that we use to smooth over the harsh realities of life. It is subtle and full of nuance and an emotional rather than a logical language. We Japanese often use the passive voice and the negative verb forms because they are less direct than the active voice and positive verbs. Nouns in Japanese are very important, especially those connected with personal relationships. We have different words for "my father" and "your father" and for "my elder brother" and "your younger brother." I use the humble form when I am referring to someone on my side and the honorific form when I am speaking about someone related to the listener's side. That way I show sincerity on my side and respect for the other's side. But we are very loose in our use of verbs. We have one word that can mean "to come" or "to go" or "to be here" or "to be there."

We Japanese are particularly careful in the form of address we use. You would say "Mr. Smith" (if you didn't call him by first name, something I can never get used to) to the president of your company, a salesman from another company, or the clerk in the shoe store. But I call an older, venerable man *sama*, my teachers *sensei*, my superiors and people I meet *san*. My superiors and close friends call me *kun* and I call my wife *kimi* and children *chan*. Many times we Japanese also use titles. I would never call the company president "Suzuki-san" but always address him as *shacho*, "company president."

We Japanese have different levels of language. Laboring men use rough, familiar words, we in the middle class speak a sort of standard Japanese, and in the Imperial Court they still use a classical, highly stylized language that most ordinary Japanese find difficult to understand. We Japanese men like to be masculine by talking abruptly and with guttural sounds while Japanese women, especially those well brought-up like my wife, speak a lovely, melodic language. We Japanese can tell in a minute where a foreigner learned to speak Japanese, particularly G.I.'s who learn some from Japanese girls. They talk like women, which sounds very funny to us.

We Japanese are known for our politeness because we are always bowing and smiling and saying the right expressions of humility about ourselves and praising others. It may appear that we treat all people the same way, but inside we have very different feelings. When I am deferential to my father or to my *oya* or to some other superior, I am expressing my genuine respect for them. If something goes wrong in one of those relationships, I reflect on myself and try with all sincerity to discover what I have done to offend or displease them. When I discover what it is, I adjust my thinking so that I may please them and show my sincerity.

But I must admit that when I am polite to people who are not close to me, I don't really feel it and am just performing the ritual that is expected of me. I am respectful to senior people because of their position and not necessarily because I feel respectful sentiments for them. My foreign friends here tell me that we Japanese can sometimes be extremely rude to other people, not just to foreigners, but to other Japanese. That, I regret to say, is true. Every day during the rush hour, you can see thousands of people shoving each other to get on the subway. Nobody here lines up in a queue the way they do in England, for instance. That is because, outside of the circle of people to whom we have obligations, we feel no particular obligations and think only of ourselves. We would not do anybody harm or steal, but we do not feel any obligation to allow somebody else to get on the subway first just because he arrived at the platform first.

We Japanese, it must be said, do not really respect the rights of other people and are motivated only by our obligations to them. If we don't have obligations, then our relations are determined mostly by power. We don't believe that Might makes Right, but whenever there is no obligation or loyalty or other ethic involved, the person who has the upper hand is the one who succeeds. Our word for "skillful," *jozu*, is composed of two ideographs, one meaning "upper" the other meaning "hand." The opposite is two ideographs, read *heta* and meaning "lower hand." Our word for "power" is *chikara*, an ideograph that has been drawn from the shape of a sword. We Japanese do not have much respect for law, as we think power is more effective.

234

I read a good explanation about Japanese thinking on law in one of our newspapers, *Yomiuri Shimbun*, which said: "The Japanese are of the opinion that a law is an edict made by the ruling power to restrict the freedom of individuals rather than regarding it as an agreement among men to keep public order." The newspaper editorial went on to say: "The public is often very tolerant of violations of 'bamboo basket laws' (i.e., laws with many loopholes such as the Public Election Law and the Road Traffic Law) and this is somewhat of a problem." *Yomiuri* wrote that: "It is said that the Japanese are the least law-abiding people in the world." I must agree with that. I know in my own thinking that I do not regard law as important, but rather pay attention to custom and power to determine how to conduct myself.

You can see the use of power all through our daily life. One of my foreign friends was enraged one time by an experience he had. He has a rented office and a long-term contract that sets the rent. But the owner of the building called on him and announced that he was raising the rent in the coming month. My foreign friend protested that the owner could not do that as it would violate the contract. He said he would not pay the increase. The owner merely replied that he would deduct the increase from the large deposit my foreign friend's company had made when they signed the contract. They argued for a long time, but the owner won because he had the power. My friend, who has been in Japan a long time, knows that he could go to court but that he wouldn't get anything. The court would take a long time and make them compromise anyway. I took him to a bar and bought him a drink and told him not to worry about it. It happens all the time, and he must understand that it is just the Japanese way. As I said, he has been in Japan a long time. He is already plotting how to get the upper hand on the owner.

We Japanese usually aren't so obvious as the building

owner about using power, but try to apply it in a more subdued way. I remember once attending a negotiating session between my company and one of our suppliers. The supplier had recently increased the wages of his workers and wanted to raise the price of his product, which we export for him. My company officials were very much against the price increase because they knew it would not be competitive in export markets. But the supplier was insistent and hinted that he would go to another trading company if we did not agree to raise the price. The negotiators on our side ignored this comment and went on discussing something else. Then one turned to me and asked how much money we owed the supplier from earlier sales. I told him, and it was quite a sum as business the last month had been good. He just nodded and went on talking, but a little while later another man on our side happened to drop a hint that we are extending an increased amount of credit to our customers and that our funds are rather tied up now. In a few minutes the supplier said that maybe he could get by with a lower price than he thought at first, and our negotiators said they thought we might get a slightly better price than the one we are charging now. After more discussion, they all agreed on our new price. Our side, of course, never said that we wouldn't pay the money we owed the supplier, but he caught the hint that we might delay payment for a long time. We knew that he had little cash reserve and needed the money. So we had the power to resist his proposals, even though we did not use it in a blunt manner. We didn't want to have him lose face, so we compromised a little.

My foreign friends have sometimes remarked to me that we Japanese seem to lack compassion, as they define it in Christian terms. It may be so. We are not a Christian people and the Christian religion has not had much influence here, though we are very tolerant, I think, of anybody who wants to become a Christian. We Japanese do not

think we are obliged to help a stranger who is hurt as we
have no connection with him. To help him means to take
on a new responsibility and we already have many responsibilities. It is not that we Japanese think we should help
the injured man and don't because we don't want to be
involved. It is rather that we don't consider compassion
to be any particular virtue. Nor do we Japanese think
compassion is a weakness. It is just not part of our ethical
way.

Yet I read many letters to the editor in the newspapers
and hear from my foreign friends that we Japanese are
very hospitable to foreigners. They praise us for our
politeness and for the little kindnesses we have shown
them, like finding their way back to the hotel when they
are lost. (Foreigners are always getting lost here. But I
suppose I shouldn't be surprised. They can't read Japanese,
and Tokyo is a confusing city. I have lived here all my
life and even I have been lost two or three times.) We like
to have the thanks from the foreigners, but they don't
really understand why we do it. It is not really kindness
or compassion, but obligation. We Japanese feel that a
foreigner in our country is a guest of the Japanese people
and we are obliged, when we meet one, to act as proper
host. Hotel clerks and shopkeepers and travel agencies, of
course, want the tourist to be pleased. But ordinary Japanese feel it is important that foreigners think well of Japan.

We Japanese are a rather tense people, especially compared with relaxed Americans. When I have been in
America, I sometimes envy Americans because they never
seem to worry about whether they are saying the right
things or have paid proper respects to their elders. But we
Japanese always have to be thinking about whether we are
doing the proper thing. I become anxious, too, if I think
some other people do not think highly of me. There are
so many obligations to think about, and I worry whether
I have repaid a favor in just the right amount. If I do not

do enough, the other person may be insulted. If I do too much, he will be offended because he will think I am trying to show him up and am insincere. It is important to repay a favor with another favor just a little bit more than the favor that was done for me. But this is difficult as I am never quite sure how my repayment will be understood. Of course, this keeps on going, and we are always building up greater obligations that require greater repayment. It is very worrisome.

I think we Japanese are tense because so many of us live in such a crowded country, and especially in the big cities like Tokyo. There are 100,000,000 of us, or about half as many people as in America, packed into a country the size of California. My foreign friends say that having so many people around them all the time, just on the street, bothers them. It doesn't bother me, but I must admit that I think the struggle for space makes us somewhat tense. We have some good ways of getting rid of tension, like the hot bath.

We also get drunk. When we Japanese are drunk, I may say that we are the happiest people in the world. We forget our inhibitions and we become very sentimental and we say things and do things we would never do if we were sober. I love everybody when I have had a few bottles of *sake*, our rice wine. It is served warm and it doesn't take much of it to make life look pleasant. The best part is that nobody criticizes me if I get drunk and act a little foolish. Everyone knows that when we are drunk we are getting rid of our tensions, and that is a good thing. One time I was out drinking with some men in my section from the office and the section chief was there. Nobody really likes him because he is cold to us. He knows he will not go any higher in the company but that many of us will, and he is jealous. Anyway, we were all rather drunk and I laughed at the section chief for pinching the fanny of one of the office girls when he thought no one was looking. I told him he was a lecherous old fool. The next day he greeted me as usual and had forgotten all about it. Of course, he was drunk too and maybe he didn't remember.

I would like to tell you something about my wife Akiko and about Japanese women. They have a somewhat different role in our society nowadays because of the change in our country from an agricultural to an industrial society, because we live more and more in big cities, and because we have absorbed some Western ideas about women. But they have not changed so much as you might think, and they are still much different from Western women, from what I have seen.

When my foreign friends have visitors from their home countries and we go out to the Ginza bars or the night clubs in Akasaka, the newcomers to Japan often say that Japanese women have become Western. They see a stylishly dressed cabaret hostess who speaks some witty English (not many do, but the visitors only see the ones who do) and they think Japanese women are no longer subservient to men. But the girls in the bar are not really typical of Japanese women. They are in a special class and, unfortunately, not a very happy class. They are entertainers, like geisha, and maybe have a special patron (I am not rich enough, so I don't have a bar girl, but there is one I have in mind), but mostly they come from poor families and are in debt to the bar owner or *mama-san*. They live a gay life for a few years and then have a long and lonely struggle without a family or home. Most of them try to save a little money so they can become *mama-san* and own their own bars.

My wife Akiko is really much more typical. Her main responsibility is to make a good home for me and our children, to be a respectful wife and a dutiful mother. The way marriages are made has changed somewhat. Nowadays, more young men and women find their own marriage partners because women move around more freely, go to school, work, and go out on social dates. But the parents still really control marriage. I am sure my sons would never marry anyone Akiko and I didn't approve of. We might try to find wives for them, and they would have to say yes. Or they might find their own, and we would say yes or no. Not many young Japanese will go against the wishes of their parents in marriage, no matter who finds the prospective husband or wife.

When our sons want to marry, we will examine the girls very carefully to see that they have good families, are healthy so they can bear children, have good educations and a good character. We will probably do as many middle-class Japanese do and hire an investigator from a marriage agency to look into the background of the girls. There is nothing shameful in this, we think, only good judgment and prudence. It only costs about 20,000 yen (a little over $50). Things like this make marriage in Japan rather stable. We Japanese believe that divorce, although legal, is a disgrace because it means everyone failed to judge correctly the prospects for success.

We Japanese men like to think that our wives are submissive to us, but it's not really that way. Akiko keeps our house the way I like it and she defers to me on the food I like and things like that, and she never complains when I go out in the evening and leave her home. But we share the responsibility for raising the children and I listen to her opinion most of the time. We do many things together, especially on Sundays when I do not work. And, I must admit, she has the control of our money. I bring my pay envelope home each week and give it to her, and she gives me my spending money for the week. She makes out our budget, pays our bills, and puts money in our savings account. When it comes to buying an appliance or something more than the routine daily items, we discuss it and she has the last word.

Akiko is clever. She never argues with me or nags me

for anything. But she has her way in almost everything because she is so sweet about it that I cannot refuse.

We usually go to the beach, as I always did with my parents, in the summer for a week's holiday at my company's *besso*, or villa, which is cheap and convenient. But one summer Akiko decided that we should go up to a resort in the mountains where she had been once as a girl. That meant we would have to pay for it ourselves. She started about the end of the winter talking about the mountains and how cool it is there and how much the boys liked them when we went skiing and things like that. She never mentioned the place she had in mind or even that it might be a nice change. I noticed later that the times she mentioned the mountains were always after she had prepared something to eat that I especially liked and had a little *sake* to go with it. She read aloud to me about mountains from the women's magazines she takes and once even composed a little *haiku* poem about mountains in summer. She also did some other endearing things, but they are kind of private and I won't go into that, if you don't mind. Anyway, I started thinking a trip to the mountains might be nice, and I said so one evening. She said, yes, it might, but nothing more. Then one day she said she had been downtown for shopping and happened to see a brochure in the travel bureau window and brought it home because she thought it might please me, after what I had said. It was about the place she had gone as a girl, but I didn't remember about that then. Finally I suggested that we go there for our holiday and I would take some money out of our savings. Akiko blushed a bit and said she didn't think that would be necessary, as she had saved a little out of her spending money, and with part of my bonus we could afford it. Then I caught on and laughed at her, but she never admitted anything. We had a wonderful vacation and the boys loved it. Akiko is a good wife.

I have told you mostly about my family, our life, and the relationships we Japanese have with one another. I should now tell you, although it is a delicate subject, something about our attitude toward people who are not Japanese. We Japanese, it must be said, are rather race-conscious. One of my foreign friends thinks we are racists like some American whites or the South Africans, but I do not think that is true. We Japanese are more nationalistic and feel that we are a unique people. You may have noticed that I use the expression "we Japanese" quite often. That is a translation of *ware-ware Nihonjin*, which is a phrase we use in daily conversation as sort of a subconscious way of reaffirming that we Japanese are a special people unlike any others. Some American newspapers said we Japanese opposed the Vietnam war because white Americans were dropping bombs on yellow Asians, but that is not so. I have been against the war partly out of human sympathy for all the people—white, black, brown, and yellow—who have been killed or have suffered there, but mostly because I did not want it to spread to Japan. Skin color has not so much to do with it.

The people we Japanese dislike the most are the Koreans, which may seem strange as they are our nearest neighbors, have a language and culture something like ours, and look the most like us of any other people. We Japanese also do not like Okinawans, even though the Okinawa reversion problem has become a big political issue between Japan and America. We have rather mixed feelings about Americans and Europeans, setting political questions aside. As a people, we Japanese really don't like any foreigners because we think they cannot understand us, and, frankly speaking, we think we are superior to them.

Yet, as I have mentioned, I have several foreign friends and a couple of foreigners who are particularly close friends. But it has taken many years for these friendships to grow. I trust them and I believe they trust me, and we have had many good times together. But I must admit to myself that I would not be happy if one of my sons wanted to marry one of their daughters. That is not so much because she would be from a different race, although that has something to do with it, but because she might not know our language and our customs and would not fit into our way of family life.

Another of my foreign friends, the one who has been in Japan a long time, is married to a Japanese girl from a very fine family. He told me that his parents were opposed to the marriage but eventually accepted it. His wife, however, has been completely cut off from her family. They refuse to allow her to visit them, and her family has had her name taken off the family register—which is a terrible thing for a Japanese. He also told me that his children, who are Eurasians of course, have a difficult time. They speak Japanese, but they look and act different and Japanese children make fun of them. He said they have a more difficult time here than they do in America when he takes them to visit there. But he must stay here because his company values his services here highly. It is too bad in many ways, but particularly because his children and most of the other Eurasian children I have seen are very handsome. They seem to bring out the best in both races.

I would not be Japanese if I did not close with the right words. I must apologize for my inadequate description of my people. There is so much more I would like to tell you of what we Japanese are like. But I hope you have understood a little about Japan from what I have told you. Please come someday to visit my country, and I will be the first to greet you *"Irasshaimase"*—"Welcome."

TOKYO

Tokyo is the head and the heart of modern Japan. It *is* Japan, the soul of a restless and energetic nation even though many Japanese are nostalgic for the ancient and gracious capital in Kyoto. But Kyoto was made the repository of the deeds of another day when the young Emperor Meiji was carried away from there a century ago. The history of modern Japan has been and is being written in Tokyo. It is there that the national decisions are made and it is there that the cultural life of the nation thrives. Tokyo is the home of the Establishment, the political and bureaucratic center, the home office of business, the headquarters of labor unions, the site of most major universities. It is the home of the abstract painters and the woodblock artists, the novelists and poets, the masters of the *koto* (a type of harp or lyre) and the conductors of concert orchestras, the Kabuki theatre and the Western-style drama, the national newspapers and the scholarly journals, the *noh* plays and the motion picture industry.

Tokyo is Japan's social laboratory. It is the crucible in which swirl the urgent forces that course through the nation. Through the gates of the city enter the ideas and artifacts from the West that are scrutinized, accepted, adapted, assimilated, or rejected. The rest of Japan gets only what has passed the skeptical test of Tokyo. And what Tokyo determines, whether in political doctrine or ladies' fashions, Japan will do as the verdict pulses out through the country.

Tokyo, more than anything else in Japan, portrays the illusion that Japan has been Westernized. The architecture of the glass-encased buildings, the department stores and specialty shops, the offices and factories, the subways and commuter railroads, baseball and movies, business suits and chic gowns, the glare of neon and the screech of taxicab brakes, the garish night club and the smart restaurant, and the hustle of people intent on their daily lives and the affairs of their nation make it seem like New York or London or Paris.

But the mood and the style of the city is somehow different. Some of this is tangible: For every Western innovation, there is something that has its legacy deep in tradition. The solemn dignity of a Shinto shrine, the musty dark of a tea store, the craftsman who turns out trim *tatami* mats or the seamstress who hand-sews exquisite kimonos, the *bunraku* puppet shows and the street entertainer delighting the children, the gay chatter and tinkling *samisen* of a lantern-lit geisha teahouse, the *soba* noodle vendors on the street in the evening and the *tofu* bean curd man in the morning, the *sake nomiya* where friends meet for a few quiet cups of *sake* after work, the lusty *sumo* ritualistic wrestling, the artistic *yabusame* archery from horseback, the serenity of a tiny pebbled garden, the tranquility of a *ryokan* inn—these bespeak the essence of Tokyo. More is intangible: An Oriental philosophy holds that the whole is the sum of two opposite parts: light and dark, male and female, earth and sky. Tokyo is a city of contrasts and cohesion, and it is this completeness that gives it a special tone and character. Tokyo is ancient and modern, Japan and the West, conflict and consensus, motion and stillness, a city full of the passions and the apathies of life.

It is difficult, maybe impossible, to write about Tokyo except in superlatives. It is the biggest, most populous, most chaotic, busiest, ugliest, noisiest, most expensive, gayest, and most fascinating city on earth. It is a cosmopolitan city, with everything to offer. It is a city of art, of myriad museums and galleries, of music and theatre. Tokyo is home for half a dozen Western-style concert orchestras, several opera companies, musical revues, and all manner of traditional Japanese music. It has ancient and modern plays, serious and frivolous, adaptations and translations of Western drama. It is a city of sports: of professional baseball and boxing, of the martial arts and horse racing, and of those superb facilities built for the 1964 Olympics. Tokyo is temples and shrines and festivals, some known to every tourist but the better tucked away off the beaten track. It has zoos and gardens and the Tsukiji fish market, where a flock of wildly chattering auctions take place every morning at five. It is night clubs and neighborhood bars, cabarets and clip joints. It is daytime shopping in swish department stores and the tiny electronic shops of Akihabara that comprise a ten-square-block discount center. It is a nighttime of illicit pleasures in brothels and Turkish baths and "gay" bars. Tokyo is restaurants: Maxim's of Paris and Chinzanzo of Mongolia, Indian curry and Chinese banquets, succulent *tonkatsu* deep-fried pork cutlets and *yakitori* skewered roasted chicken, of delicate *sushi* raw fish and steaming *unagi* eels.

Tokyo is superbly appointed hotels, though Frank Lloyd Wright's grotesque Imperial has succumbed to the march of time and the pressures of economics, depriving Asia of a great landmark. Tokyo is red-brick buildings, an 1890 vintage known as Japanese Victorian and also succumbing to time and the dear price of land. The city has the world's tallest steel tower, built expressly to top the

Eiffel Tower of Paris, and underground movies to appeal to the most way-out taste. Tokyo is Kanda bookstalls, row on row, where a serious student can get an entire education if his legs hold up, since the rules say one can browse as much as he likes so long as he does not sit down. Tokyo is pretty girls dressed in vivid kimonos and fluttering like twittering birds in brilliant plumage under the cherry blossoms on a Sunday afternoon.

Tokyo is chaos. It was a fishing village when the Tokugawa shoguns came and built it into a fortress and castle town. When the men of Meiji made it the center of their modernizing efforts, the government and entrepreneurs put up buildings, filled in land, brought in electricity, constructed railroads, erected steel bridges, and paved streets to give the city the first touches of its Western façade. There appears never to have been any comprehensive plan for the city, no Major L'Enfant with a concept of what it should be, no commission to lay out streets on a rectangular grid. Tokyo in the modern period just grew in roughly concentric circles out from the Imperial Palace, with radial roads stretching out as the city pushed out. Twice in the last half-century Tokyo has been nearly destroyed, in the 1923 Great Kanto Earthquake and in the 1945 Allied bombings. Each time, it was rebuilt helter-skelter with no evident thought to bringing order to its layout. One Western observer several years ago called it "unplanning for ten million." With the population of Tokyo proper running close to 13,000,000, and adding in the greater metropolitan area including Kawasaki, Yokohama, and smaller outlying cities and towns, it is now "unplanning" for about 20,000,000, or one fifth of Japan's people. The construction spurt of the last few years, stimulated by preparations for the Olympics and the nation's economic growth, has simply dumped confusion on top of existing confusion.

Tokyo's chaos is compounded by the lack of street

names or systematic building and house numbers. There is no 1227 Main Street or 489 Cherry Blossom Lane. Just before the Olympics, the city authorities gave a few thoroughfares names and put up some signs in English and Japanese to guide people around. But most people living in Tokyo did not pay much attention. They continue to rely on the old system of locating places by area names and major crossings. Yurakucho ("Town of Having Pleasure") is an amusement area in the center of the city. Nihonbashi ("Japan Bridge") is a bridge from which all distances in Japan are measured. Kasumigaseki ("Vale of the Morning Mist") is the site of government ministries, Ginza ("Silver Way") a major downtown shopping district, Meguro ("Black Eye") an outlying railroad station. In a residential area, the first house put up in a district was number one. The second one, even if a quarter-mile away, was number two. And if several houses were put up on the same plot, they all took the same number. There are ten houses all with the address 33 Otsuka-machi. The only way to get around is with a map, memory, asking directions, and luck.

Tokyo is an ugly city, perhaps the ugliest in the world. It is flat and concrete-gray and covered much of the time with silvery smog. The threat of earthquakes—an average of ten mild tremors hit the city every day, and a good rocking comes along every few weeks—led to construction ordinances decreeing that no structure would be more than ten stories high. New techniques have been developed by Japanese engineers so that thirty- and forty-story buildings are now going up. Rather than the rigid construction of earlier days, the new buildings are erected with flexibility built-in. As one engineer put it: "We can erect them so that they sway like willows in the wind." They do, so much so that construction workers building the first skyscraper got seasick when a tremor started it vibrating. Most Tokyo buildings are purely functional concrete architecture, dreary and undistinguished. The city lacks grassy parks and trees and boulevards, with a couple of exceptions, and residential areas are mostly a jumble of nondescript houses crammed one next to the other.

Yet there are particularly Japanese spots of beauty among all that is grotesque in Tokyo. The Meiji Shrine, dedicated to the spirit of the Emperor Meiji, lies deep in a heavy wood that shields it from the frenzy of the surrounding city. It is a magnificent edifice, white-pebbled courtyard and natural-grain wood, with sweeping eaves and simply appointed altars. It has an air of serene mystery about it, since only priests and invited guests are allowed past the hanging veil into the outer shrine and only higher priests and the Imperial Family permitted in the Inner Shrine. The Yasukuni Shrine, though not secluded from the city, has something of the same ambiance. It is dedicated to the spirits of Japan's war dead.

Most of Tokyo's beauty, however, is hidden in small things: a dainty gate to a home where only a corner of carefully tended garden may be seen from the street, a burnished sword and its cracked and polished lacquered scabbard laid in a museum niche, a finely sculpted *ishidoro* stone lantern standing in the moss garden of a teahouse, a clump of bamboo sitting beside the recessed door of a *sushi-ya* raw fish shop, a tasteful display of kimono material in the window of a seamstress' shop in a quiet alley. To the Japanese mind, beauty in large things occurs in nature: the ever-changing moods of Fuji-san, the winds in the cypress high in the hills, the placid pond that reflects the pagoda of a temple, the rush of a mountain stream flowing quickly toward the sea. Man-made beauty is intricate and small.

Every major city conjures up in the mind's eye its own image: New York and its towering skyline, Paris and its tree-shaded boulevards, Rome and its fountains. Tokyo is a city of streets, narrow, twisting, wandering lanes that serve as the lifelines and playgrounds of the city's vibrant existence. Few streets have sidewalks, except in major shopping and business areas, and the houses and store fronts come almost to the edge of the road. Because homes and shops are so cramped, much of life is forced into the street, where children play, neighbors meet, vendors pass by, and shopkeepers carry on the day's work. The inescapable fact of life in Tokyo is life itself, for it is all around and ever-present. The resident of the city is never out of sight or hearing, not of one human being but of tens and hundreds of human beings. Life is an unending struggle for space to live, to work, to move, to eat, to sleep, to have fun, to love. The morning and evening rush hours are the worst. Subways are so jammed that a commuter must decide before he is shoved in whether he will stand with his hands up or hands down, since he can't change once the door is closed. Tokyo subways can make New York subways seem as spacious as the Kansas prairies. The multiplication of all the movements and the frictions over space makes for immense pressure on the individual and has a direct impact on the personality of Tokyo people. They are more tense, more competitive, more vital, more everything. People in Tokyo even talk faster than other Japanese.

As cosmopolitan as it is, Tokyo is really a cluster of small cities and towns within a bigger city; it is governed as a special political entity, a sort of superprefecture. As the city has sprawled out from the central area, other business, shopping, and amusement districts have sprung up. By day they are drab, filled with office workers and shoppers and the humdrum of commerce. By night, they are gaudy baubles of flashing neon signs and paper lanterns. With the first brush of dark, the *pachinko* pinball parlors and the tiny stand bars twinkle to life, the night clubs resound with too-loud bands and the teahouses with twanging *samisen*, the coffee shops and the movie houses are filled. Surrounding these subcenters, and washing up against them like waves against a rock in the middle of the sea, are the towns that make up the patchwork of the city. They are all much alike, and if one of them could be picked up and put down in another part of the city, it would fit right in.

A Tokyo neighborhood is a mixture. If the city authorities ever heard of zoning laws they have not adopted them; if they have been adopted, nobody pays any attention. A big house of a prominent politician or company executive sits next to the small house of a laboring man. Other houses of all nondescriptions, food shops and sundry stories, an auto repair garage, a machine shop, a school, a maker of *geta* wooden clogs, a coffee shop, a small business office, more houses, a doctor's office, the man who sells bamboo poles, everybody and anybody is all mixed up together. A few neighborhoods are a bit distinctive. Asakusa, outside the raucous working-class entertainment district, is where many laboring men live, Seijo-machi is an intellectual and artists' colony, Shiba Shirogane is the home for many big businessmen. But the rest are almost identically jumbled.

Each Tokyo *machi*, or town, is economically self-contained. A few supermarkets have been put up, but most shopping is done in neighborhood stores, each of which sells only one or two items. Rice comes from the rice man, milk from the milk store, meat from the meat shop—and maybe beef from one and chicken from another—fish from the fish store. The housewife picking up the daily menu for her family has to stop at half a dozen places. But they are all close by. Older housewives, out of habit formed before refrigeration, shop three times a day, or for each meal. Younger women, having got used to owning a small refrigerator, go every other day or so. Vendors bring around bean curd in the morning, noodles at night, hot roasted sweet potatoes in the winter, and, just like Peoria, Good Humor popsicles in the summer.

Tokyo is a city of smell. Through the alleys of any neighborhood are wafted the aroma of *yakitori* roasted chicken, the delicate scent of fresh sliced fish, the pungent odor of huge *daikon* turnips, the tingling sniff of curry, the pervasive and slightly sharp fumes of *shoyu* soy sauce, the light and multiflavored scents of tea leaves, the ever-alluring smell of freshly sawn sandalwood. Tokyo no longer has so many collectors of night soil in what used to be called "honeybuckets." They have been replaced by trucks that pump human waste from buried receptacles into sealed trucks. But Tokyo, like other Asian cities, still has open sewers that give off an immediately recognizable stench.

In sound, Tokyo has many of those in any Western city: the blare of horns, the rumble of trucks, the clang of the streetcar bell. Only it has more, in quality and quantity. The decibel rating in Tokyo must be the highest in the world. Tokyo also has its own sounds. Each of the street vendors has a distinctive cry of his trade: some a sonorous horn, another a clack of heavy scissors, others the rhythmic beat of sticks. Some of the sweet-potato men have taken to the transistorized bull horn to let loose their three-toned cries of *"yah-key-moh."* There is always something reassuring in one particular sound, that of the fire watchman clopping through the alleys on his wooden *geta* in the quiet of the night, beating two sticks and calling out the equivalent of "All's well." With Tokyo's flimsy wood and paper houses sitting hardly an arm's length apart, fire is more dread than plague. And there is something serene about being awakened in the morning by the deep-throated "bong-bong-(pause)-bong" of the neighborhood temple bell.

Neighborhoods, like so much else in Japan, are organized. A central point is the *koban*, the police box that is the clearinghouse for information. The *koban* has a map of the neighborhood and who lives where, and is the source of countless directions each day to people looking for other people's houses. People in the neighborhood look to the *koban* for all sorts of help: to report a fire, an accident, a crime. When a policeman leaves the *koban* to wander through his district, he becomes *o-mawari-san*, "Honorable Mr. Walk Around." He keeps his eyes on the territory for which he is responsible to see that things are as they should be. The self-government of a neighborhood is the function of the *tonarigumi*, or neighborhood association. The head of each household is his family's spokesman on this council, which is usually headed by the senior residents of the area. The *tonarigumi* tries to handle the small problems that a distant and overburdened metropolitan government never seems to get around to, such as making sure there are light bulbs in the street lights, or asking Yamamoto-san to stop letting his dog run loose, or seeing that the stop sign run down by a dump truck is replaced.

Tokyo's *machi* are fairly cohesive units and retain some of the small-town atmosphere of rural Japan. Each has its own shrines and festivals, besides the national holidays. On a hot summer's afternoon, young men of the neighborhood, stripped to all but loincloths and headbands, will prance through the streets carrying overhead their *o-mikoshi* (a portable shrine) chanting and twisting capriciously, stopping now and then to catch their breath and pass around the *sake* bottle. That evening, they will set up a big drum atop a stand in a vacant lot and begin beating out a call for the neighborhood to turn out. Everyone does, and the traditional dances go on until the early hours, though the very young are bundled off to bed, much against their will, at a respectable hour.

The social pressures inside a *machi*, like a rural town, are intense. Privacy is impossible in such cramped quarters, and there is some pretense by everyone of ignoring what does not concern them. Japanese housewives, however, are notorious gossips, perhaps because they stay home so much and their daily companions are other housewives. Thus everyone knows what everyone else is doing, and woe to the one who does not conform. When a new-comer moves into the neighborhood, it is up to him to make the first approach to his neighbors. Within the first few days, the new housewife is expected to go to the local noodle shop and purchase gift coupons for each member of the families on either side of her new house and for the three families directly across the street. She then goes around to each home, introduces herself and, in the most formal and polite language, offers the coupons and asks the established residents to honor her family with their good wishes. The recipients, at their leisure, call the noodle shop to deliver the goodies. The newcomers, for many months afterward, must be sure to take a low posture and to defer to their neighbors until they give signs that the new family is accepted into the community.

Homes in Tokyo reflect the cohesion of family life. Most, except the poorest, have walls around them and are oriented inward rather than facing the street, with a southern exposure onto a small garden so that the winter sun gives a bit of warmth. In many homes, three genera-tions, the retired grandfather and grandmother, the rice-winning father and mother, and the grandchildren live in three or four rooms. This pattern has begun to change under the pressures of population growth and urbaniza-tion, and more apartment houses are going up. Among the deepest desires of a Japanese is to live in his own home, but Tokyo has become so crowded and land so dear that apartment living has become a more accepted way of life.

These *danchi* apartments are even smaller than the houses, usually two rooms and a small kitchen. Much of the company-furnished housing for young marrieds is in *danchi*, which adds to the cohesion of the company as men who work together live together. It also increases the social pressures and gossip of an ingrown group. Parents usually do not live with the couples in *danchi* as there is not enough room and they do not wish to give up their own homes. Further, when the young man has progressed enough in the company to warrant a private house, he does not invite his parents to come live with them. This, however, does not relieve him of his obligations for filial piety. The sons of a family, particularly the oldest son, must see to it that the parents are cared for, sending them money if they need it, visiting them often, and especially spending the holidays with them. Family ties have been strained by urbanization, but they have not been broken. Instead, new forms and manners of fulfilling the old responsibilities have evolved.

Urbanization, the rise of the middle class, and the influence of Western ideas since the end of the war have combined to produce some changes in the role of women in Japanese life, especially in Tokyo and other major cities. A growing number of women today attend universities; some, the major schools; more, the smaller women's universities. Some graduates work for a while before they are married. A few go into the professions, including medicine, or into business, although businesswomen are still a rarity. More go into journalism, where they become commentators or social critics but rarely news reporters. Some are active in political organizations and several have been elected to the Diet, but not many go into the bureaucracy. High school graduates work for a while as secretaries or saleswomen in department stores. Girls with middle-school educations work in textile mills or electronics plants for about four years before they marry. Japanese women have deft fingers and are patient, which makes them especially good at jobs that require painstaking care. Many women, after marriage, help their husbands in the small shops that are a mainstay of daily commerce, tending the store out front and keeping house in back at the same time. But for all the changes and the new political and economic rights women have acquired, Japanese women mostly become wives and mothers and are the center of the family life that has been extremely important to the Japanese since time began.

One of the paradoxes of Tokyo life is the fetish for personal cleanliness and the diligence with which homes are kept clean, as opposed to the sloppiness and often filth of the city. The streets are usually littered with paper, the alleys can reek with garbage strewn about, and the sight of men urinating against a wall in downtown Tokyo is common. Part of this is due to the lag in public services. Garbage collection, though improved in recent years, has not kept up with the population growth of the city. Neither have public rest rooms. Part of this appears due to a lack of public consciousness: As an architect participating in a conference on urban problems once noted, there is no word in the Japanese language for "citizenship," in the Western sense. The Japanese appear to feel no obligation to the general public good, beyond the obligations to their own group. Streets in a *machi* may be swept clean, each family being responsible for that section immediately in front of his own home. But nobody feels responsible for the thoroughfares or public places.

To continue the paradox, however, Japan has an extremely efficient public health service and strict enforcement of its regulations. It has eradicated cholera, the scourge of most Asian nations. A visitor from the Philippines, where cholera is chronically rampant, once came down with cholera several days after entering Japan, despite having had the required inoculations. He was in a mountain resort outside Tokyo when he called in a doctor. The physician recognized the illness, treated him, and immediately notified the public health authorities. They visited the patient and obtained from him a list of everyone with whom he had had the slightest contact since he entered the country. The authorities then reached every person on that list, made sure he had had cholera shots or gave him the injections, and ordered each to report immediately any symptoms of the illness. Because of this thorough approach, Japan is probably the only Asian nation free of cholera.

Tokyo has its share of slums and poverty-stricken people, though they are probably fewer than most of the world's big cities. Tokyo also has ghettos in which reside a class of outcastes little known to the outside world. They are called *eta*, an impolite word, or more often *burakumin*, or "village people." The *burakumin* may be as many as 3,000,000 in Tokyo and other large cities, but no one knows for certain. They are descended from people who in ancient times did the unclean work of skinning animals, tanning hides, and cremating corpses. Gradually they were segregated into their own communities, where they developed their own customs, mannerisms, and ways of speaking. Although class distinctions were supposedly abolished after Japan started modernizing, there is still strong prejudice against the *burakumin*. They are often not permitted to attend schools other than in their ghettos, they have a difficult time finding work outside the community, and most of all, no ordinary Japanese will marry one. The *burakumin* look like other Japanese, but many Japanese maintain that they can identify one instantly by speech or gesture or even by facial expression. Some try to pass as ordinary Japanese, the way light-skinned Negroes attempt to pass as whites in America. A social psychologist who has done a thorough study of these people reports that they live in constant fear of being discovered. The family registers in which all pertinent information is recorded in one's home town are checked by prospective university officials, employers, and spouses and give away the passing *burakumin*. Some had their records destroyed by the fire-bombing during the war and were able to start new lives in other parts of Japan because no one could investigate the registers. In recent years, the *bura-kumin* have organized an association in an effort to eliminate the discrimination and to put themselves on an equal footing with other Japanese, but have had little success. So far, there has been no mass movement even remotely akin to the civil rights movement in the United States.

No description of Tokyo would be adequate without a word about its incredible traffic, which rates mention not only because it is such a distinctive feature but because it shows how thin is the veneer of Westernization. Tokyo's streets are clogged with every imaginable vehicle, from huge trucks to three-wheeled pickups, from limousines to two-cylinder passenger cars, buses, streetcars, motorcycles, bicycles, animal-powered and man-powered carts, even a few jinrickshas which haul tourists around in front of the Imperial Palace or a geisha to her appointed rounds. Mass driving is relatively new to Tokyo, having appeared in the prosperity of the last ten or fifteen years. Tokyo's streets are inadequate to accommodate the vehicular population explosion, though the recent construction of expressways has alleviated the congestion slightly. Much more of the problem is that the Japanese have not had enough exposure to heavy traffic to know how to control it, drivers do not understand the machines they propel through the streets, no one innately has much respect for law, and there are no native Japanese customs to regulate traffic. There is little regard for the rights of others and no set of obligations to govern driving habits, leaving to the application of power the determination of how traffic shall move.

Japan has become the world's second-largest producer of vehicles, turning out over 4,000,000 a year, exporting 10 per cent of these and turning the rest loose onto pot-holed roads with little room to maneuver. Traffic control is almost nonexistent. Signals are usually on the far, rather than the near, side of the intersection where drivers cannot see them till the last minute. Even then signals are often lost in the jungle of surrounding neon. None are timed to allow traffic to flow smoothly. Traffic police, who rarely appear at all, seem eternally bewildered about how to prevent a traffic jam or to clear one up. Finding the entrance to an expressway requires the clairvoyance of a spiritual medium, as they were put in no place that a driver would logically expect. Directional signs on expressways and at ordinary intersections have improved, but they are still rare and inadequately marked. (Most are in Japanese and English, so the problem is not language for the non-Japanese-reading driver.)

A far greater problem are Japanese drivers, commonly believed to be the reincarnation of the wartime *kamikaze* pilots. It can be said with little fear of contradiction that they are the world's most incompetent. They are reckless, totally lacking in driver courtesy, and simply do not know what they are doing. The worst are taxi or truck drivers, most of whom are young and do not understand the workings of the machine under them. Their incompetence is pointed up by the few older cab drivers who own their cabs and who show a modicum of sanity. Having learned over the years the damage that can be done, and the loss of income they can suffer, they drive with some moderation. The rest have little regard for traffic laws, run red lights with regularity, drive in the opposing lane, ignore stop signs, exceed speed limits by huge margins. Traffic law aside, the average Japanese motorist has even less common sense in driving. He weaves from lane to lane, charging into a stream of cars with quarter-inches to spare. The driver who has his bumper just a bit in front of the next car's bumper has the upper hand and, therefore, the right-of-way. The driver behind must either get out of the way or fight to get in front. Thus, a driver usually follows another as close as he can to keep other cars from

JAPAN: Images and Realities

diving in front of him, either from a side street or another lane. The abuse of cars is terrific. A standard tactic is to roar along and hit the brakes hard at the last minute to stop, then gun the engine and let the clutch jump in to get off to a racing start. A ride through Tokyo streets in a cab is a series of head-snapping jolts as the driver careens his way through traffic.

The accident rate in Tokyo is probably the highest in the world. But the death and injury statistics show a different pattern from other major cities. Truck and car drivers kill or injure other drivers far less than they bump off motorcyclists, bicycle riders, and pedestrians. Storming through the narrow and sidewalkless streets, Tokyo drivers knock over cyclists and walkers by the score. In one bad but typical accident, a truck driver plowed into a line of school children and killed ten, even though they were being shepherded across the street at the proper crossing. People being killed while asleep in their own homes is not uncommon. A driver racing through a narrow alley comes to a sharp turn he cannot make and crashes into the garden wall right beside the street and the flimsy house wall a few feet inside, ending up atop the hapless resident. American soldiers visiting Japan on leave from Vietnam have been known to go back to combat more shaken by Tokyo traffic than by the carnage of war.

The Japanese behind the wheel of a car has a first-class opportunity to let his ego rule. The "me-first" thrust of Japanese life comes fully to the surface. Overtaking another driver, cutting sharply in front of him, and forcing him to jam on his brakes gives a driver a flush of self-satisfaction. He has successfully applied power and forced his will on another person. He has no obligations to the other driver and is free to compete with him with no holds barred. He has little respect for another's life, his property, or his rights. And because every driver instinctively recognizes that others have the same absence of

260

obligation, life in Tokyo streets is something of a revealing return to a primeval state of an otherwise civilized
people. Motor vehicles as an artifact of everyday life are
still so new to Japan that no customs exist to control them.
Nor do the police see any reason to enforce the few weak
laws on the books, nor the courts to sit in judgment.

If driving is the least civilized aspect of Tokyo, the
city's holidays are the most civilizing. They represent the
most enduring of Japanese traditions, especially at New
Year's. Tokyo and, indeed, Japan, simply close for a week.
Government and business offices shut down, factories stop
producing, essential services are manned by skeleton crews,
stores close. Even newspapers do not publish on January 2,
giving the staffs New Year's Day off. Closing out the old
year starts about three weeks before the New Year and
ends about three weeks after. Hundreds and maybe thousands of *bonen-kai* ("year-forgetting") parties are held
as business and government people entertain their associates, clients, customers, and friends in geisha houses.

About December 28, things begin to close down and
a mass exodus begins as people return to their home towns,
meaning their ancestral places, for the holidays. The
Edokko ("Children of Edo" whose native place is Tokyo)
scrub their homes, pay their debts, and reconcile their
quarrels to start the new year with a fresh slate. Special
rice cakes and other holiday foods are prepared. On New
Year's Eve, everyone bathes and the women have their
hair done. Before midnight, hundreds of thousands of people stream toward the Buddhist temples and Shinto shrines
to make their first obeisances of the new year. At the
stroke of midnight, those close enough to the front of the
shrine hurl coins into huge nets spread to catch them. The
shower goes on well into the dawn and the next day as the
hordes keep coming. Some temples are patrons of certain
types of people, such as the Inari O-dera in Akasaka, where
the district's geishas go to give offerings for another good

year. The temple is dedicated, with obscure symbolism, to the fox, statues of which are adorned in red bibs during the holiday.

On New Year's Day, people visit their relatives bearing gifts and call on people to whom they have particular obligations, such as the official go-betweens of their marriage. On January 2, thousands of people file through the Sakishitamon gate of the Imperial Palace to greet the Emperor by signing registry books put out for them. This is one of the few times during the year when the public is allowed inside the Imperial Palace grounds. Downtown Tokyo during this season is an eerie place, nearly deserted instead of being packed as it is the rest of the year.

Around January 4, offices and shops reopen, but not much gets done. Office girls come to work in their holiday kimonos rather than Western-style dresses and everyone visits everyone else in the company to exchange good wishes. Then, having forgotten the old year with *bonen-kai* parties, it is only right that the new year be ushered in with *shinnen-kai* new-year parties. Along about mid-January, the Japanese concede that the year has really started and that they must settle down to work. Besides, all are too exhausted from having a good time and need the work to catch their breath.

A measure, perhaps in counterpoint, of Tokyo's subsurface lack of Westernization is the isolation of the largely Western international community there. Tokyo is East Asia's center of commerce, diplomacy, and communication, attracting several thousand American and European businessmen, diplomats, journalists, and scholars to the city, some for long periods. But the cultural gap between the international and the Japanese communities is so wide that few foreigners ever bridge it. The international community, perhaps unlike any other in a modern industrial society, participates little in the life of the city. It is an island floating in a Japanese sea, attending its own churches, educating children in its own schools, forming its own social centers, patronizing stores that cater almost entirely to its needs. Most Westerners have a few close Japanese friends and the Japanese generally are cordial to foreigners in their midst. But the international community, for the most part, mixes with the Japanese only under well-defined circumstances. Almost every night of the week there is some sort of business entertaining or diplomatic reception to which foreigners are invited. Westerners are often invited to the golf course and to formal social occasions. But foreigners are rarely asked to Japanese homes and have only cursory contact with most of their neighbors.

Part of the reason is the Westerner's choice. He, like the Japanese, is bound by his own culture and cannot or does not make the effort to discover and understand the Japanese. For most, Japan is just too bewildering, in good measure due to the language barrier. Japanese is difficult, and most foreigners do not make the effort to learn; and of the few who do, even fewer ever reach any sort of proficiency. The Japanese, despite having studied English, the international language of Asia, rarely learn to speak well enough to carry on conversations with Westerners. But a good part of the foreign community's isolation arises because the Japanese are not comfortable with Westerners and do not want outsiders involved in their society. The Japanese believe that their customs and ways are unique and that no one else can learn them. They fear that the foreigner will make all sorts of social *faux pas* and embarrass them in front of their friends. They also fear ridicule from the foreigner who may laugh at them for manners and customs he considers quaint or outlandish.

Curiously, the Japanese have mixed feelings about the foreigner who does learn Japanese and takes a genuine interest in Japanese culture. They are complimented by his interest, for they know the hard work needed to learn the language, and they are tolerant to a fault of his linguistic and social mistakes if the foreigner has shown sincerity and good will. But the Japanese are also suspicious of this sort of foreigner and wonder if he is not prying into their lives for some unspecified ulterior motive. A Japanese rarely takes anything at face value, and certainly not the foreigner who claims that he is interested in Japan for the sake of that interest alone.

Every Westerner and his family going to Japan suffers from some degree of "culture shock," the experience of living among a people whose religion, customs, language, attitudes, ethics, values, routine of daily life, and physical environment are so radically different from those in America or Europe. As one American in Tokyo put it several years ago: "If you think you'd enjoy living on another planet, you can do it here. You don't have to wait for the astronauts to get to the moon." Said another: "The most difficult problem for Westerners in Japan is just living here. You have to start from scratch, like a child, and learn how to live all over again." These were telling commentaries on how Japanese, and not Western, the Japanese really are.

Chapter II

NARA:
PAST and
PROLOGUE

In central Japan, not far from Kyoto and Osaka, is the small city of Nara. It is not much known to Westerners, though some tourists take a side trip there from Kyoto. Nara is lovely and serene, a town filled with temples and pagodas and parks with tame deer, set in a countryside of natural beauty. It is a town crossed with quiet lanes, a place for walking and thinking and the sort of a town in which one would like his children to grow up. Outside the city proper is the gleaming white Horyuji, a stately temple whose pebbled court is enclosed by long, straight walls and whose open spaces give it an air of contemplation. One can almost sense the presence of the builder, the scholarly statesman Prince Shotoku, who sat and pondered religion and politics in his Yumedono, the Hall of Dreams. Not far from the Horyuji is the Yakushiji, a temple dedicated to the God of Mercy and Healing. The Yakushiji's three-tiered pagoda is gracefully proportioned and the bronze statue of the Yakushi is breathtakingly beautiful, slim and flowing and tranquil. In Nara itself, nestled against the side of a hill at the edge of a park, is the Kasuga Jinja, an exquisite shrine of vermilion gates and green grass and white walls, a combination of Chinese Buddhist and Japanese Shinto architecture that reveals the eclecticism of Japanese religion. A few steps away is the weathered wooden Nigatsudo, the Hall of the Second Month, part of what was once the most powerful Buddhist monastery in the land. Each year, at just about the Christian Eastertime, twelve monks gather in an upper room for a private supper and ritual. The origin of the ceremony is lost in obscurity, but it has made religious scholars wonder if perhaps a whiff of Christianity and the Last Supper blew across Asia to Japan a thousand years before the first European missionaries arrived. Down the hill is the Todaiji temple with an immense wooden hall housing the towering and imposing Daibutsu, the Great Buddha, painstakingly molded during the flowering age of Japanese Buddhism. These and much more make a walk through Nara an excursion in a time capsule back to the seventh and eighth centuries.

Nara, founded in 710, was the first permanent, settled capital of a unifying Japan. Nara is more a city of China than a city of Japan, for it was, and is, the mirror of Japan's great infusion of culture from China in the days of a magnificent Chinese civilization. What happened then is of more than academic interest or more than a pleasant sight-seeing trip through quaint antiquity, because an inquiry into the cultural impact of China on Japan thirteen centuries ago turns up significant clues to what is happening in Japan today.

Historical generalizations are among the riskiest of intellectual exercises since there is always the temptation to work out a neat theory and then fit into it all the facts that prove it. Even with this caveat, however, the theories can be useful instruments in trying to understand what a people are like, how they got that way, and where they are probably headed. This is especially true of Japan, where the parallel between the events and the flow of history in the seventh and eighth centuries and the nineteenth and twentieth centuries is so striking. It is possible and even profitable to read passages from standard works on early Japanese cultural history and to substitute the words "nineteenth and twentieth centuries" for "seventh and eighth centuries" and "the West" for "China" in order to come up with a helpful and sometimes revealing insight into Japan and its historical movement during the last hundred years.

It is not stretching reason too far to speculate that the trends that developed in the ninth century may well be paralleled by those of late-twentieth- and twenty-first-century Japan. The culture, institutions, and items that Japan borrowed from China were different from those taken from the West, but the motivations, the methods, and the processes of adaptation are remarkably similar. The time sequences are foreshortened in the modern period because Japan was more unified at the start of the process and because transport and communication have been much faster. But these differences do not invalidate the proposition.

Japan before the coming of Chinese culture was a land of clans, one of which migrated from western Japan east to the central plains near the Inland Sea. This clan, the Yamato, gradually became pre-eminent. Its family of high priests became the Imperial Family and evolved the legend of descent from Amaterasu-o-mi-kami, the Sun Goddess. Their Shinto religion, the Way of the Gods, was a rather simple and naïve belief in the spirits of nature. The Yamato and other clans knew how to work bronze and build simple thatched homes, to farm the land and to organize their society along family lines. They were an unlettered people and did not develop a written language from their spoken tongue. They had occasional contacts with Korea and China but were mostly isolated from the outside world.

China in the sixth century was in disunion, the earlier

Han Empire having fallen into ruin and the country having been partially overrun by nomadic invaders from Central Asia. Late in the sixth century, however, a powerful general reunified China and established the short-lived Sui Dynasty. It was overthrown and the T'ang Dynasty, with its capital at Ch'ang-an, was established in 618. This became China's and perhaps the world's most splendid civilization, its power and cultural influence spreading across all Asia. The government of the T'ang rulers was effective, the economy prospered, arts and letters were brilliant, philosophy and education flourished, and religion, especially the Buddhism that had reached China from India, was fervent.

As China unified and word reached Japan, the Japanese began to take an interest, gradually at first, then in a rush. Prince Shotoku, who had become a zealous Buddhist, sent the first mission to China in 607. Over the next two hundred years, twelve more official missions, plus a stream of individual monks, scholars, and ordinary travelers, followed. They brought back with them descriptions of Chinese culture that enthralled the Japanese ruling class and inspired a reformation intended to result in a nation organized along Chinese lines. The Japanese also invited Chinese, and Koreans who had been influenced by the Chinese, to come to Japan to instruct them in the Chinese ways.

Some time after Shotoku's death in 622, a set of seventeen injunctions governing court and official behavior was issued as a memorial to the Prince, clearly the most influential man of his times. The Seventeen Injunctions showed strong Chinese, especially Confucian influence. This was followed by the Taika Reform of 645, to which some of the Meiji Restoration edicts later bore marked resemblance. It attempted to withdraw the right to own land from the clans and to put it in the emperor's name, to determine rules by which outlying provinces would be governed, to revise the system of land tenure and rice allotments, and to institute a centralized system of taxation.

A new capital was established in Nara in 710. The city was laid out on the pattern of the Chinese capital Ch'ang-an, facing south, with the Imperial Palace at the north and the city on a rectangular grid spread out before it. The Imperial Court was organized along Chinese lines, and the bureaucracy was patterned after that in China. Buddhism overshadowed Shinto in imperial favor. Art and architecture, which were essentially religious as was Western art in the early Christian and Middle Ages, followed Chinese principles closely. Perhaps most important, the Japanese took over wholesale the Chinese form of ideographic writing and for the first time began compiling their own written history and official documents.

Chinese forms, however, did not fit exactly around the Japanese substance. From the earliest stages of the borrowing process, the Japanese were selective and adaptive. They were less changed by Chinese culture than the Chinese ways were changed and Japanized to suit the needs and thinking of the Japanese. Though the Japanese took over the court dress, titles, and manners of China, their fundamental thinking about the emperor did not change. The Chinese emperor ruled by the Mandate of Heaven, which meant that he could rightfully stay on the throne only so long as he was virtuous. Overthrow of the Chinese emperor was not only permissible but has recurred repeatedly through Chinese history.

The Japanese emperor, in contrast, retained his throne by right of dynastic succession that had little to do with his virtue or ability to rule. To depose the emperor would be to cut the line of the Imperial Ancestors that, according to legend, went back to the Sun Goddess. Japanese emperors through history have been subjected to all sorts of indignities, including assassination and being ignored, but the Imperial Family has not been deposed by the actual rulers of Japan. These rulers have papered over their manipulation of the emperor so that the imperial line, while bent at times, has remained unbroken and is today the world's most ancient continuously reigning house.

Further, the Chinese emperor was usually the actual ruler of his country, though subject to the intrigues and machinations that have always surrounded royal families. The Japanese emperor has rarely been the true ruler. Even in the days of strong Chinese influence during the Nara period, powerful clans exercised their authority and continually struggled for actual political supremacy. Religion quickly became a major weapon, some factions advocating the continued growth of Buddhism, others the revival of the native Shinto as the religion of the Imperial Court. This quarrel may have been among the reasons that the capital was moved, first in 784 to nearby Nagaoka, and then in 794 a little farther away to Heian-kyo, or Kyoto.

The establishment of Kyoto as capital opened the Heian (Peaceful Tranquility) period, which lasted until 1160. The theme that ran through the history and cultural development of that era was the adaptation and assimilation, or the rejection, of Chinese culture and the reversion to Japanese cultural patterns. The duality of politics, in which real power is separated from symbolic rule, developed fully as the Fujiwara clan became supreme. The centralized Chinese system of land tenure never really took hold, being too much for the jealous clans to accept. Over the years, land tenure moved in the opposite direction and gave rise to the particular forms of Japanese feudalism that dominated land holding from the mid-tenth century to the Meiji Restoration. Since taxation was based on land tenure and rice production, that too passed back into the hands of the clans. Buddhism continued to flourish and some sects retained loose communication with their counterparts in China, but all took on a Japanese coloration and manner of exerting authority. Japanese artists moved away from the forms of their Chinese tutors and evolved a style distinctly their own. The assimilation process was most evident, and most important, in the modifications of Chinese writing. Language and writing are completely intertwined with thought and a cast of mind. Had the Japanese accepted Chinese writing without change, they might have eventually changed their way of thinking and have become like the Chinese in the fashion in which they organized their institutions and led their lives. But they did not. Instead, they drastically revised Chinese writing to fit the Japanese language.

Of all the mysteries of the Orient—and they are legion —surely none is more puzzling to the Western mind than the intricate and elaborate writing of China and Japan. The Chinese and Japanese write in ideographs, idea and sound pictures originally drawn with a brush and ink in a maze of vigorous strokes and graceful curves. Because the two written languages look alike, many Westerners assume they are related. They are only in that the ideographs have the same origin. Beyond that, the two are as dissimilar as, say, English and Russian. Chinese, in technical terms, is a monosyllabic, uninflected, tonal language, a root tongue evolved over thousands of years first as a spoken and later as a written language. Chinese characters usually have two components, one giving a clue to meaning, another a hint to pronunciation. Some are pictures of things—a man, a lake, a mountain. Others, more difficult, represent ideas —"east" is a picture of the sun rising through a tree. Grammatically, Chinese lacks the myriad declensions and genders of Latin or English. Sentences are short and fairly simple, though word order is similar to the subject-verb-object order of English.

Japanese, in contrast, is a polysyllabic, highly inflected, pitch language. It is not a root tongue, but is believed to be related to Korean, Manchu, Mongol, and, for historically obscure reasons, to Turkish and Finnish. Japanese words have many syllables, a great variety of verb and adjective endings, and an inconsistent array of post-positions (the opposite of English prepositions) to indicate a noun's case. Japanese sentences tend to be long and involved, with a word order almost opposite to that in Chinese (and, unhappily, English). When the study of things Chinese became the chief intellectual preoccupation of the Japanese upper classes in Nara, they were forced to learn Chinese, a painful and time-consuming process, or to use a clumsy approximation of Chinese ideographs written in Japanese grammatical patterns and often representing only sounds.

The urge for a native literature began in the ninth century in Kyoto and led to less dependence on strictly Chinese forms of writing. The Japanese evolved a cursive syllabary called *hiragana,* in which Chinese ideographs were simplified to represent sound only. This allowed the Japanese to move Chinese ideographs around and fit them more easily into Japanese speech patterns. Around the year 1000, two great Japanese books appeared, *The Pillow Book of Sei Shonagon* and *The Tale of Genji,* both classic in their descriptions of the court life of Kyoto. By that time, Japanese had resettled into its own linguistic patterns. Other developments over the years have led the Chinese and Japanese languages on such diverse courses that the speaker of one cannot come close to understanding the other and the written languages bear only the sketchiest resemblance to one another.

Today, after another era of borrowing from abroad, this time from the West, Japan appears to be entering what might be called the Second Heian Period. In the decades ahead, the Japanese may well repeat with Western culture what they did with Chinese culture centuries ago. It may be easier because the impact of the West has been resisted in many fields, except technology, while that from China was welcomed. In some ways, too, the Japanese have been forced to borrow from the West while their acquisitions from China were by choice. Japan is now moving with the convergence of two historical currents. One is the reaction to a long exposure to the alien West, the other the recovery from the trauma of destruction and defeat in World War II. Both have already started carrying the Japanese toward a revitalization of their own culture, including the rejection of many things from the West. The Japanese promise to intensify this process in the near future as they turn in on themselves and look to their own history and traditions to discover what kind of people they are and to search out their own national identity. The Japanese will continue to borrow from the West, primarily in technology, but the sampling of ideas and institutions appears to be over. The return to a Japanese cultural pattern will most likely be faster than in the earlier Heian period, just as the borrowing process was faster, because the modern world moves more quickly.

There is no conclusive evidence for this, by any means, but the signs are clear enough to warrant the speculative prediction. Among the foremost is the revival of the imperial institution as the central theme running through Japanese life, religion, nationalism, politics, and the social order. Reverence for the emperor and his family has gradually increased to the point where even the radical left has muted its call for ending the imperial system. The leftists appear to have accepted it as inherent in Japanese life. Scholars are reviving their interest in Shinto and the Imperial Way, seeking to redefine the emperor's role in the modern world.

Other intellectuals are also showing more concern. Perhaps the most outspoken has been novelist, playwright, and actor Mishima Yukio, probably the Japanese writer best known in the West. Mishima has written that a renewal of faith in the emperor is a renewal of faith in Japan. He has said that the emperor must be revered not so much as a person but as a "cultural concept." The emperor, in Mishima's view, is the arbiter of poetry, elegance, and ethics in Japanese life. Mishima has particularly urged that the bonds between the emperor and the Army be revived. He has contended that Japanese culture is an indivisible totality of the chrysanthemum of art and ceremony and the sword of courage and sacrifice. He believes that the chrysanthemum and the sword are joined in the emperor as the symbol of both beauty and honor in Japanese life.

Japanese educational requirements are being revised to emphasize ethics in which the emperor is the model of correct behavior and sets the standard to which all Japanese should aspire. The national myths and gods are being revived to point the way in ethical training that stresses the ancient Confucian virtues of loyalty, duty, obedience, harmony. Among the younger, moderately conservative politicians who will be coming to the fore in the next decade is a growing feeling that the emperor's role in politics is the true source of political legitimacy. They talk in terms reminiscent of their Meiji forefathers—but not of the ultranationalists of the 1930's. The resurgence of nationalism is based on and contributes to the symbolic centrality and unity of Japan in the imperial institution.

The Ministry of Education's document called "The Image of the Ideal Japanese," already mentioned in Chapter V, was part of the revival of the imperial cult. But it went beyond to repeat much of the social philosophy contained in the seventeen injunctions dedicated to Prince Shotoku in the seventh century and the Imperial Rescript on Education in the nineteenth century. "The Image" departed from its antecedents to consider the individual rights and freedoms, but quickly exhorted the Japanese not to succumb to other ideological imports from the West. It warned against the materialism that has gripped Japan in recent years, contending that if the "lack of ideals in spirit continues, while material desires grow, we cannot hope for true economic prosperity or the elevation of human nature." It lamented that new ideals after the war remained abstract and have not been converted into reality. "The Image" asked that Japanese have more confidence in themselves. It conceded that Japanese have characteristics that should be remedied, but said that the Japanese have overlooked many of their own fine points that should be passed on to posterity.

In a sentence that presented the essence of the document, the authors wrote tersely: "We should not forget that we are Japanese."

"The Image" had a Western tint, saying that Japan should, ideally, become a democratic state in which the majority rules without being arbitrary and the minority is neither servile nor rebellious. It called on the individual to develop his talents and human qualities, as might be urged by an advocate of the Protestant Ethic in America, and not to follow others blindly but to become a brave person of strong will. "The Image" moved on quickly, however, to the Confucian virtues of responsibility, duty, loyalty, and harmony. The portrayal of the traits expected of the Japanese as a member of the family, society, and the nation diminished the Western touches and drew from the Japanese heritage. The treatise defended the family as the source of education, the purification of love, and the foundation of society and the nation. The report was critical of the low standard of ethics in the postwar era: "The major defect of Japanese society is the weakness of the social standard and the disregard for social order." It pleaded for a return to traditional ways and for all Japanese to acquire a correct sense of patriotism.

The introspection of the Japanese is evident among the young people who, in twenty years, will be working their way into the lower reaches of the Establishment. The Japanese sometimes speak of three generations alive today. The prewar generation is that of the present leaders in the Establishment, all of whom were educated and had chosen careers before the war. They are aware of the outside world because Japan in their youth was expansionist and their daily lives were caught up in it. The midwar, or "lost," generation are those whose educations were interrupted by the war and who emerged into an adult world dominated by the Occupation and the struggle to stay alive amid the rubble of the war's destruction. This generation is also aware of the outside world, but with a pain and an anxiety seared into their consciousness by the experiences of their youth. The third, or postwar, generation are today's youngsters who have no memory of the war and little of the grim days immediately after. They have grown up and have been educated during a time when the eyes and the efforts of their nation were turned to the goal of economic prosperity. These young people appear to be far less aware of the West, except for its fads, than the two older generations. They seem largely uninterested in Western ideas or in Western people.

The clues slip out more in nuance than in blunt assertion. In a high school English-speaking contest one would have expected the young people who had the interest and the diligence to learn an especially difficult language to be outward-looking. To the contrary, the contestants chose subjects that dwelt on Japanese history and custom and how, as Japanese, they could contribute to their nation's search for identity. An English-speaking university student, on another occasion, said that he regretted studying international law and wished that he had spent more time on Japanese history. He said he hoped his training would not be held against him when he applied for a position in the bureaucracy (not the Foreign Ministry). A young woman who had majored in English literature, primarily Shakespeare, said she wished she had studied Japanese literature instead. She found herself more interested in what

Japanese writers had to say about Japan than in the ideas of Western authors.

University panel discussions and study groups in which foreigners participate rarely discuss the outside world. The students are not concerned with picking the brains of the Westerner to learn more about the West but with getting his views on Japan and impressing on him the differences between their views of themselves, the world, or a particular issue, and those held by the Westerner. Similarly, Japanese youngsters often approach Westerners in subways or parks or on the street to ask whether they might practice their English with a native speaker for a few minutes. But the conversations are rarely about the Westerner's homeland. The youngsters usually want to know what the foreigner thinks about Japan and to express themselves about Japan, not the rest of the world. Even this has dropped off in recent years as more youngsters either ignore foreigners or, surprisingly, are pointedly rude to them in a few instances. Japanese young people often give the impression that they want to be like their Western counterparts, picking up the rock-and-roll fads and miniskirt fashions that ripple out from America. But these pass even faster than in America and leave little permanent mark. The Japanese youngster today is intent on finding his niche in Japanese society, not on Westernizing himself.

Much is sometimes made of the generation gap between today's young people and their parents. In Tokyo on any night of any week, youngsters can be found breaking every rule of conduct their parents taught them, which makes them little different from their parents before them. Students often take to the streets in protest and rebellion against the old order. Or so it seems. The protest about the inadequacy of higher-education facilities and the indifference of professors is both real and justified. But the students are not saying "change the order"; they are saying "make it work the way it should." Those students who proclaim themselves the vanguard of a movement that would overturn the social order are noisy and sometimes dangerous. They are also a small minority. The trouble they have caused and will cause cannot be dismissed lightly. In perspective, however, the overwhelming majority of students are more concerned about passing the examinations and entering Mitsubishi or the Ministry of Finance than they are about remaking Japan. And the majority are much more often than not joined by the demonstrators once the second year of the university course is over and the need for establishing oneself as a candidate for the business or bureaucratic world has become more immediate and compelling. The rioter of five years ago wants to be the Mitsui salaryman on his way up five years from now. With its element of "the thing to do" for the excitement of it, the protest of most Japanese youngsters ends up being little more than a political and intellectual panty raid. When the time comes for entering the mold, it is a rare one who tries to break it.

For all the inward turning and retrospection, Japan neither can nor wishes to return to the isolation of pre-1868. Japan needs its trade and economic ties with the West to continue its prosperity. It must have some form of collective security arrangement, probably with America but possibly with other Asian nations or even in a neutral, nonaligned force. Japan's political interests are intertwined with those of all nations whose shores are washed by the Pacific and, to a lesser extent, with the major industrial powers of Europe. Japan's interplay with the West will continue, and the West will continue to leave its imprint on Japan. But an imprint is exactly what it will be, an engraving on the surface and not the deep probe of the cultural lance.

Some historians maintain that the essence of history is change. Others say the essence is continuity. Both are probably right, at least in the case of Japan. The changes have been and will be on the surface of Japan, in the forms in which the Japanese organize and operate their institutions. The continuity has been and will be in the inner workings and the substance of Japanese life.

An especially perceptive Japanese once described his homeland as a bamboo pole sheathed in steel and wrapped in plastic. The image is a good one. The Westerner can see the colorful wrapping that is the tinselly, imitative veneer of Japan. He can see through the plastic to the steel of modern, industrial Japan. Both look like the West. But inside, and often obscured, is the bamboo reality of the enduring Japan.

The Japanese have a tale:

Once upon a time, in the skies above ancient Japan, there lived a handsome young shepherd named Kengyu and a beautiful princess called Orihimé. They met, fell in love, and were married with the permission of her father, the Celestial King. Now, Orihimé was the most skillful weaver of silk in the heavenly kingdom and Kengyu was entrusted with great herds. But they were so much in love that Orihimé neglected her weaving of the King's garments and Kengyu allowed his herds to stray. They were admonished by the King, but to no avail. In anger, he separated them and cast them into the endless sky, doomed to wander forever as stars on either side of the Amanogawa, the River of Heaven.

The King, however, later took pity on them and relented slightly, permitting Kengyu and Orihimé to meet once a year. But there is no bridge over the Amanogawa, and the princess, on her first attempt to visit her husband, wept so bitterly that she evoked the sympathy of the *kasanagi*, or magpies, who spread their wings over the river so that Orihimé could cross. And so it came to pass that on the Seventh Night of the Seventh Lunar Month, Orihimé and Kengyu met on the banks of the Amanogawa, which Westerners call the Milky Way. Every year, the legend says, they meet on the same night and here on earth the people rejoice and celebrate the festival of Tanabata, the calligraphy for which means "Seventh Night."

One summer not long ago, the town of Asahi celebrated Tanabata with a burst of color like the explosion of a rainbow. Asahi is east of Tokyo, in the rolling farm country near the Pacific coast, where there are few factories and community life has not been caught up in the tumult of the city. This is not to say that Asahi, a town of 31,000 people, is not modern. Its shops were filled with television sets and cosmetics, the farmers had tractors and power tools, and the young people sported the latest styles in haircuts and clothes. But life is simpler than in Tokyo and people are not so jaded that they cannot find simple joy in a festival.

On this particular Tanabata, the main streets of the town were strung with banners and bunting of every imaginable hue and each store displayed streaming colored-paper decorations hung from tall bamboo poles. To these, and to the bamboo set before the shrines and homes, were hung strips of white paper with short poems commemorating the love of Orihimé and Kengyu. They fluttered in the gentle breeze for three days and then were taken down and floated away in a stream to the sea. The girls of Asahi went to the shrines to present their supplications to Orihimé to improve their sewing and their talents for art and music and poetry. The young men asked Kengyu for good fortune and bounteous harvests.

On one evening, the people dressed in *yukata*, the summer kimonos, to join their neighbors and dance in a parade through lantern-lit streets. First came the young girls followed by their older sisters, then the young boys and their older brothers. Behind them pranced the women and men. The girls and women dancing that night reconfirmed the conviction that Japanese ladies have the most graceful hands in the world, whether opening a sliding door, or serving tea, or performing a dance. They can put more beauty into a delicate and expressive motion of the hand than the finest artist into a masterful painting. Even the youngest girls could make proper motions by imitating the older ones, and girls in their teens were polished and pleasing to the eyes of the mothers who taught them.

Each neighborhood group was followed by an ornate cart carrying a drum on which several husky lads boomed a rhythm strange to Western ears. Not all was traditional. The sound of the drum was accompanied by music from a transistorized tape recorder and carried to the dancers through a transistorized amplifier system. A papier-mâché figure of the Japanese version of Batman drew giggles, as did another of Oba-Que, a gay TV ghost popular with children. Interspersed with the dancers were floats carrying Daikoku-sama, a god of merchants, and other symbols of the town's prosperity. Hyottoko the Clown cavorted through the crowd, and the inevitable dog that adorns every parade roamed at will.

The legend of Kengyu and Orihimé says that if it rains on Tanabata, the *kasanagi* will not spread their wings for Orihimé to cross the river. That summer, Tanabata was a brilliant day and a clear starlit evening. And so the *kasanagi* formed the bridge and the people were happy that Kengyu and Orihimé could meet once again for their night of love.

The old ways persist in Japan, and for those who are enchanted with them, this is good.

INDEX

A NOTE ABOUT THE AUTHOR

Richard Halloran was born in Washington, D.C., in 1930. He attended Dartmouth College (A.B. 1951), where he majored in government and international relations, and the University of Michigan's Center for Japanese Studies (M.A. 1957). He received a Ford Foundation Fellowship in Advanced International Reporting to attend the Graduate School of Journalism at Columbia University, 1964-5, where he studied at the East Asia Institute. As a first lieutenant and paratrooper, he served in Korea, Japan, Okinawa, Taiwan, and Vietnam during 1954-5. He was with Business Week *from 1957 to 1964, first as a staff writer, then as Assistant Foreign Editor, and later as Far East Bureau Chief in Tokyo. He joined the Washington* Post *as a specialist in Asian affairs in 1965 and was Northeast Asia correspondent, based in Tokyo, during 1966-8. With his wife and their three children, he now lives in Washington, D.C., where he covers diplomatic affairs for* The New York Times.

A NOTE ON THE TYPE

The text of this book was set on the Linotype in Janson, a recutting made direct from type cast from matrices long thought to have been made by the Dutchman Anton Janson, who was a practicing type founder in Leipzig during the years 1868–87. However, it has been conclusively demonstrated that these types are actually the work of Nicholas Kis (1650–1702), a Hungarian, who most probably learned his trade from the master Dutch type founder Kirk Voskens. The type is an excellent example of the influential and sturdy Dutch types that prevailed in England up to the time William Caslon developed his own incomparable designs from these Dutch faces.

The book was composed, printed and bound by The Book Press, Brattleboro, Vermont. Typography and binding design by Virginia Tan.